Blood to Remember

# Blood to Remember
*American Poets on the Holocaust*

*Edited by Charles Fishman*

Texas Tech University Press

Copyright 1991 Charles Fishman

All rights reserved. No portion of this book may be
reproduced in any form or by any means, including electronic
storage and retrieval systems, except by explicit, prior written
permission of the publishers except for brief passages
excerpted for review and critical purposes.

This book was set in 10 on 13 ITC Garamond and printed on
acid-free paper that meets the guidelines for permanence and
durability of the Committee on Production Guidelines for Book
Longevity of the Council on Library Resources. ∞

Jacket and book design by Cameron Poulter

Printed in the United States of America

Library of Congress Cataloging-in-Publication Data
    Blood to remember : American poets on the Holocaust / edited by
    Charles Fishman
        p.   cm.
    Includes bibliographical references and indexes.
    ISBN 0-89672-214-7 (cloth). — ISBN 0-89672-215-5 (paper)
    1. Holocaust, Jewish (1939-1945)—Poetry. 2. American
    poetry—20th century. I. Fishman, Charles M., 1942-
    PS595.H64B57 1990
    811'.54080358—dc20                                    90-24009
                                                              CIP

92 93 94 95 96 97 98 99 / 9 8 7 6 5 4 3 2

Texas Tech University Press
Lubbock, Texas 79409-1037 USA

IN MEMORY OF
Jacob Fishman [Yakov Szyfman], 1908–1935

Uncle, may you rest at last.

The more we know of the Holocaust, the more *we* change, the more we find ourselves circumscribed by the event we sought to transcend and from which we had hoped to pull free. . . . The more we know, the more we shall remember.

*Terrence Des Pres*

No gravestone stands on Babi Yar;
Only coarse earth heaped roughly on the gash.
Such dread comes over me; I feel so old,
Old as the Jews.  Today I am a Jew . . .
And I too have become a soundless cry
Over the thousands that lie buried here.
I am each old man slaughtered, each child shot,
None of me will forget.

*Yevgeny Yevtushenko*

It is blood to remember; it is fire
to stammer back.

*Hart Crane*

# Editor's Preface

Seeking to forget makes exile all the longer;
the secret of redemption lies in remembrance.
*Israel Ba'al Shem Tov*
*18th century, Eastern Europe*

Our time is marked by the Angel of Forgetfulness, not by the
Angel of Memory. Our machines are constructed with obsoles-
cence in mind, not perpetuity. We revise truth daily in our news
rooms, eviscerate history in our schools, build new models of the
universe in our laboratories before the old are fully understood.
In editing Blood to Remember, my purpose has been, in part, to
counter this inclination toward obliteration and distortion. I have
been guided by my belief that an anthology of Holocaust poetry
must not be simply another collection of contemporary poems. In
truth, one does not collect poetry for such an anthology: the poems
gather; the darkness gathers.

I believe that what is required is a book of memory and vision,
the record of our human refusal to forget what has wounded us
beyond repair. For memory is the voice that calls to us from the
other side of time, and blood is the truth we remember—the news
that reminds us who we have been and who we are. At the same
time, I believe that art should not mute the voices crying out to us
from the past: that the poet's voice, in particular, must not speak
too easily, too quickly, too knowingly, of the sequence of events
and reverberations we have learned to name the Holocaust, the
*Shoah,* the Kingdom of Suffering and Death.

As many have realized before me, the Storm was too intense to
register accurately on the delicate seismographs of art, the magnitude
too great. It follows that no single poem or book of poems could
hope to capture more than a few moments in that shattered chron-
ology. The Storm composed itself from innumerable bits and tend-
encies, from fields of force and eddying maelstroms of power: it
was history's darkest child brought full term, to everlasting birth.

*Blood to Remember* is my belated attempt to speak to that darkness,
to honor the dead and the living, to listen long and closely to the
voices of American poets who have also needed to speak and to
write. I have made this book for them and for myself, for our
murdered sisters and brothers, and for the souls who were denied
being in this life. *I have made this for you.*

*

The special nature of this anthology spoke directly to a group of extraordinary individuals, all of whom deserve my highest praise: Yala Korwin, for her great skill in tracking hard-to-find poems and elusive facts; Richard Michelson, for his assistance with preliminary editorial decisions; Dr. Robert A. Raab, Rabbi of Suburban Temple (Wantagh, New York), for his swift and illuminating clarifications of Hebrew and biblical allusions; Marina Roscher, for her expert advice concerning German references, and for her sustaining friendship; and Reva Sharon, for her important contributions to early phases of the editing.

To the writers who offered their help, and knowledge, and who brought to my attention the work of other poets: all of you enabled me to learn and gave me renewed determination to see *Blood to Remember* completed. *Camerados,* I salute you!

My heartfelt thanks, too, to Dr. Robert V. Mark, Dean of the School of Arts and Sciences at SUNY Farmingdale, and to Dr. Michael J. Vinciguerra, Provost, and Dr. Frank A. Cipriani, President of the College, for their faith in me and for their generous support.

Finally, for my family—and, most deeply, for my wife and life-companion, Ellen, my abiding love, my unreserved admiration.

# Contents

# CONTENTS

CONTENTS

# CONTENTS

CONTENTS

# CONTENTS

CONTENTS

# CONTENTS

# CONTENTS

# CONTENTS

# CONTENTS

# CONTENTS

I

**After the Holocaust—
No Poetry?**

Even an outcry is now a lie,
even tears are mere literature,
even prayers are false.
                              Aaron Zeitlin

David Koenig

# After the Holocaust,
# No Poetry

After the Holocaust,
No poetry—
That is what they say—
But I write poems about it.
What's that?
You do, too?
Come then,
Let us sit down together.
How do you spell your name
In this country,
With an *umlaut* or a vowel?
Shall we speak a bit
In the old tongue?
The one they tried to cut
Out of our parents' mouths?
Forgive me.
I'm not unstrung.
The poems keep me sane.
I guard them
Like torn and injured pages
From buried books of prayer.

Linda Pastan

# Response

a ban on the following subject matter:
the Holocaust, grandparents, Friday night
candle lighting . . . Jerusalem at dusk.
      from the poetry editor of *Response*

It is not dusk
in Jerusalem
it is simply morning

and the grandparents have disappeared
into the Holocaust
taking their sabbath candles with them.

Light your poems, hurry.
Already the sun is leaning
towards the west

though the grandparents and candles
have long since burned down
to stubs.

Gary Pacernick

# Why I Write about the Holocaust

When I was a boy I lived among people
Who wore the SS insignia
Branded on their arms,
And I felt the presence
Of those who disappeared
In the flaming dark;
Could hear them crying out
For help that never came;

Could feel their shame as they
Stood naked in gas chambers
Pounding against walls—
Reduced to integers in
A mad equation for murder.
Kneeling to the earth, I blotted
Out my shadow with my body
And felt darkness drawing me down
Because mankind's machinations
Meant nothing to me now.
As I walked among survivors
I saw smoke rise in their sad eyes;
I tasted the bitter herbs of their memories;
I heard their silent screams.

James William Chichetto

## Etchings

for Ursula Niebuhr and Sylvia Weisberg
The twentieth century man who has not meditated on Auschwitz does not
yet know the meaning of meditation or the meaning of his own times.
                                        Thomas Merton

Perhaps there is a better night than this or better dream
          off the etchings of despair . . .
Perhaps pushing through the grass in the distance, some high
          wind of feeling will suppress this
          and the knowledge of the soul that thoughts take
          will fall without exaltation.
Perhaps in some dark mind memories will point back to joys,
          lost colors of a coast, fragments
                              breaking them to pieces. . . .
          And they buried the dead
                    out of folds of dust
                    out of powdery thistle

out of white ashes to gain them back.
And they buried the dead
    cuffed by their bunks
      tugging the designs of cloud,
        the silken smoke.
And they buried the dead
    before their adulthood and dreams, amid
    crossfire, and a thousand churches of God.
And they buried the dead
    like white leaves,
      washing themselves under Abraham, Isaac,
      and Jacob.
And they buried the dead
    in blanketing fog
    in high grass
      to put a rock down on their graves.
      . . . and they buried the dead.

Joan Jobe Smith

## Hollow Cost

My mother told me about the hollow cost
one Saturday morning as I lay
in her bed beside her where I read
comic books while she moaned
for just forty more winks, it her
day off from the Payless Cafe,
and when she finally yawned,
stretched and woke, after I'd
turned the Little Lulu pages
as loudly as I could, sometimes
she told me stories about when
she was a little girl in Texas
riding horses, milking cows,
cooking on a wood-burning stove.
But that one morning she cleared her throat

the way she always did before she scolded me
and she told me she had something to tell me
that I should hear first from my mother
hunger
gas showers
shaven-headed women
sixty-pound men
human-skin lampshades
the war so much more
than white oleo
F. D. R. speeches on the radio
letters from my father in Algeria.  Oh,
how you wish you had never heard
some of the things your mother told you
that six million were more
than all the stars in the sky
on a clear, winter night

Frank Finale

## Digging

She went to the local library, found
Dante's *Inferno* in the Travel section, heard
three girls giggling by open books, "We're
writing ours on Hitler."
                              *Quiet, please!*
The library, stacking so many
lives   deep   dark   dormant
seeds on dusty shelves, has
its winter hours—TIC   TIC   TIC

In a photograph, 1942, a German
snow, large as doily flakes on school windows,
floats down past the chimneys and stacks
of old shoes, down over the cattle cars of
Jews, down through the hissing puffs of black

locomotives that furnace the dark, down
over the open trenches in a field
where evergreens bristle the wind, listen, SHHH
                    SHH.


Emily Borenstein

# I Must Tell the Story

I press my face to the pane of death to witness
the slaughter of Jews in Warsaw.
I must tell the story of this tragic event.
I write for my friend Pesha.
I write for my cousin Perelke who was going to be
an actress
for my nephew Wiernicka who wrote poetry
for Chaim Kaplan and his *Scroll of Agony*
for half-witted Nathan who was hanged from a tree
for Hinda, the bride, who died in her husband's arms
for Motl, the tailor
for Bruno Schulz, his stories, his dreams
for Emanuel Ringelblum who preserved for posterity
the record of the slaughter.
Names pile up like pebbles on tombstones.
To forget you is to let you die twice.
To forget you is to hear forever blasting in my head
the single long note of the Shofar sounding in the houses
of the dead.

Cornel Adam Lengyel

# Independence Day: Eureka

1

Celebrating a Fourth of July in Eureka,
I moved with the crowd in the street, loud and alive
with flags, bunting, band music; boys shooting firecrackers;
bearded cowboys and lumberjacks; oldtimers in regalia,
marching toward the wharf or trooping toward the tracks.
On Humboldt Bay a warship, decked with planes;
at Redwood Acres the horses are ready to run.
"Place your bets!" the barkers shout from loudspeakers.

Scoreboards change; the crowd in the bleachers roars,
roars like the sea; near the tracks a ferris-wheel
is turning forever slowly; livestock judges
peer into sawdust pens with appraising eyes;
ranchboys with electric shears trim their pets;
shaggy lambs are baaing mournfully.

2

I enter a redwood grove to walk among
the silent giant trees; survivors of chaos,
enduring witnesses: huge, mute
many-armed messengers from a younger world.
I hear a fresh burst of cheers from the bleachers,
from the children of free men at play in a promised land.
I think of another people in another land
where children are burned in roaring ovens.

I touch a tree and think of Israel,
survivor of world-storms, a tree of promethean promise.
Again her branches are broken; her roots are torn.
Yet the tree will stand. Though charred and blackened,
leafless among the rocks, still fed by a spring of light,
Israel shall send green shoots to the sun again.

Derek Walcott

## XXXVIII, *from* Midsummer '81

The camps held their distance of brown chestnuts and grey smoke
that coiled into thorns. The industry of guilt continues.
Wild pigeons gurgle, the squirrels pile up acorns like little shoes,
and moss, voiceless as smoke, hushes the bodies
of abandoned kindling; in the clear pools, fat
trout, rising to flies, bubble in umlauts.
Over forty years ago in the islands, I felt
that the gift of poetry had made me one of the Chosen,
but that all mankind was one kindling to the fire of the Muse,
now, I see her again, on that pine-bench where she sits,
the nut-brown ideal, in silence, with her coppery braids,
the blood-drops of poppies embroidering her white bodice,
essence of smoke and autumn, the spirit of Keats,
whose gaze raked the level fields where the smoky cries
of ravens were almost human. I knew then she was
goddess of the golden stubble, of the cornflower iris,
the winnower of chaff for whom the flashing blades
fell in whole harvests. Had I known what I know now,
the palm-fronds of my island would have been harrows, and
the sand of the beaches as warm and white as ashes,
and at fifteen I would have put down my pen,
since this century's pastorals were already written
at Auschwitz, Buchenwald, at Dachau, at Sachsenhausen.

Sister Mary Philip de Camara, V. H. M.

## Yellow Starred

Approach the Holocaust
only with synecdoche:

not six million Jews—
just Anne Frank,

not hundreds of concentration camps—
but Buchenwald,

a single freight train,
one oven—

not millions of emaciated corpses,
but piled high human hair—

the unique color black
will stand for boots—

one madman—Hitler,
a lone symbol—twisted cross

one God,
one sound—silence.

# II
# The Terrified Meadows

The facets of the Holocaust are many, many,
and each drips obscurity. . . .

                              J. L. Kubiček

Geraldine Clinton Little

## Meditation after Hearing the Richard Yardumian Mass, "Come, Creator Spirit"

in memory of Daniel Varoujan,
Armenian poet killed by the Turks
Beginning in 1894, nearly 200,000 Armenians
were massacred within two years.

**Kyrie:**
Last week a showing of Holocaust films.  The familiar
structures of bone, some still walking, the snapped-out
"Heils" and hands, the irony of twisted crosses.

Last night, bones and heart bruised
by a sweep of notes, time on a page transformed
in air to moving statement moving the mind

to wind humming in fruit trees near a stable
by a hut.  A family breakfasts on cheeses,
olives, whispered talk: *Turkey, War.*

In the maydan a platform, a hangnoose holding
sun, a circle of birdsong, then a prisoner's
neck.  After the snap, limbs dance in air.

At night in the hut, words barely spoken: *An Armenian
Revolutionary; Turks are never hanged.*
The body dangled three days in an insect elegy.
                              *Lord, Have Mercy On Us.*

**Gloria:**
Laud, laud the mule's sure feet
bearing the burden of household goods.

Laud, laud the donkey's ears
wreathed with the chatter of fleeing families.

Laud, laud the receptive brooks
gathering in blood of slain children.

Laud, laud the earth's wide arms
mothering bodies scimitared still.

Laud, laud the way of a leaf
swaying, soundless, its simple knell.

*Glory Be to Thee, O Lord*

**Credo:**
The wrestling of a moth
from its cocoon

The green chanting of a root
through mud

The bright victory of geese
high in dark wind

The thrust of a forming grape
through vineskin

The rising of a star
out of storm

The spinning, kicking, writhing, wailing fight:
survival—

*I believe*

**Sanctus:**
Sultans' "holy wars." When is war
holy? Leaning over a lake I see
my face, falling away behind me, shadows
of other faces. How we ripple in winds
too twisted for any untangling to beginnings.

A film flicks on in my head. Once more, Holocaust.
*Armenian* holocaust long before Hitler, the same
fragile sculptures of bone, the same unheard
litany of lamentations. Wild strawberry
at my elbow. Blood for sipping. So sweet.

Look. In a whirlpool a twig turns, turns.
Hitler, about to invade Poland: "Who
still talks nowadays of the extermination
of the Armenians?" What force starts the whirlpool?
What hand can stop the swirl, rescue the twig?

Over me, the clarity of a budding bough. I see
how we must pray for fading
each into the other face, I
in you, you in me, holy. See
we are one in the current tumbling past pebbles, weeds.

*Holy, Holy, Holy, Lord God of Hosts*

**Agnus Dei:**
Bright on the peak of Ararat, snow
in the distance, splinters,
driftwood, remnants of hope.

I pluck a cup of flaming flower,
cup brimmed with spilled blood.
Yes. But blooming, blooming, blooming.

I think of how a single apricot
drops on the grass its unique shadow
while the mountain claps hands.

I think of one lamb's gentle feet
writing a poetry of passage
on meadows of butterfly and rue.

Above the whine of the slaughterer's weapon,
canticles ride winds
of final peace.

*O Lamb of God, O Lamb of God*

David Ignatow

# 1905

While my father walked through mud
in shoes borrowed from his sister,
all Kiev attended *Prince Igor* and cheered,
and while he worked in a cellar bindery
and slept on workbenches rats leapt over
at night, Dostoevsky's *White Nights*
and *Anna Karenina* were being read avidly
amid joy, tears and protests.  My father
was the silent one, walking through the streets
where the hot arguments went on about poverty
and guilt.  He walked, his work bundle under arm,
from cellar to monastery, to bind holy books
and volumes of the Russian classics,
and when they had had enough of classics
and needed blood, he fled,
for his blood was real to them; only he
had worked and starved.  All others were
but characters in a novel or a play,
bless Chekhov, Gogol and others for their genius,
but my father was the one who had not been
immortalized and made untouchable.
Only he was real in Russia's torment.
Only he stood for life.  All else was books,
and that was the torment.

William Pillin

# The Terrified Meadows

My nights are haunted by footsteps
on the wind.  The sky, the trees
are kisses of memory on my forehead.
I hear my uncle's laughter

on terrified meadows that threaten with firebrands,
on a highway that flowers with knives.

A long time ago, in a far land—
the sky immensely blue over sunflower steppes—
my young aunt walked like April
through the house.  I was in bed and singing.
Little swallow, she whispered
and kissed my forehead.  But my dark uncle
with white teeth wickedly flashing
laughed and threatened to bounce me
up and down till I begged for mercy.

A long time ago in a far land
they journeyed to see us
past the white elm trees,
past meadows of rye and barley
swept by a green moon-fire.
They journeyed to be with us
on the feast of the candles.
The wagoner cracked his whip, he urged his horses.
Why did the beasts rear up, why did they neigh?

Past the meadows that blossomed
with knives and axes,
past the terrified meadows
that threatened with firebrands,
to a little wooden house they journeyed,
to a little whitewashed room
where the yellow wax of death
blazed and sputtered.

On a wooden table
lay their young bodies.
The peasant axes
were pulled from their cleft skulls,

the bloody hair was washed
the stabs of Black Hundreds
artfully covered.

Aunt Dora lay on the table
as lovely as when her laughter
edged the winds with silver.
From a hundred cuts bleeding
Uncle Dusia lay there,
who gave a blow, praise God,
for each of his gashes.

Everything looked so clean
for the feast of the candles.
Everyone was so silent.
Only my grandmother's wails
were whirlwinds of terror,
only her screams
stabbed the blue vastness.

A long time ago.  In a far land.

Leo Hamalian

## Boghos Sarkissian, a Watchmaker of Karpet, Remembers the Turkish Atrocities of 1915

I
Doors ripped off houses,
Rifle butts smashing flesh.
Hamadiyeh cavalry
Driving men like cattle

Hands and feet nailed to horseshoes.
Jammed with women,
The church aflame.

Telegraph wires crackled
Wild sparking words erupted—
Unbelievable.
Inventions and lies,
Say Turkish officials.
One by one radios click off.
Silence.
Aydin Bitlis Malatya Kharpet Moush. . . .
We died there
Them and us.
Together we died.
No monument to mark
The massacre.
Only the archaeology of bones
Buried in the Syrian sand
And the little museum of Deir-e-Zhor
With the pyramid of skulls.
For me, after such death
There can be no other.

II
Children weave rugs in Aleppo
Broken branches, roots unwatered.
Later, for some the crescent,
For others, the red star.
For others, the ghettos of the New World
Where they may dream a reconstructed voice.
But neither busy fingers nor dreams
Can change the truth:
A whole generation lost, lost,
Gone forever, vanished.
They cannot speak
Not even through the tongues of these young.

III
Yet they have their kingdom
Where once our children roamed.
They, they abide.  They do have
Their steps, walks, doors, and shapes
Which unlock them.
They breathe the familiar dust,
Their destiny, their life.
We look to heaven for ours.
We see the past.
We confront it.
It consumes us.
It consumes us.


Irving Feldman

## Scene of a Summer Morning

Scene of a summer morning, my mother walking
to the butcher's, I led along.  Mountains
of feathers.  My breath storms them.  Angry feathers.
Handfuls.  The warm gut windings stinking.
Here, chickens!  Yankel, the bloody storeman,
daringly he takes the live animals
in vain.  Yankel, a life for a life!  Eternal
morning too young to go to school.  I get
a hollow horn to keep.  Feathers, come down!
Gone.  The world of one morning.  But somewhere,
sparkling, it circles a sunny point.
Incredible the mazes of that morning,
where my life in all the passages at once
is flowing, coursing, as in a body
that walked away, went.
                              Who writes these lines
I no longer know, but I believe him
to be a coward, that only one who escaped.
The best and bravest are back there still,

all my Ten Tribes wandering and singing
in the luminous streets of the morning.
Unsounded the horn! And silence shudders
in the center of the sunny point,
heart-stopping at dawn.
Enormous my thieving hand in the ancient sunlight
no longer mine. Littering through my fingers,
drifting, the Ten Tribes there, lost forever.

Hans Juergensen

## The Scar—August, 1934

The clearing ahead shimmered
In the wealth of August
When summer hangs heaviest
In the branches.
The trail's moss yielded
Underfoot; everywhere emerald
With a mere edge of rose.

This I recall seeing,
As my older friend and I
Walked those uneasy steps,
Aware of being stalked.
Boots crackled through decay
Hardened in Prussian seasons.
We dared not speak.

The Death's-Head men
Felt sinister:
Their holstered purpose moved

Sure, well trained . . .
My friend and I were Jews.

The clearing smelled
Of mown grass
Acid-sweet—
The afternoon had
Almost stopped.
My friend's head inclined—
Fate flecked his eyes.
I meant to run.

. . . a sharpness of flame
Spewed toward me.
One black arm jerked back
With the report I never heard:
It was my friend who died.

He lay face down.
I waited for my moment—
No longer quite afraid,
Or making thoughts.
The executioner approached
Unhurried—not unkindly—
Weapon slack, to warn:

> "Sag' nichts davon;     "You understand
> Sonst weisst du,          You must not
> Was passiert."            speak of this."

They left me there.
Proud backs and crunching heels
faded in the woods . . .

That's all I can remember
. . . over thirty years ago.
   —1966

Kirtland Snyder

# City Children at a Summer Camp.
## Slonim, 1936

The naked girls
lift their arms
above their heads.

Are they under
arrest?

No, they are showering
at the Jewish camp,
hands held up

deflecting drops of water.

Light makes of their arms
fine porcelain.

They could be Dresden
dolls
were they not
living children.

Heads bowed,
they stand on wooden
planks
on porcelain feet,
one girl up on tip-toe.

Water sparkles
in their hair,

shines on their fine
skin.

Porcelain dolls,
easily broken.

No fruit to come,
ever,
from their plump vulvas.

Van K. Brock

## The Hindenburg

for Sarah Swenson
This early showpiece of the Thousand
Year Reich used 850,000 skins of cattle
for hydrogen bags.

It is said that the night it burned
the thunder of panicking hooves
drowned the screams of passengers.

As far away as the buttes of Asia,
one old Siberian woman says that merely
the echo of their lowing still stirs
immense winds and whirlwinds.
                                        All the small
meadows of Europe remember their grazing,
a thousand days per beast, half-a-billion
days.  Cattle-cars and railway platforms—
from Malta to Finland—still shudder
at their foreshadowings.  Untold cobblers
recall the million seams glued and stitched
on screaming machines before its pockets
held enough hydrogen to kindle that conflagration.

The war on nature begun,
eventually, every country in Europe
and many in Africa and Asia were gutted:
millions died in bombings, in battle, at sea,
and we do not know how many millions in the fires,
filth, hunger, and madness of unimaginable slave pens.
But we know it was all only the outward rendering
of an ageless accumulation
sucked up from all over Christendom,
and the ruins run in and out of us all—
before, behind, and in each direction,
stretching for far more than a Thousand Years.

Kenneth Fearing

## AD

*Wanted:* Men:
Millions of men are *wanted at once* in a big new field;
*New, tremendous, thrilling, great.*
If you've ever been a figure in the chamber of horrors,
If you've ever escaped from a psychiatric ward,
If you thrill at the thought of throwing poison into wells,
have heavenly visions of people, by the thousands,
dying in flames—

*You are the very man we want*
We mean business and our business is *you*
*Wanted:* A race of brand-new men.

Apply: Middle Europe;
No skill needed;
No ambition required; no brains wanted and no character allowed;

*Take a permanent job in the coming profession*
Wages: *Death.*
—1938

Kirtland Snyder

## Selma . . . A Pot of Soup . . .
## A Bottle of Milk.  Lodz, 1938

Look
how Selma holds
the bottle
out to us.

Shall we sip
the milk,
so white!
so cold!

Look
how she holds
the soup
beneath her shawl,

keeping its warmth
for the walk home.

Can you smell it?  Barley!

Selma's smile
is all we need ·
to know her happiness,
the happiness
of all her family
who today will eat and drink.

But what of the swelling
sleeplessness
about her eyes,

the mark above her brow
that seems
a bullethole—

what of that?

David Zucker

## Entrance to the Old Cracow Ghetto

After a Photograph by Roman Vishniac, 1938

Symmetry of alleyways and courtyard
arches caught his harried eye, and mine.
Appia and Reinhardt dreamed the massive planes,
the rainslicked cobblestones.  Such shabby weight
must come from the newsreel's black and white country
of hunching men and eternal sleet.  I've
seen it, in dream sweat of a March alley
far from the ball field's green.
Now it reemerges, a monumental texture
in the ruined places, overcoats barely seen,
gray shapes part of the eye's structure.

Of course they knew their disaster, like Isaac,
but having little to resist with hugged
the soaring walls, ignored the upturned cart,
the crumbling steps.  No heroes or villains
on the unlikely scene.  All belongs to form.

A caged pigeon, left foreground, white enough
to call dove.  Three figures, another's leg,
indifferent through the crosshatched streaks.
In circular purpose they bend toward
railed upper walks.  A perfect photograph,
union of shadow and matter clicking into place.
One of the three climbs the stairs to a mumbled
prayer, a cold meal, a broken business.
Little wine or oil of the promised good land here,
the black and yellow Silesia just beyond his eye.
Yet all takes a foggy grace from light
soaring in pillars beyond the arches, upper right.
The dove preens, aims now into my sight.
One of the shadows certainly will turn
to spring the cage, plunging the bird
into a shining field.

Shelley Ehrlich

# Vilna 1938

On a Photograph by Roman Vishniac

A woman leans in
the entry, wooden
door open to
the cobblestone street.
She dresses all
in black.  Her face,
a distant star.  Below,
her neighbor flings
open shutters to
a cellar shop.  Carrots
glow near a burlap
sack of grain.  No one
else on the street.

These two are not
strangers.  My aunts
lived lives like these.
If I were to cross
the cobblestones, step
over the threshold,
where would the darkness
lead?

# III
# Crystal Night

The Holocaust is a sacred realm. One cannot enter this realm without realizing that only those who were there can know. But the outsider can come close to the gates.

Elie Wiesel

Denise Levertov

## *from* During the Eichmann Trial

*iii Crystal Night*
From blacked-out streets
      (wide avenues swept by curfew,
       alleyways, veins
        of dark within dark)

from houses whose walls
       had for a long time known
the tense stretch of skin over bone
as their brick or stone listened—

    The scream!
The awaited scream rises,
the shattering
of glass and the cracking
of bone

a polar tumult as when
black ice booms, knives
of ice and glass
splitting and splintering the silence into
innumerable screaming needles of
yes, now it is upon us, the jackboots
are running in spurts of
sudden blood-light through the
broken temples

the veils
are rent in twain
terror has a white sound
every scream
of fear is a white needle freezing the eyes
the floodlights of their trucks throw
jets of white, their shouts
cleave the wholeness of darkness into
sectors of transparent white-clouded pantomime

where all that was awaited
is happening, it is Crystal Night
it is Crystal Night
these spikes which are not
pitched in the range of common hearing
whistle through time

smashing the windows of sleep and dream
smashing the windows of history
a whiteness scattering
in hailstones
each a mirror
for man's eyes

Charles Fishman

## Weltanschauung

Where is the lightning to lick you
with its tongue? Where is the frenzy
with which you should be inoculated?
                                    Nietzsche

The *Sieg! Heil!* Victory! Salvation!
jackboots out the last flame of reason.

The lightning comes later: the blazing
arms of the sun twisted clockwise
toward pain, glittering on the dial:
little flares—each with its face,
its annihilation.

                    *

You refused to believe the bearded
faces, eyes that had seen into the nerve-
ends of civilization, had seen Kafka

shrivel in that holocaust, Einstein
reduced to a small cupful of ash.

Blond hair curled in the bookish heat.
Blue eyes cheered to see Marx char.
Freud blistered and blackened and cracked
like a burnt up child.

*

In the *shtetls* chess tables filled
with cooked fish. Prayer shawls grumbled
with fire in the wooden *shuls*. *Kristallnacht*
knocked the teeth from your skulls.

The vault clicked shut and Churchill
sipped his tea. You wore the star
and time would make you free.

*

Death wagons gouged through the ghetto
like a rich man's purse.

Each Yid was corpse and hearse.

*

You were artisans, poets, actors, teachers,
coopers, cut-throats, dreamers, debaters.

You loved, hated, feared death, feared failure.
You lied to yourselves, to God, to each other.

You had nowhere to go, yet a train waited.

*

No food. No water. No air.
Wheels whacked against your feet
like rifle butts.

When they unbolted the car you stared
through the Butcher's door.

\*

*Himmelstrasse:* the last tick of the clock.

And you moaned, and you cried out.
And you went singing, and you choked
on courage.

And God was there, and there was nothing.

\*

In winter, ashes from the crematoria
were spread like a gray smudge
over the frozen roads.

Elaine Terranova

# 1939

A woman takes a small girl's hand.
The leaves pull away and fall,
separate, stiff with color.
Out of the smoky, distant forest
the train brings its load of passengers,
the passengers, their burdens.
A horse nuzzles the fence of every field,
at peace within its boundaries.
There is the woman's beautiful fair hair,
a certainty that's braided into it.

At the crossing, the stationmaster's wife
aligns the bars
of any misdirected night.
A girl is walking by her mother's side.
She knows from fairy tales
the shape that evil takes—
stretched in shadow, giants, witches,
wolves—the weight of poisoned fruit,
the irrevocable claim of fire.

The hill twists and flattens.
The little girl tugs at the funny hooks
of weeds like fingers pointing down,
down.  She hears the snap of branches
underfoot, the whistling stalks
that pull the air into
their tubular, dry bodies.  Sometimes
in the wind the trees reach up
on tip-toe to the sky like tall, lost girls.

These are the easy days.  Heaven
comes to meet the earth
in such a bountiful accord.  The sun
so neat it pulls the water taut
until the river shines.  The two walk on.
They walk into the clouds, an ample white,
into a sky that has already forgotten them.

Jeffrey A. Z. Zable

## To the End

I remember the guns
the barbed wire
the little children without eyes
their bodies like sacks of dust
waiting to be thrown into fire

headless birds
soaring through smoke
an ocean of blood
waves crashing onto shore
rootless trees
devoured by wind
leaves jabbed into the earth:

*This the beginning!*


Emily Borenstein

## The Shoah
### (Whirlwind—Holocaust)

Under an ominous sky trees uprooted themselves.
Dead branches whizzed by.

An old woman fell forward blood dripping from
her forehead.

Great oaks bent down.  They prayed like willows.
Their leaves streamed forward all in one direction.

Then everything fell on top of everything else.
The trees fell crown first.

The bark exploded.  The trees screamed.
They split apart.

On the edge of town trees fell on their knees
reciting the *Hineni.*

The wind blasted the trees.
It whipped, pounded, stripped them of leaves.

It trumpeted like a shofar:
*TEKIAH! SHEBARIM! TERUAH! TEKIAH!*

Houses fell, mangled and twisted, under a sky
clenched like a blackened fist.

In a demolished synagogue a voice cried out,
"Ovenu Malkenu!"

It was the voice of my mother praying for redemption,
chanting the *Yaahleh* and the *Shema Kolenu!*

It was life rising in outbursts into meaning
stumbling over the roots of trees.

It was my mother on her knees chanting the last
*Shema Yisroel* of the dying.

Elaine Mott

## The Last Visa for Palestine

for my cousin, Gitl Frost,
who did not survive the Warsaw ghetto

For a moment I saw my lover at the train station,
the yellow star blazing up
on the dark fabric of his jacket.
They were moving us along, children and old people,
pushing us into the train like cattle. The leaves
on the trees were opening out of winter.
Windflowers blown to the ground
were spreading a pale carpet under our feet.
My lover looked at me for the last time,

doors closing between us, and in the darkness
the answer in my eyes was lost.

Even over the smell of death
I can smell the green fields we are passing through,
near, yet further from me than the primal, locked bones
of my mother's pelvis, or the river of her
that I slid out of into the light.
In one green field the clouds were high and racing.
We ate apples and bread and wine,
and I let my lover's hand move under my dress,
white linen like a bride's.
The grass was our first bed
on which we dreamed our children, three small ghosts
swimming into the sun.
In a mirror I saw our breath mingle.
The mirrors have flown to the sky. The rivers
have carried away our breath.

Carole Glasser Langille

## Babi Yar

for Anatoly Kuznetsov

They say the woman with the black hair
shivered as she turned; the soldier
called out to her in German, told her to wait,
while others lined the front of the ditch, stripped off their clothes.
Body after body, limb upon limb.
That by the time he reached the woman
(a matter of minutes)
her hair had turned completely white
and when she was finally shot

the bullets only wounded her
and she was buried like that, still breathing, an old lady,
not quite twenty.

This happened thirty-nine years ago
and every woman who knows about her
has gone to sleep, one time or another,
hugging her shadow.

What substance do we have?

Gizela Spunberg

## Memories of December

Like a very fine, white dust snow was falling
that memorable December night, when we were saying "Good-bye."
We walked the desecrated, violated streets
of our conquered city and knew
that we were parting forever maybe.
I held you under arm, pressed to your shaking body.
In the soft lights of the city lamps I saw your eyelids trembling,
tears were running down your cheeks.
You stopped, turned facing me and said:
"So you are leaving me, that I cannot believe!"
"I must go, my destiny is calling me, Mother!"
And destiny it was—it led me towards life and
yours brought you to your untimely death.
It did not seem that way then—
yours was the safe road, mine the dangerous one.

We returned home, sat holding hands.
You stroked my head, I kissed you on the cheek.
The softness, the feel of it is still on my lips.

Your face is before my eyes, the straight chiseled nose
the generous chin.  I have your mouth and
hairline, exactly to the thinnest angle.

Did I fail you?  Did I betray you by my absence?
Would I have been of any help?
There is so much to regret, so much to be sorry for.
You have never been in my home—
I have never cooked a meal for you—
And what is most regrettable, you never saw him,
your grandson, and he never knew you.
There is so much of you in him in looks and traits.
That happiness you deserved—it was torn away from you.

When again in December, four years after we parted,
they, the cold-blooded killers, took you
for your last walk, you left a message, a legacy:
"Tell my daughters, I was not afraid. . . ."

Ruth Whitman

## The Death Ship

*The Struma.*
It lay in the harbor at Istanbul
without food or coal.

Don't let it land,
said the Ambassador.

Jews are enemy aliens,
said the British.
Tow them out to the Black Sea,

send them to Crete, Mauritius,
to Rumania, Germany, Jamaica,
but don't let them come to Palestine.

That was December 1941.

Safe in my kibbutz at Sdot Yam
(meadows of the sea),
                        I looked
at the peacock-blue Mediterranean
and cried, let them come,
we have room.

No, said Lord Moyne,
if one ship comes
they'll all want to come.

Let the children come.

Children?
What will we do with children?

The hold was airless.
Sickness, filth,
layers of excrement, vomit.
The ship could not sail.
The ship could not stay.
No land would take them.

In February the ship exploded
outside the harbor at Istanbul.
Eight hundred lives flew up,
their rags, arms, legs, hopes,
falling like rain.

One was saved.
He was allowed to enter
Palestine.

Yala Korwin

## Passover Night 1942

not a crumb of leavened
or unleavened bread
and no manna fell

no water sprang out
of the bunker's wall
the last potato was gone

we sat and munched
chunks of potato-peel
more bitter than herbs

we didn't dare to sing
and open the door
for Elijah

we huddled and prayed
while pillars of clouds
massed above our heads

and pillars of fire
loomed like blazing traps


Maurya Simon

## Letter to Vienna from Paris, 1942

Grandmother,
your face is dangerous,
is a chameleon blushing
the color of red onions.

You missed the last exodus:
it's obvious your teeth
won't last.

Look at the world's compass.
The needle's nose trembles.
Here, children cut yellow stars
from old scarves, their topaz
eyes turn brass and tarnish.

Grandfather,
they left your white dish
dark with foreboding.
You're too cold to carry fire:
all your weapons sold
for fake diplomas.

The iron wings stretch out
across France, Poland, Russia.
The thin hand of each man
is clasped to fodder.

Carol Ganzer

**Taking Leave**

When they came
for us, it was
the middle of the
night, their sirens
wailing. How carefully
we had covered the
windows with tar-
paper so our shadows
would never lean
out. On the floor
where we left them—

open books, the list
of friends who
vanished.  *You were
the last to leave . . .*

We slept hundreds
of miles away, some-
where close to the
border, our camp
smoking in a haze—
blue of ash, blue
of heaven, thick
taste of chalk on
our teeth.  All
night the cries of
prisoners kept coming
back, long after
their breath had
lifted the leaves
and whirled them
in damp air.  We
never knew the
name of the place,
later pinpointed
on a map by one
side or the other.
*Your eyes, so round,
the brown flecks on
your cheek, mother,
your hand waving us
into the street . . .*

Inge Auerbacher

# I Am a Star

Only "special" children wear a star,
I am noticed from near and far.
They have placed a mark over my heart,
I'll wear it proudly from the start.

A star's a reward, so I've been told,
This custom passed on from days of old.
I know all that the star is revealing,
But, I'll try to have a better feeling.

*I am a star!*

Most people are in such a rage,
History has turned a new page.
Why do the "others" taunt me?
I don't owe them an apology.

I know my lessons well,
In my class I excel.
Why does everyone stare?
I'll pretend not to care.

*I am a star!*

Papa told me to avoid trouble,
Come home from school on the double.
To me the star's yellow is gold,
I'll try not to act so bold.

I stand tall and proud,
My voice shouts in silence loud:
"I am a real person still,
No-one can break my spirit or will!"

*I am a star!*

Pearl B. Sheridan

## Little Lamb

Stars?
There are no yellow stars
In the Lord God's heavens.
Someone must be mistaken.

One star of the promise to Abraham
Is sewn over the heart of a small child.

Where are you going, little Isaac?
Where are you going, little lamb?

The angel sent to stop
The sacrificial knife
Has been arrested at the umschlagplatz,
Has been deported as an undesirable,

Has been selected for special flight
Up the chimney.
Some say he volunteered.

Where are you going, little Isaac?
Where are you going, little lamb?

Helen Degan Cohen

## In Hiding

Poem about the many days in hiding
with a Catholic woman in a countryside
beside a place called War.

Once, in hiding, we went open-
riding in a lenient sleigh
buoyant on the lack of sound and motion

full-away from war
sleepweaving through a back country
my white-haired "lady saint" and I
our frozen faces craning
out of homespun colors:
one soft hour the sound of bells was all.
We were missed by the storm
in its silent eye:
mounds of forest meandered past us
and nearer, more intricate intrusions
fled like calendars behind
their knowledge of our presence—
nature had to wait, we folded leaves
to dream in our escape, the sleigh
was like a god-crib carried by
some fabled beast across her snowy haven
and it hazed the deep green to a waiting green
where animals we knew of kindly
slept unblessed. Our war went still
and deep, around the weightless sleigh.
And now, in a trembling present,
tense with the lunacy of peace
such as it is—a masquerade in blooming
shades of sacrifice, of comfort jaws
and love-drops like the red of war—
I crane my turtle-head for frozen air,
then burrowing
into the soft escape, the easy ride,
I hear, beside the child I was,
those solitary bells of joy
pulling her lonely sleigh.

Gregory Orfalea

## The Poacher

He stole us out of our lives
tonight, the beret black as an olive
hopping on his head like a price.
And we are glad his slate
hangs over our heads
that the mutton blisters
on the spit
for it is cold and wet tonight.
But forty years ago
this little hotel owner
stole sheep
and hid them in caves
while the fire forked
to warm his hands
and snapped the water
on the shivering wool.
He drank by animal light
smelling all the grassy oils
of the Pyrenees.
If any sheep caught fire
he cursed and ate it himself.
They would butt their horns
in the dark when feet
came snooping
and he could pray
someone was in need
of a ram.  When the war started,
his caves fissured with rain.
He knew them all, and all
the travesty of the law,
the chance to live by the skin
of the teeth,
and when they began their long trek
from Danzig to Copenhagen
to Paris to Pau, his ears picked up.
He smelled singed flesh

and the screams
of the flock of innocents
and they bled for him
they clawed at his door
till he hid them away
in the sockets of his heart
while the rain dropped
like liquid slate and kissed
their wounds in the caves.
Long past sight
he took no one to Spain
who didn't know what it means
to die in the eyes of another.

Arlene Maass

## Opa the Watchmaker

Casper ten Boom's crime: "I will open my door
to any man in need who knocks."

Don't tell me the signs of the sky are against my back
and the rouge of the evening bears down on the mind's watchworks.
All of our lives now
are but rationed bones, like slivers of dice,
like blue bread rancid.
Life is in the palm of machinists.

He made me stalwart, but like Jacob the Patriarch
I move slower, leaning on the Maker who watches all,
leaning on the Maker for what I can't comprehend,
leaning on the Maker who personifies all wisdom
but I can't ask why this.

A babe arrives, smuggled into our home, unaware
that it is poor timing to be born Jewish in civilized Europe.
A soft spot crowns his head that a lifetime is meant to fill.
And I, an old man with hoarfrost beard tumbling,

51

caress the baby that must be wise and know not to cry!
I grasp the brass-bound Book
a watchmaker seeking precision
a watchmaker who looks to the One who created time
but is not bound to the brass moments—like the babe, like me.
Wisdom for understanding when there is no justice in the streets,
strength to love when there is no bread—
these are my requests clenched in the palms of the numbered days.
Love is numbing,
fields are barren even of turnips and squirrels,
bread is gold, worshipped in dug-out root cellars
and love goes hiding in the forests
like wild herbs against the wind
like a prophet's words rustling the reeds.
Charity is regarded as madness, or the play of fools.

I'm empty-handed now—
even the brass-bound Book is left behind
in our house guarded by the watchmen of the Third Reich.
They liked our watches, but not us.
Thrown like sandbags in a cart, we leave Haarlem's market.
I carry nothing but what is buried in my heart—
how psalms are burnished in my eyes when I dare close them.
How resonant the words of King David
in the private conclaves of an old man's head!
How comforting the words of Jesus
to a Dutchman's burning heart.

They kept shoes, yanked gold from corpses,
burnt scrolls and flesh.
But they could not enter the hiding place
where the root of Jesse, the bruised reed, dwells.
No, they could not approach Moriah.

So many bones in this field of clay,
like a camp storeroom full of eyeglasses to the ceiling
from eyes that see the other side of time.

George Bogin

# Pitchipoi

So it was that through late July and August [1942], four thousand Jewish
children, already orphans, some only a few months old and none above
the age of twelve, were accumulated at Drancy [a concentration camp
outside Paris]. Georges Wellers . . . witnessed the scene. 'They were
dumped from buses in the middle of the courtyard, as though they were
tiny beasts . . . the majority of the gendarmes did not hide sincere emotions at
such a sight, nor their disgust at the work they were made to do.'
Nonetheless, not one gendarme refused to carry out the assignment. Many
children were too young to know their names and were entered as
question marks on the train lists. They were in a constant state of panic;
they were often screaming. Nobody could comfort them, nobody could
tell them what their destination was, and they invented among themselves
a name for the fearful place for which they were bound: 'Pitchipoi'. The
word lingered in Drancy long after the children had been killed in Auschwitz.

David Pryce-Jones
*Paris in the Third Reich*
*A History of the German Occupation, 1940–1944*

After such words
what further words?
The poem should stand as tall as the Eiffel Tower
and as wide as the city of light
and deep as the guilt of the French police.
The words must flame and smoke
like all the hells on earth,
the only hells we travel.
And fabulous should be the guilt
of a single gendarme
and fabulous the innocence
of the child plucked from its parents—
guilt perhaps like a dragon in the viscera,
innocence like a raindrop on a leaf.
And Pitchipoi? Pitchipoi?
Should the poet enter the imagination
of the child boarding the freight car?
But the least cannibal in New Guinea
has seen Pitchipoi.
And the poet, will he be this sad American

who is sinking under the weight
of the guilt that has been
and the terror to come?
Let these notes be incinerated
and the ashes scattered from the Arc de Triomphe
for the poem died in the epigraph.
Pitchipoi.


Yala Korwin

## The Little Boy with His Hands Up

Your open palms raised in the air
like two white doves
frame your meager face,
your face contorted with fear,
grown old with knowledge beyond your years.
Not yet ten.  Eight?  Seven?
Not yet compelled to mark
with a blue star on white badge
your Jewishness.

No need to brand the very young.
They will meekly follow their mothers.

You are standing apart
against the flock of women and their brood
with blank, resigned stares.
All the torments of this harassed crowd
are written on your face.
In your dark eyes—a vision of horror.
You have seen Death already

on the ghetto streets, haven't you?
Do you recognize it in the emblems
of the SS-man facing you with his camera?

Like a lost lamb you are standing
apart and forlorn beholding your own fate.

Where is your mother, little boy?
Is she the woman glancing over her shoulder
at the gunmen by the bunker's entrance?
Is it she who lovingly, though in haste,
buttoned your coat, straightened your cap,
pulled up your socks?
Is it her dreams of you, her dreams
of a future Einstein, a Spinoza,
another Heine, or Halevy
they will murder soon?
Or are you orphaned already?
But, even if you still have a mother,
she won't be allowed to comfort you
in her arms.
Her tired arms loaded with useless bundles
must remain up in submission.

Alone you will march
among other lonely wretches
toward your martyrdom.

Your image will remain with us
and grow and grow
to immense proportions,
to haunt the callous world,
to accuse it, with ever stronger voice,
in the name of the million youngsters
who lie, pitiful rag-dolls,
their eyes forever closed.

Charles Reznikoff

## *from* Massacres

2

Her father had a shop for selling leather
and was one of the notables in a Polish Jewish community
when the Germans entered.
They put their horses into the synagogue and turned it into a stable.
On a Saturday afternoon, peasants from neighboring villages
came to tell the Jews of the town
that the Germans were killing Jews: they should run away and hide.
But the rabbi and other elders of the town
thought running away useless:
besides, they thought the Germans might take a few of the young men to
    work for them
but that no one would be killed.

The next day, before sunrise, a Jew from a neighboring village
ran into the town shouting:
"Jews, run for your lives!
The Germans are out to kill us."
and the townspeople saw the Germans coming in.

The young woman's grandfather said, "Run and hide, children, but I will
    stay:
they will do no harm to me."
Those who could hid in a neighboring forest.
During the day they heard shooting—
single shots and cries;
but towards evening they thought the Germans would be leaving the town
and, sure enough, peasants from the neighborhood met them
and said: "You can go back now.
The Germans killed everybody left behind."

When the Jews came back,
they found that the Germans had rounded up about one hundred and
    fifty Jews,

including the rabbi and other notables.
They told the rabbi to take his prayer shawl along—
the other Jews had been gathered in the center of the town—
and he was told to put on his prayer shawl
and sing and dance. He would not
and was beaten up. And so were the other Jews.
Then they were driven to the cemetery.
Here a shallow grave had been dug for them.
They were told to lie down in fours
and were shot. But her father remained behind in the town—alive:
he had said he was cutting the leather in his shop for shoes
and was registered as a shoemaker.

Later, the Germans went into the town to take whatever they could find;
the place was swarming with Germans—four or five to every Jew.
Many were put upon a large truck;
those who could not climb on themselves
were thrown on; and those for whom there was no room on the truck
were ordered to run after it.
All the Jews were counted and the Germans searched for every missing
     person on their list.
The young woman was among those who ran,
her little daughter in her arms.
There were those, too, who had two or three children
and held them in their arms as they ran after the truck.
Those who fell were shot—right where they fell.
When the young woman reached the truck,
all who had been on it were down and undressed and lined up;
the rest of her family among them.
There was a small hill there and at the foot of the hill a dugout.
The Jews were ordered to stand on top of the hill
and four S. S. men shot them—killed each separately.
When she reached the top of the hill and looked down
she saw three or four rows of the dead already on the ground.
Some of the young people tried to run
but were caught at once

and shot right there.
Children were taking leave of their parents;
but her little daughter said to her,
"Mother, why are we waiting?  Let us run!"

Her father did not want to take off all of his clothes
and stood in his underwear.
His children begged him to take it off
but he would not and was beaten.
Then the Germans tore off his underwear
and he was shot.
They shot her mother, too,
and her father's mother—
she was eighty years old
and held two children in her arms;
and they shot her father's sister;
she also had babies in her arms
and was shot on the spot.
Her younger sister went up to one of the Germans—
with another girl, one of her sister's friends—
and they asked to be spared,
standing there naked before him.
The German looked into their eyes
and shot them both—her sister and the young friend;
they fell
embracing each other.

The German who had shot her younger sister
turned to her
and asked, "Whom shall I shoot first?"
She was holding her daughter in her arms and did not answer.
She felt him take the child from her;
the child cried out and was shot.
Then he aimed at her: took hold of her hair
and turned her head around.
She remained standing and heard a shot
but kept on standing.  He turned her head around again

and shot her;
and she fell into the dugout
among the bodies.

Suddenly she felt that she was choking;
bodies had fallen all over her.
She tried to find air to breathe
and began climbing towards the top of the dugout,
and felt people pulling at her
and biting at her legs.
At last she came to the top.
Bodies were lying everywhere
but not all of them dead:
dying, but not dead;
and children were crying, "Mama! Papa!"
She tried to stand up but could not.

The Germans were gone.
She was naked,
covered with blood and dirty with the excrement of those in the dugout,
and found that she had been shot in the back of the head.
Blood was spurting from the dugout
in many places;
and she heard the cries and screams of those in it still alive.
She began to search among the dead for her little girl
and kept calling her name;
trying to join the dead,
and crying out to her dead mother and father,
"Why didn't they kill me, too?"

She was there all night.
Suddenly she saw Germans on horseback
and sat down in a field
and heard them order all the corpses heaped together;
and the bodies—many who had been shot but were still alive—
were heaped together with shovels.

Children were running about.
The Germans caught the children
and shot them, too;

but did not come near her. And left again
and with them the peasants from around the place—
who had to help—
and the machine-guns and trucks were taken away.

She remained in the field, stretched out.
Shepherds began driving their flocks into the field;
and threw stones at her,
thinking her dead or mad.
Afterwards, a passing farmer saw her,
fed her
and helped her join Jews in the forest nearby.

## *from* Mass Graves

3
In the morning the Jews were lined up by an officer
and the officer told them:
You are Jews, unworthy of life,
but are now supposed to work."
They were put upon trucks
and taken away to a forest
and set to digging.
After two or three spadefuls of earth,
the spade of one hit something hard,
and he saw that it was the head of a human being.
There was also a bad smell all around.
He stopped digging
and the officer in charge came towards him shouting:
"Why did you stop?
Didn't you know there are bodies buried here?"
He had opened a mass grave.

There were about ten thousand dead in that grave.
And after they had dug up the bodies
they were told to burn them.
Planks had been brought and beams—long and heavy.

The Germans also brought a grinding machine to grind the bones
and the ground bones would be sieved
for the gold fillings of teeth.
The dust of the bones would then be spread over the fields,
and the smell was dreadful.

They kept on working three months
opening mass graves;
and opened eight or nine.
In one those digging saw a boy of two or three,
lying on his mother's body.
He had little white shoes on
and a little white jacket,
and his face was pressed against his mother's.

One grave would remain open for new corpses
coming all the time;
a truck would bring bodies, still warm,
to be thrown into the grave—
naked as Adam and Eve;
Jewish men, many of them bearded, and Jewish women and children.
The graves they had opened would be refilled with earth
and they had to plant grass all over them;
as for the dead—
a thousand bodies would be put on a pyre;
and there were two pyres of bodies burning all the time.

Anthony Hecht

## "More Light! More Light!"

Composed in the Tower before his execution
These moving verses, and being brought at that time
Painfully to the stake, submitted, declaring thus:
"I implore my God to witness that I have made no crime."

Nor was he forsaken of courage, but the death was horrible,
The sack of gunpowder failing to ignite.
His legs were blistered sticks on which the black sap
Bubbled and burst as he howled for the Kindly Light.

And that was but one, and by no means one of the worst;
Permitted at least his pitiful dignity;
And such as were by made prayers in the name of Christ,
That shall judge all men, for his soul's tranquillity.

We move now to outside a German wood.
Three men are there commanded to dig a hole
In which the two Jews are ordered to lie down
And be buried alive by the third, who is a Pole.

Not light from the shrine at Weimar beyond the hill
Nor light from heaven appeared.  But he did refuse.
A Luger settled back deeply in its glove.
He was ordered to change places with the Jews.

Much casual death had drained away their souls.
The thick dirt mounted toward the quivering chin.
When only the head was exposed the order came
To dig him out again and to get back in.

No light, no light in the blue Polish eye.
When he finished a riding boot packed down the earth.
The Luger hovered lightly in its glove.
He was shot in the belly and in three hours bled to death.

No prayers or incense rose up in those hours
Which grew to be years, and every day came mute
Ghosts from the ovens, sifting through crisp air,
And settled upon his eyes in a black soot.

Emily Borenstein

## The Excavator

The engine of the excavator rumbles
and pants
clawing graves out of the sand
biting the sand
plunging its steel arm into the sand
digging with its hand
scraping up sand
readying the sand while waiting for
columns of stooping prisoners
to fall dead in the sand
the cold yellow sand.
Oh! The grinding of metal on sand.
Oh, the excavator!
May it smash its hand!
May it fall apart!
May it fall into quicksand!

R. M. Cooper

## Rebecca 1942

We stole a glass and hung the canopy
Between two bunks.
Life is ancient beauty
Still in this.
The bride and groom are happy,
The ceremony small,
Every duty properly done.
We managed a rabbi, the ring,
Several cakes, a cantor,
Three bars of Swiss chocolate, one harmonica—
By arrangement with the other blocks,
Two jars of marmalade
And a set of lookouts.

In the solitude of witnesses,
Here stand the consecration of rags and doubts,
The jesters, matchmakers, lovers—
Near enough solemnity to say, "Behold Thou,"
"Blessed Thou," "as the stars,"
And "grow old."

Alfred Van Loen

## Auschwitz #6

Tortured, sick, and hungry,
yet as long as there was the sun
and the moon at nights feelings
were alive
and even in this place of horror
and death
people hoped, prayed, and loved.

A man found a woman he had known
years ago when there was food,
when there was peace and life,
and love blossomed for each other.

Men and women were separated
and looking was punished
with burned out eyes
and talking meant a slashed tongue.
But love knows no fear
and they were surprised
in each other's arms.

Endless tortures . . .

The woman was raped, the man forced
to watch,
and she was sentenced as a prostitute

to burn at the stake he
had to build
and to which he had to put the fire.

Refusing, he was tied
to the same stake
and the flames leaped with the laughter
of the Nazis.

John Z. Guzlowski

## Cattle Train to Magdeburg

She still remembers

The long train to Magdeburg
the box cars
bleached gray
by Baltic winters

the rivers and the cities
she had never seen before
and would never see again:
the sacred Vistula
the smoke haunted ruins of Warsaw
the Warta, where horse flesh
met steel and fell

The leather fists
of pale boys
boys her own age
perhaps seventeen
perhaps nineteen
but different
convinced of their godhood
by the cross they wore

different from the one
she knew in Lvov

The long twilight journey
to Magdeburg—
four days that became six years
six years that became forty

And always a train of box cars
bleached to Baltic gray

Ephim Fogel

## Shipment to Maidanek

Arrived from scattered cities, several lands,
intact from sea land, mountain land, and plain.
Item: six surgeons, slightly mangled hands.
Item: three poets, hopelessly insane.

Item: a Russian mother and her child,
the former with five gold teeth and usable shoes
the latter with seven dresses, peasant-styled.

Item: another hundred thousand Jews.

Item: a crippled Czech with a handmade crutch.
Item: a Spaniard with a subversive laugh;
seventeen dozen Danes, nine gross of Dutch.

Total: precisely a million and a half.

They are sorted and marked—the method is up to you.
The books must be balanced, the disposition stated.
Take care that all accounts are neat and true.

Make sure that they are thoroughly cremated.

Frieda Singer

## Saving the Children

to Gizelle Hersh

They had taken away
her hair
her shoes
her name a bluish numeral
under the skin
her gender denied
in a sea of men
yet something of her
as she was remained.

In the barracks
where work makes one free
she learned to stand
motionless from five to ten
for Zeile Appell
camouflaging her skin where
blemishes meant selection to the left,
urging her sisters
who refused
the moldy soup
the sawdust bread
that to eat was to resist
to eat, even to eat
the pain.

To eat, even when
the throat gagged
from the disinfecting stench;

to eat, even with
swollen ears
and frozen feet
in cubicles too narrow

to stand or sleep
where one worn blanket
was assigned to cover ten;

to swallow
even the teeth marks
of the snarling kapo guard
doubling back upon them
the injuries from above.

To remember always
that first day
when a flick of the wrist
sent her to the right
her parents to the left.

*Mother, where are you,*
twelve year old Katya would scream
night after night.
At sixteen, more adult than child,
she had promised
to care for the children
the promise that kept her
and them alive.

Stanley Cooperman

## The Children of Terezin

They smelled like grandfathers,
those children,
like *zaydeh* who died
in Prague one evening,
dignified
with candles . . .
they smelled of old thighs,
old laws, and wine
turned black as graves.

From the fragile web
of their midnight dawn
they learned
to fashion quills,
dipping the tips of their bones
into the sweet
liquid
of many dreams . . .
making small tracks
on paper
like winter birds.

They sang of butterflies
and mice,
jellied quince, fleas,
cats with yellow
fur, and blossoms
forever as the sun;
they accepted
the coloring-book of the world,
knowing only that
landscapes are bright,
that trees
have many arms,
and that corpses are green
as grass.

Inge Auerbacher

## Something to Remember Me By

He was a stranger; we had never met.
He wanted me to recall him, not to forget.

He handed me a box filled with treasure
And hoped it would give me much pleasure.
Odds and ends up to the brim,

For dreams of any child's whim.
      "Something to remember me by!"

I was startled and full of surprise,
A rainbow of color before my eyes.
Things made of threads attached to eternity,
Knitted by loving hands without identity.

His eyes looked hopeless; in a daze,
He walked restless, as if in a maze.
He was a humble man—without fame,
Staying unknown—never stating his name.
      "Something to remember me by!"

He rode away on the death train,
filled with desperation and pain.
He rests with the ashes in sleep,
His memory I will forever keep.

The little girl, now fully grown,
Remembers him, though still unknown.
To this day his words sound loud and clear,
His presence assured from year to year.
      "Something to remember me by!"

Martin Steingesser

## The Three

for Miroslav Kosek, Hanus Löwy & one Bachner,
three children who died in German camps.

Koleba, you signed your dreams,
   raids over the wall
               for green meadow smell
and the warm hum of bees.
You craved these, not like sweets,
   but the way fawns forage snow for shoots

and so under one name
                    wrote other lives, brilliant as air
burning like a star
               over Terezin, over Prague.
And your voices—such thin arms!
                  straws across the Holocaust,
       reeds weaving into light—
under this sign, your star
       pulses
           Ko.le.ba
                pulses
bright yellow, a burr
            —your star in the throat of Death


Michael Blumenthal

## Juliek's Violin

Was it not dangerous, to allow your vigilance to fail, even for a moment,
when any minute death could pounce upon you? I was thinking of this
when I heard the sound of a violin, in this dark shed, where the dead
were heaped on the living. What madman could be playing the violin
here, at the brink of his own grave? It must have been Juliek. . . . The
whole of his life was gliding on the strings—his lost hopes, his charred
past, his extinguished future. He played as he would never play again.
                   Elie Wiesel, *Night*
Ahnest Du den Schöpfer, Welt? (World, do you feel the Maker near?)
              Friedrich Schiller, "Ode to Joy"

In the dank halls of Buchenwald,
a man is playing his life.

It is only a fragment from Beethoven—
soft, melodic, ephemeral as the sleep
of butterflies, or the nightmares of
an infant, but tonight it is his life.

In one hand, he holds the instrument,
resonant with potential. In the other,
the fate of the instrument: hairs
of a young horse strung between wood.

Each note is a flicker of the lamp of his life,
and his father, an old conductor, listens
with the rapt attention of someone who knows
the finality of all moments, the power of music.

The bow glides over the strings, at first,
with the grace of a young girl brushing her hair.

Then, suddenly, Juliek leans forward
on his low stool. His knees quiver,
and the damp chamber fills with a voice
like the voice of a nightingale.

Outside, the last sliver of light weaves
through the fence. A blackbird preens
its feathers on the lawn, as if to the music,
and a young child watches from the yard,
naked and questioning.

But, like Schiller crying out—
*Ahnest Du den Schöpfer, Welt?*,
Juliek plays on.

And the children,
as if in answer,
burn.

R. M. Cooper

## Eli 1943

One of the visiting dignitaries
Slips film into his Leica and starts to tell
A little joke about Wehrmacht fairies
And the twenty-minute brothel bell.
Everybody laughs together
As they walk past shaved and naked women
In line to be gassed.
The commandant leads the way himself,
Pausing to comment on the fine points
Of "special treatment."
He gives the tour technical balance.
The women are gassed,
Removed, searched, burned.
The officers wonder
If there's still enough daylight for one last
Picture: leaning slightly forward, at ease,
Smiling—a group-shot standing near some trees.

Laura Kasischke

## For Malka Who Lived Three Days Dying

Through long days and nights, he went
from one Jewish house to another, telling
the story of Malka.
                    Elie Wiesel, *Night*

Half the lamp is lit tonight.
A dream passes your face like
a pale bird resting
on an electric wire. I am afraid
to wake you to the great
stillness of me. The long swim
I cannot make.

*

There among the other bodies
she took three days to die.
Tell me, in your dreams,
does she pray?
Slow and silent
Hebrew syllables sung
and saved
for the Holy Land.

*

Half the lamp lit and I run
through the water of your dreams,
my arms full of living children,
daughters who will live
to sing to your sleep, *It
cannot happen here.*

A blessing rests on the mountain.
The promise of something strong.

*

A woman I love
presses my hands, tells me
how it is to be raped.
The dark road.
Wanting to fight and afraid to fight.
She whispers, *The danger
is in believing
you are safe.
Never believe they cannot
come for you.*

*

In your half sleep, the lamp
still lit, tell me how it is.

The water-thinness of her veins
sliced by bullets in her neck.
The songs sung
do not reach her.
No bird resting there.
No path through the mountains
to the woods.

In this dream, tell me,
does she whisper where the strength
comes from?

Liliane Richman

## To My Mother Who Endured

Bergen-Belsen, 1942–1945

This is the tale
Our foremothers told
Because the soil
Is drenched with sorrow
Just a few miles away
From coves warmth-hooded,
From houses thrifty,
Where everyday housewives
Brewed herbed *pot-au-feus.*

Just a few miles away,
There was barbed-wire hell
Where mud turned to soiled ice
While calcinated bones
Swirled into Munch's scream.

This our ritual meal
For our tears are salty,

Our lives bitter
With recollections,
Blisters, boils, hunger, typhus.

Features melted to essentials,
Bird-face Marcelline was
Luckier than Anne Frank.
She told her story
As we sat in a cubicle
Far from lovely light.
I cried,
Drank the host of tears
She shed in the death canal
When after dark tunnel walk
She met her father.

"Father, papa!"
She told me she screamed.
"Now I walk on the Champs Elysées,
I never again loved any man.
In the camp he kissed me
Till my heart was thawed,
Spring blossomed with his touch,
We held each other
' Until the nazi
Kicked us apart.
'Oh please don't,' Papa cried,
'She is my petite fille!'
He pressed an onion in my hand.
I wish I could see him again!"

This is a tale
Our foremothers told
So that we never forget.
For this our tears
Are made of salt.

Esther Cameron

## Exposure

Supine in the rough grass,
above you gray-white emptiness.
Around you the smoke trails climb the sky:
some optic makes them seem
to converge before vanishing.

Somewhere, not far off,
there is shouting,
they are sorting the others:
some to the right, some to the left,
some to gradual, some to immediate death.

How is it they overlooked you,
lying here like old iron,
like a piece of slag from their ovens,
unidentified object with fused glass eyes?

Those whose faces in the archived
photographs will show grainy,
neither horrified nor stigmatized
but like any crowd in transit,
and who will be bent, broken, injected
with foreign substances, taken apart—
these are the extras, the properties.
It's those others who are the persons of this drama,
they are acting out the lives of the gods
like battered children who break their toys,
like children who act with their dolls
what they see done around them, in all loud
parliaments where mute life is disposed of.

Will you rise, throw yourself between?
You know when you walked among them
you had neither hands nor voice.
Lie here for dead.  Stare upwards.
If your mind can bear the emptiness no longer

let your madness rioting in the clouds
create gods to slaughter, instead of human beings.
This lying here pinned by knowledge, this staring upward
into gray-white emptiness where the smoke-trails
seem by some strange optic to converge before vanishing:
this is your destiny, your vigil,
your service.


Helen Degan Cohen

# I Remember Coming into Warsaw, a Child

out of a sheer, sunlit countryside,
where sometimes a goat made the only sound in
all the universe, and a car engine would certainly
tear the wing of an angel.  Entering burnt Warsaw
and the Sound of the World, how strange, how lonely
the separate notes of Everything, lost in a smell of
spent shots still smoking, a ghost of bombs, a silence
of so many voices, the ruined city singing not only
a post-war song but an Everything hymn of dogs wailing,
a car, a horse, a droning plane, a slow, distant
demolition, hammers like rain, the hum, the hum,
bells and levers and voices leveled and absorbed
into the infinite hum in which the ruins
sat empty and low like well-behaved children,
the ruins, their holes like eyes secretly open,
passing on either side, as we entered Warsaw, an air
of lost worlds in a smoky sweet light ghosting
and willing their sounding and resounding remains . . .

Vince Clemente

## From the Ardeatine Caves

Nazi war criminal Herbert Kappler, 71, former police chief of Rome, died
yesterday of stomach cancer. He had been serving a life term for the
execution of 335 Italians, mostly Jews, in reprisal for the ambush killing of
32 German soldiers by Italian partisans in Rome. The execution was staged in
the Ardeatine Caves, just outside of Rome. German engineers assisted in
sealing the caves that entombed the victims. The execution was carried
out on 24 March 1944, now observed in Italy as a national day of mourning.

*New York Times:* February 1978

I
*Above the Giardino Alla Francese*

From your window above the Giardino alla Francese
you muse through the cypress grove
to the pond, the footbridge
and think of Monet at Giverny—
the water lilies like floating candles.

From your window above the Giardino alla Francese
you record in meticulous columns
your *todeskandidaten,*
these "candidates for death"
for the order that read:
"Ten Italians for every German dead
in today's ambush."

You've been up all night
listening to Wagner
remembering your boyhood in Stuttgart,
at 6 AM a vireo's song woke you
to the list incomplete—
and you had run out of Jews.

You have no stomach for this, Herr Kappler,
but a soldier like a monk
takes his solemn vows.
Out of some bizarre logic

you tell yourself that somehow
what you are doing is God's work—
this god redeyed
all in pieces
seeding the fall harvest.


II
*Inside the Ardeatine Caves*


You learn, Herr Kappler
how one of your young officers
refused to shoot:
he looked too deeply
into the eyes of a boy,
the baker's helper from Rimini,
and saw for a second
his own brother
home from Dresden.
He could not fire.
The pistol froze
at the boy's temple.

At the bottom of the hill
you think you smell death.
It is only the mountain ash,
berries hemorrhaging.
The young officer is there
waiting for you at the cave's mouth,
double-lightning bolt
on his helmet.

"Better I at your side
when you fire," you say,
then walk him
arm around waist
into the chamber.

Once inside, it is easy,
the cognac helps—
even the baker's helper falls.

The bodies are piled in rows
stacked like bread
and the caves are sealed tight.
"No resurrection here,"
you tell yourself,
"none tonight."


Arlene Maass

## In Remembrance of the Children of Izieu

Subject: The Jewish children's home in Izieu. In the early morning hours
the Jewish Children's home "The Children's Colony" was terminated. A
total of 41 children from 3–13 in age were removed. Cash or any other
kind of possessions could not be secured. Transport to Drancy is
arranged on April 17, 1944.

Klaus Barbie's telegram

French cognac 1944 is death
nazis keep pouring trains
snapping bones
"those who devour my people
as men eat bread"
the beast of Lyon
*obersturmführer*
sends those unblinking frozen eyes
chosen children
to the ovens
yeast rising
men turning to bones and then to ashes
the haste of death
like the haste of redemption
the night of eating lamb roasted in fire
when the people gathered their kneading bowls

into their garments and ran
fleeing into darkness      exodus
to those waters that rushed and      parted

the children of Izieu
delivered to flames never parting
smoke knotting through trees
searing the clouds
Rachel weeping
if they could have been trees
or been concealed in sheep wool
deported
caught in the horns
gathered into silent forests
*where is the afikomen?*
the children of Izieu
gathered unto their fathers

Carolyn Forché

## *from* The Angel of History

This is Izieu during the war, Izieu and the neighboring
    village of Bregnier-Cordon

This is a farmhouse in Izieu,

Itself a quiet place of stone houses over the Rhone Valley

Where, between Aprils, forty-four children were hidden,

For a year, in full view of the mountains

Until the fields were black and snow fell all the night
    over the little plaque which does not mention that
    they were Jewish children hidden April to April
    in Izieu near Bregnier-Cordon

*Comment me vint l'écriture? Comme un duvet d'oiseau*
    *sur ma vitre, en hiver.*
In every window, a blank photograph of their internment

Within the house, the silence of God. Forty-four bedrolls,
    forty-four metal cups.
*Et le silence de Dieu est Dieu*

In *Pithiviers* and *Beaune-la-Rolande,* in *Les Milles, Les*
    *Tourelles, Moussac* and *Aubagne,*
*the silence of God is God*

The children were taken to Poland
The children were taken to Auschwitz in Poland

Singing *Vous n'aurez pas L'Alsace et la Lorraine*

In a farmhouse still standing in Izieu, *le silence de*
    *Dieu est Dieu*


Willis Barnstone

## Miklos Radnoti

*Because time is a fiction in the mind,*
I don't want to die, that is, in July
or Friday or last year. Farms and haystacks
are burning today. I Miklos Radnoti
write you a postcard with a poem. Darling,
I say to myself I won't lie down. The ox
drools blood. The shepherd girl is an orphan
when the troops stray over the wheatfields.
Wife, after they beat me to death, look through
my trenchcoat, in the mass grave, for the poems.

*Maybe in two years, by 1946,*
you will find our bodies. Today all over

Hungary and Poland I am dying.  In taverns
I am already forgotten.  How could the smell
of my hair linger?  I hid in cellars too,
smoked in darkness, kissed kisses of the taste
of blackberries.  When peace comes I won't be
at the Writers' Club.  Angels drink artillery.
Peasants dream among fleas, among worms.  Wife,
the poems are time's wings.  Spread them darkly.

Charles Fishman

## September 1944

variations on a theme
by Arnost Lustig

I stood in the gypsy camp
by the high-voltage wires,
around us the bare Polish
plains and forests.
A thin transparent fog
enveloped the ground, the people.
It penetrated the soul.
A purple fire flashed
from the chimneys,
glowing a deeper purple
before turning into black
smoke.  Everything stank.
The smoke became a cloud,
and slowly a black rain—
ashes—dropped down.
Like everyone else, I wished
the wind would shift
or the earth reverse its
direction.  The ashes had

a bitter taste.  They were
not from coal or burnt wood,
rags or paper.
They fell on us—mute, deaf,
relentless ashes, in which
human breath, shrieks and tears
could be felt.
I stood at a concrete fence post
with white porcelain insulators,
taking it all in like
an hallucination.
A tune from Strauss's *Die Fledermaus*
ran through my mind.

———————

Based on the translation from Czech by Josef Lustig

Alfred Van Loen

# Auschwitz #1

With gradual rhythm snowflakes
Fell on barracks and roads,
Covering trees, surrounding
With merciful cold.
Within the white blanket,
Death and peace:
Wintertime and soon expected
Christmas.
Christmas without candles
Without music
Without food and without warm clothes.

At this time a young woman
Dragged herself into the field
Through the cold snow

To be alone,
To give birth to her first child
Without help, without love.
The crying infant came into life.

Along came three drunken Nazis
And watched with amusement
This miracle happening before their eyes,
And they took the baby
And threw it in the oven—
A sacrifice to their Führer.

This happened while the young mother
Froze to death:
Around Christmastime,
After nearly two thousand years
Of Christianity.

R. M. Cooper

## Rebecca 1944

It's only one nightmare—a girl returns
After the camp gestapo used acid
To scald her nipples off.
The whitish burns are open,
And the sight of what they did
Soaks through her shirt.
She's one of the lucky ones.
Those taken for interrogations
Seldom come back,
And there's nothing we can do
But know they die.
Operations performed in the political block
Take on the permanence of concrete walls,

Scarred bloody by electric shock—
And souls break quicker than bodies die
Inside that barred darkness.
Part of her survived.


Mark Pawlak

## Unforgettable

The struggle of man against power is the struggle of memory against forgetting.

Milan Kundera

A man who, in his youth in Poland,
was once publicly whipped, receiving 30 lashes
for refusing to salute a Nazi soldier,
tells of the dogs used by S.S. guards
to terrorize Jews at Auschwitz: German shepherds
that would, on command, bite and tear the buttocks
of anyone wearing the prisoner's striped uniform.

Some of these dogs were specially trained,
at a signal, to grab a man by the collar
and drag him to the ground.
Given a second signal, the dog
would pin the man down
with its muzzle to his throat;
and, given a third signal,
bite.

40 years later, he cannot forget
how the guards made a sport
of setting these trained dogs on prisoners;
he cannot forget the third signal.

Alfred Van Loen

## Auschwitz #5
### "Devilish Tortures Invented by Humans"

A man torn from his home
Separated from his wife
And children,
Ready to die.
But not before a struggle—
Fists in the face of devils
Who guarded Auschwitz.

For making a fist
They invented a torture:
The one who had dared
Had to make a fist forever.
They cut his fingertips,
And made an incision in the palm
Of his hand into which
They forced his fingers to grow.

A mouth that spoke
Would be robbed of its tongue,
And someone who did not obey
Immediately
Would have to sit all day
With a loudspeaker blasting
Into both his ears
Until he went deaf and crazy.

Someone who tried
To steal a slice of bread
Would be tied to a tree
And food put before him
Until the heat of the sun
And the cold of the night
Hurried his starvation.

Ronald William Pies

## Voices

*after Elie Wiesel's Night*

One hundred men,
 they marched us from Birkenau
to Buno.
 One hundred of us,
they lit our way
 with machine gun,
closed our eyes
 in the closing snow.
Rabbi Eliahu,
 the radiant one,
scratched the snowbanks
 for his son,
pushed the mangled
 from the snows
to clear his son's throat
 of unshod feet
and newspapers
 advertising strudel.
We ran,
 and dreamed of soup.
We ran from the guns,
 from the myriad dead tales
of mercy,
 ran for a wall
to sleep against,
 to fold our idiot shoulders,
ran from our sons
 who fattened
the piling snow.

  When they took Hepzibah
   to the ovens,
  I walked out
   to the edge of camp
  so that the sun

could scald my eyes
and the frozen ground
    swell
and fold me in
    like a gullet.
But the Kapo found me,
    lurched my shoulders up,
striking my face.
    They were good,
those nubby fingers;
    sharp and sweet,
pungent as chimneys.
    I thought of cabbage broth,
the Shabbas,
    the lemon and the lemon rind.
Do you recall,
    my husband,
how on Shabbas
    Hepzibah would wear
that velvet dress,
    teaching you to dance?

I recall
    that they marched us
from Birkenau
    to Buno.
One hundred men,
    we stopped
when the Gestapo pissed
    or the sirens thickened,
the Americans
    bombing around us,
that steel
    dropping sweeter
than manna.
I recall
    that through the sirens
I heard singing:
    My father
who knew Talmud and Midrash,

who tore no paper
on Shabbas,
   who washed his hands
before wrapping tefillin.
   For me, a boy of nine,
it was a worship of smells:
grape wine brimmed in a goblet,
   damp books lining
the cedar shelves.
   Father,
in my nostrils
   there is only the human bread
of Birkenau.

     Before they shaved our heads,
       I would think back
     to the parties in Krakow;
       to a boy
     neither husband
       nor lover,
     before the signs went up,
     before they searched us
       for prayer books,
     when there was breeze
       and garden
     and rowing in the park.
     My husband,
       they have stopped
     giving out potatoes
       here.
     The ink on my wrist
       is heavy.
     Do you remember
       the balloons
     with chocolate inside?

I remember
   that on the train
to Buchenwald

            a son
clawed his father
        for a crust of bread.
A father lay singing
        in a pool of urine,
and the living lay
        in the trousers
of the dead.
        When we stopped
at Breslau,
        the workers
threw rolls at us;
        through the slats,
we watched businessmen
        in long furs,
sleek ladies
        in German hats.
Rabbi Eliahu,
        the radiant one,
was still singing
        in the corner:
"If there is a God,
        if there is,
        he should be strangled
        slowly."


Susan Dambroff

## There Were Those

There were those
who escaped to the forests
who crawled through sewers
who jumped from the backs of trains

There were those
who smuggled messages

who smuggled dynamite
inside breadloaves
inside matchboxes
inside corpses

There were those
who were shoemakers
who put nails
into the boots
of German soldiers

There were those
who wrote poetry
who put on plays
who taught the children

There were those
who fed each other


Ruth Lisa Schechter

## The Hungarian Mission

Based on a first-hand account by Marika,
a member of the Children's Cadre, January 1945

I forged I.D.'s to rescue Jews
who escaped to Tungsram, a lightbulb factory
on the outskirts of Pest.
I hid four I.D.'s in my warm, Halina boots
made of lamb.  I travelled many hours.
The weather was zero.

I headed away from the Danube
past The Road of Martyrs
where thousands marched

adrift in wind and fog
to die.  The snow was deep.

I had no choice.
I moved in gunfire and fear
of Germans running the other way.
I scooped snow into my mouth.
I felt no hunger.
I kept humming some Hungarian folksongs
learned in grammar school.

I followed instructions
and gave the four I.D.'s
to four Jews
who had no papers, no food.
I don't remember their names.

On the way back, I heard sounds
in a ditch.  A Russian soldier
was mumbling: *Tovarish.*
He was dying.  I washed his face
with snow.  He turned over like
an animal and opened his coat, reaching
for my hand.  His intestines,
red and bleeding, spilled onto the snow.

When I returned to report my mission
I passed out after shouting:
"I have been to Russia!"

Elaine Mott

# On the Wings of the Wind

In Memory of Hannah Senesh

A man straps on her harness,
the parachute is folded back,

a bird, a butterfly, a white wing
tucked against her body.
She sways forward under the weight of the equipment
she carries. There are so many lives to save.
The airplane stops, and darkness draws her in.
She thinks of her father, her mother,
of going back to the beginning of herself,
of being small and curled and wet,
with solid lungs that won't breathe.
She hears her own thin cry,
sees the birth-stains on the sheets,
the placenta that fed her
stretched between the midwife's hands.
The cord is cut and slips off. She drops
out of the opened hatch. In the blue air
she falls free. There is no floor,
no ceiling, no wall to hold her anymore.
Her house has opened like petals and dissolved.
At the moment the cities below her
are being emptied of Jews, she falls
burning in the cool air. Her parachute unfurls.
Taking to the current,
she floats on the rushing silver light,
the airstream, home.

Joan Campion

## To Gisi Fleischmann
### Rescuer of Her People

Courage in battle is an easy thing,
Compared to your gift—
You, who never would bow down
To your tormentors, and whose hand
Was always quick to save:
Though surely you endured

a million secret deaths
Before your own turn came,
Dying with those you could not
    help.

When I imagine you, I do not
    dwell
Upon your end, so common to
    the times, yet
So wretched in its loneliness.
Instead, I see your spirit
Burning as faithful as a candle
Whose flame is buffeted
But never quite put out.
For long and blood-drenched years
    that candle gleamed:
For multitudes, the only light
    there was.

Those who will not bend
End by being broken,
And you were. Yet they could do
    no more
Than murder you. The radiance
    that was yours
Will glow forever in the hearts
Of those who search for righteousness.
And even if your very name should
    fade,
Wherever there is love, there you
    will live.

Burton D. Wasserman

## 1945, The Silence

It was a letter
From Poland,
Delivered simply
With the junk mail
And the butcher's bill,
Yet breathing the bristle
Of military commands
And commanding the sight
Of dragging, bleeding feet.

The letter seized my mother
Read itself aloud in her quivering
Voice, on and on
And on
Until she fell;
Father, speaking in his father's voice,
Emptied its final silence
Into our mouths.

My little sister asked
"Why did the Nazis kill mama's family?" Father
Would not or could not answer, instead
Kissed his child's eyes full of tears.

I, almost thirteen,
Suddenly saw my parents
As smaller than life.

We all carried mother to bed;
For months after, we tried to reason,
To love her, to beg—but she
Would not listen
Or become part of us again:
She had become
The Silence.

Leatrice H. Lifshitz

## A Few More Things about the Holocaust

Not only their money
was taken
a few more things
like beds and bathrooms
songs and stories
air

Not only their furniture
was taken
a few more things
like hallways and windows
bags and babies
hair

Not only their time was taken
a few more things
like hinges and handles
brothers and sisters
prayer

Not only their breath
was taken
a few more things
like shame and shadow
space and spirit
God

Florence Weinberger

## The Dancing Dog

I am the placid animal
that walked unwittingly into ghettoed cities,
stood unnaturally erect on packed trains; their cold metal walls

burned my skin, their wheels gouged my body.
I waited while a sorter tried my strength
and sent me left or right, to die or live.

Beside a hill of rocks I tried to live,
drawing from my ancient depths the force of the animal
that does not think, bargains only strength,
lays down rage so he may dwell in cities,
soothe himself at night, mend his body
and listen to the others baying at the walls.

When no one watched, I scanned the walls.
Imagination would not fail. To live
outside again, alive again in mind and body
both, to turn my wrath upon the animal
that caged us while it burned our cities
was dream that drove my strength.

It needed all my strength
to fade like lichen into the surrounding walls,
into this community become the worst of savage cities.
I let concerns of mind and spirit die to live
within my calloused flesh, an animal
bred to swift accommodation of its body.

I learned to recognize the wasting of my neighbor's body,
the departure of mind, will and strength
to survive, the loss of animal
instinct, the moment he was ready to mount the walls,
activate the bullets, ignore the call to live,
bring down lightning into our forsaken cities.

I raised him up, and still I dreamt of civilized cities.
I ate his unfinished bread, picked vermin from my body.
I wore his shoes another day, to live.
I touched his brittle limbs, and found my strength

again, I peeled him off the barbed walls,
I dug his grave. I denied he died a howling animal.

I built his monument with bestial strength:
with anguished voice, shook down the walls.
I stepped into the day: a well-trained animal.


Gerald Musinsky

## Drawing the Blinds

If you have seen the tan-shell beetles
piled high around the window screen,
then you have seen the bodies at the fences
of Auschwitz and Treblinka.
And if you have seen dry leaves on the sill
turn to dust,
then you know how the ash pits at Babi Yar
were stirred by the wind.

I see an alley in Warsaw
where waxy faced children look on with
button eyes from an old coat,
the dye on their arms that same blue
as their veins pushed taut against skin.
From the depths of black rooms
the parents sit, stooped and broken;
they sag, empty sacks of cracked leather.
Even at noon, shadows are everywhere.

What can you do with the dead?
But leave the chair, close the windows,
and draw the blinds.

Barbara Helfgott Hyett

## You Know the Funny Thing Is

You know, the funny thing is
the memories I have—
I'm not sure that I could say
where I was, what I was doing.
The only thing I have
is the picture that I know
I took. I took the picture.
I had the camera. I had to
have been there. Otherwise
I wouldn't have known.

From an interview with Warren Priest, former Surgical Technician,
120th Evacuation Hospital, Buchenwald

## In Some of the Bunks

In some of the bunks, the men
didn't beat on their tins
and at all and just lay still.
Some of their eyes were open and that was terrible
and some of their eyes were
closed and that was worse.

From an interview with Curtis Mitchell, Retired Colonel,
Special Messenger for the War Department, Belsen

## And There Were Pits

And there were pits,
I would say about fifty
yards long, and people
buried alive in there.
And they had German
civilians digging them
out—but they wouldn't
touch the bodies—with
shovels. Two at a time.
You could see that the
bodies were still warm.
The soldiers, the infantry
men were so angered by
what they had seen that
they made the civilians
throw the shovels away
and take them out by hand
and lay them gently down.

———

From an interview with Nathan Futterman, Corporal,
U.S. 8th Infantry/Wobbelin, 1945

Richard C. Raymond

## And Nothing Moved

I know I saw those things.
Cunning in self-defense, the brain
Has kept its shutters tight,
But the eye knows.

I stood there and stared and stared:
At piles of sprawling shoes,
At sacks of hair, tagged for color,
At drawers of teeth with gold fillings;

At whitewash walls of a barren room
Black with stains of desperate palms
High as hands could reach;
At crouching rows of ovens,
At stakes for target practice live;
At bones in pits and trenches
And drums of lime;
At artificial flowers in a vase,
At curtains in a window.
And nothing moved.
Skeletons, breathing still, lacked strength
To crawl in rags from barracks,
No trees grew leaves for the wind to stir,
Stenches defeated the wind,
The barbed wire hummed.

I know I saw those things,
Stranded for years in my eye,
Marooned there, denied their full belief,
Although the cock has crowed, and more than thrice;
And now, against their pressure for entry,
This continual straining to strike for home,
Will the brain weaken,
Too long on guard grow slack,
And into screaming ducts and crannies
Sterile horror ooze for a thousand years?

Helen Degan Cohen

## A View from the Ghetto
(Or, On Either Side)

Here I stand at the edge of the field.
Before me, wildflowers.
Behind me, dark children,
like myself. In the pure spaces
between knotted wire, far off, I see

bits of clothing fluttering
toward us.  Nearer.
Behind me, they are staring, some
go home. Others swallow.
Brushing wildflowers they come
closer, picking up stones.
The sun shines on them.
Mama? I am running, running.  Away from
their blue shirts like the sky,
their hair like the wheat,
their mended dresses ripped by sunlight,
spitting, cursing.
Down the curb, around walls.
Day after day.
Until we are gone.
All the dark ones are gone.
They have no one.


Ber Green

## The Martyrs Are Calling

The village ruined, its people dead;
the synagogue empty, its prayers unsaid.

Where are the grandparents, sisters and brothers, the children safe amid
    dreams?
Dead, brothers, dead they lie in meadows and streams.
Where are the shoemakers, tailors, tinsmiths, capmakers, teachers,
the bathhousekeepers, locksmiths, beggars, cantors, preachers?

Where is the inn, the bathhouse, the reading hall, the mill?
A hill of ashes, brothers, a skeleton-hill.
Over the holy graveyard I wander all alone;
my footstep quakes, my body becomes one heavy moan.

A door, a hinge, a picture-frame,
signs of a life that went up in flame.
A broken gate, a piece of wall—
the sands, the boards . . . grief fills them all.

I search through the wreckage of a home
and find a button, a shoe, a comb,
a rusty knife, a tattered boot,
and a Yiddish letter soiled by the brute.

Across the graveyard like a driven ghost I tread
where bayonets grew drunk and slaughter rioted;
I want to shriek, to roar, but on my tongue the word is dead.

*And let us tell the might of*—who can tell
of the heroes who hid in caves, of the martyrs who fell?
*Some in fire*—the unholy ones hurled babes into the flames
before their mothers' unbelieving screams.
*Some in water*—Don't you hear the rivers, how they thunder
with heroes drowned, with martyrs whom the tides dragged under?

And once again God's earth grows green
on the same spot where mother, child were slain.
Lush fields of cabbage and high grass arise
on the same spot where a whole city lies.
And quietly a little river flows
on the same spot where Jewish streets once rose.

And the sun shines, and leaves adorn the trees,
and the ashes are borne upon the wings of the breeze.
And everywhere wild plants take root—
and the God of Mercy is mute.

And suddenly there lifts a bitter moan
from every smoke-charred stone.
Within the holy ruins a rumbling comes alive:
"World, we shall yet arrive, we shall arrive!"

And suddenly the synagogue is filled with Jews, dead Jews at prayer:
swaying, wrapped in the white shawls they used to wear.

The holy congregation has risen at one word—
and your voice, too, my grandfather, is heard.

In the dark light of candles the ancient prayer-house gleams;
it trembles with the passion of a hundred holy screams.
And suddenly the whole earth's ripped asunder—
the skies turn black, as if with brewing thunder.

The sacred horn of the slain lamb rings out
a sob, a warning, and a wrathful shout:
over mountains of bodies and valleys of bones,
over ravaged market-places, and outraged cobblestones,

through slaughter-fields, and graveyard-neighborhoods,
through inferno-ghettos and partisan woods—
every hamlet, every little town
an altar on which grandfathers and schoolchums were cut down.

Through smoke and fire the shofar-call is hurled,
straining to reach its voice across the world.
Over grave-filled lands the notes are borne,
over corpse-filled meadows of fresh corn:

Repent, indifferent and stone-hearted ones!
Bow down at the ashes of six million daughters and sons!
Beneath ten layers of ash, bury your face:
then wash yourself, be cleansed of your disgrace!

Be cleansed at last, wash off the shame!
The martyrs' blood—can you not hear it scream?
Still unextinguished is Treblinka's flame . . .

World, wipe out forever the unholy one!
His memory begone, his name begone!
Remember: the spirit of revenge lives on.

And the notes console and cry:
Maidanek must not cause your dream to die.
Here where these ash-heaped ruins lie
there'll be a new birth to amaze the sky.

Long life to life! To death with death!
Into the dry bones is blown new breath.

Make strong, my tribe, your body and your soul!
Make yourself whole—a new life's to be charted,
oh partisans, oh Maccabean-hearted!

———————

Translated from the Yiddish by Aaron Kramer

Yuri Suhl

## . . . And the Earth Rebelled

News item: "A great number of Jewish prayer-shawls, many of them
blood-stained, were given burial in the Jewish cemetery in Yavar, Lower
Silesia. . . . Together with the prayer-shawls, there were also buried
several small cakes of soap which the nazi murderers had made out of
Jewish bodies."

The earth rebelled.
The good and patient earth,
Which knows so well
Death's varied look, its every shape and mold,
Had never taken to itself
A corpse of soap,
Enshrouded in a prayer-shawl's bloody fold.

The Grave was stunned,
And beat the earth with frantic cry:
"And where is body? Where is bone?"
But earth had no reply.
The Grave insisted: "I have always been
The confidant of Death, his trusted kin,
I know the turn of all his harrowed lines:
Death with gaping holes instead of eyes,
Death with shape of life, or cruelly torn,
And tender, cherished infants dead, new-born,
And those who died by gas, the 'peaceful' dead,

'Efficient' Death, with bullet-hole in head,
And Death imprinted with the hangman's rope.
But never have I seen a corpse of soap,
Nor heard that Jewish prayer-shawls can die!" . . .
But earth had no reply.

The earth was stark
In soundless shock
From drop of dew to mountain mass;
And all the leaves on all the trees were numb,
And all the winds arrested in their paths.

The birds in all their secret nests
Were stricken dumb,
As though the Grave, by disbelief,
Had turned the pulse of earth to stone,
And now moaned lonely in his grief:
"Whence this *talis?* Why this soap?
And where is body? Where is bone?"

But suddenly a blast of thunder split
The clotted silence of the earth to bits,
And over all of Europe's fields and seas,
From ocean beds to misty mountain peaks,
Was heard the throbbing of the Grave's demand:
"For every bit of soap there was a soul,
For every *talis* there was once a man!
Now earth and Grave must call the awful roll,
And never will the reckoning be done,
Till all the dead are counted,
One by one!"

And thus the Grave spake to the wondering Wind:
"Get ye into that land of frightful sin,
Where German nazi—forever cursed name—
Destroyed a people in a flame of pain.
Awaken all the martyrs, tortured, bled,
Bestir the crumbling ashes in the pits,
And ask the ashes, ask the restless dead,
And ferret out the traces, find a way

To recognize the *talis* and the corpse
Of human soap that came to me today!"
And thus it was that in a herald's guise,
The Wind pressed forward into Polish skies.

The grasses wept, and all the stalks of grain,
And every threshold, suffering memory's pain,
And all the splintered ruins, charred and burned,
And all the ancient hallowed streets, upturned,
And anywhere the searching Wind appeared,
Arose the sound of sobbing and of tears.

The Wind, perplexed, turned here and there.
So many graves on Polish earth!
Lublin or Lodz or Warsaw first?
Or maybe Maidanek? Or where?
"Where!" the echo came from far and near,
And from the disembodied multitude
A million-voiced reply resounded; "Here!
Our corpse, an image of six million Jews!
The tortured dead of Warsaw, Vilna, Lodz,
The bitter weeping and the tears unshed,
Each smouldering ash, each drop of blood,
Are all one corpse, one body of our dead!"

But still the doubting Wind did not believe,
And tarried, unconvinced, to hear the truth.
Again the echoes cried, "Go back!
And take along these signs as proof."
And then the heavens shook
And from the emptiness
Came forth the witnesses:

A speck of glowing ash.
A letter from a sacred Book.
A last *Shema*.
And shifting in his course, the Wind returned
To tell the waiting Grave what he had learned.

But as the Wind moved past a Polish wood,
A voice arose: "Your work is not yet done!
Add to the prayer, the ashes, and the Book,
The thunder of a Jewish Fighter's gun!"

———————

Translated from the Yiddish by Max Rosenfeld

Aaron Kurtz

## A Million Pairs of Shoes

A million pairs of shoes
lie thinking.
A million pairs of shoes, all that survived,
clambering,
creeping,
climbing to the sky.
A million Jews bore their wounds in these shoes.
A million children bore their future in these shoes.
A million pairs of shoes—forsaken, remembering
in the city of holocaust,
Lublin.

A million pairs of feet
hacked,
hewn,
charred.
But the shoes remained sound—intact
with poverty's corrosion upon them
or the patina of better days:
shoes with the sacred dust of the Warsaw Ghetto,

shoes of Viennese patent-leather elegance,
tough peasant boots that trudged hard roads,
children's shoes scuffed from childish games,
rubber boots of fishermen from the Volga, the Danube, the Vistula,
white-plastered boots of flour mill workers,
men's boots, women's shoes, children's slippers
twisted and worn,
shabby and torn.

No need to ask the coarse, clayed peasant boots
and the thick-soled shoes of toil
to what cities of the world they have been,
to what lands and why:
they speak
of ghettos and swamps,
basements and cemeteries,
blind attics and underground hideouts.
These boots are full of hopes and disappointments
from dangerous and bloody roads;
they pant, still hearing the hobnailed tread of fear,
and still pursuing hope
with faltering stride, heroic, sacred steps.

A million pairs of shoes
waiting.
These shoes will live.
These shoes will walk—over the world,
over the oceans and continents,
walk and walk
and never wear out!
They will be the shoes of history—
they will be the walking monument
of a people
on fire amid the flaming walls of hell.

Hell has fallen.
The people have survived.
The mountain of shoes
at the oven-graves of Lublin

is a mountain of rock split into a million fragments.
But the might of the rock lives on in every fragment:
a brotherhood of peoples that will arise and walk
that first day
of Genesis.
—1945

---

Translated from the Yiddish by the author and Olga Cabral

Naomi Replansky

## The Six Million

They entered the fiery furnace
And never one came forth.
       How can that be, my brothers?
       No miracle, my sisters?
       They entered the fiery furnace
       And never one came forth.

They fell in the den of lions
Of lions made like men.
       No beast that wept, my brothers,
       Nor turned to lamb, my sisters.
       They fell in the den of lions
       Of lions made like men.

The block of ice closed round them
And nothing kept them warm.
       No gods came down, my brothers,
       To breathe on them, my sisters.
       The block of ice closed round them
       And nothing kept them warm.

No gods were there, no demons.
They died at the hands of men,
The cold that came from men,

The lions made like men,
The furnace built by men.
            How can that be, my brothers?
            But it is true, my sisters.
            No miracle to spare them,
            No angel leaned upon them,
            Their bodies made a mountain
            That never touched the heavens.
            Whose lightning struck the killers?
            Whose rain drowned out the fires?
—1946

IV

Without Jews

Though the tree has been chopped down,
the root has not withered. . . .
                    Aharon Appelfeld

Bernard S. Mikofsky

# 1945

And that year
When the fires ceased
And the ovens were finally cool
A strange wind moved out
In slow, grief-laden eddies
And sooty swirls
Across Europe—
And even beyond.

And those with conscience
(And even those without)
Heard faint sounds from afar,
Echoes from an age-old abyss,
And sometimes these seemed to come
From inside one's ear—
So tiny and yet so persistent,
Echoes of the anonymous cries
Of numbered millions.

And far from the ovens,
Far from the funeral fires,
This wind still carried
Wraiths of soot
Too fine to water the eye
Yet searing the heart.

That year the strange wind
Moved slowly across Europe—
And even beyond,
Now and then pausing
To eddy into the deepest corners
Of our minds
To remind us,
To stir us for an instant
From our dream of well-being.

John Ciardi

## The Gift

In 1945, when the keepers cried *kaput,*
Josef Stein, poet, came out of Dachau
like half a resurrection, his other
eighty pounds still in their invisible grave.

Slowly then the mouth opened and first
a broth, and then a medication, and then
a diet, and all in time and the knitting mercies,
the showing bones were buried back in flesh,

and the miracle was finished.  Josef Stein,
man and poet, rose, walked, and could even
beget, and did, and died later of other causes
only partly traceable to his first death.

He noted—with some surprise at first—
that strangers could not tell he had died once.
He returned to his post in the library, drank his beer,
published three poems in a French magazine,

and was very kind to the son who at last was his.
In the spent of one night he wrote three propositions:
That Hell is the denial of the ordinary.  That nothing lasts.
That clean white paper waiting under a pen
is the gift beyond history and hurt and heaven.

Enid Shomer

## Women Bathing at Bergen-Belsen

April 24, 1945

Twelve hours after the Allies arrive
there is hot water, soap.  Two women bathe
in a makeshift, open-air shower while nearby
fifteen thousand are flung naked into mass graves
by captured SS guards.  Clearly legs and arms
are the natural handles of a corpse.  The bathers,
taken late in the war, still have flesh
on their bones, still have breasts.  Though nudity was
a death sentence here, they have undressed,
oblivious to the soldiers and the cameras.
The corpses push through the limed earth like upended
headstones.  The bathers scrub their feet, bending
in beautiful curves, mapping the contours
of the body, that kingdom to which they've returned.

Randall Jarrell

## A Camp in the Prussian Forest

I walk beside the prisoners to the road.
Load on puffed load,
Their corpses, stacked like sodden wood,
Lie barred or galled with blood

By the charred warehouse.  No one comes today
In the old way
To knock the fillings from their teeth;
The dark, coned, common wreath

Is plaited for their grave—a kind of grief.
The living leaf
Clings to the planted profitable
Pine if it is able;

The boughs sigh, mile on green, calm, breathing mile,
From this dead file
The planners ruled for them. . . . One year
They sent a million here:

Here men were drunk like water, burnt like wood.
The fat of good
And evil, the breast's star of hope
Were rendered into soap.

I paint the star I sawed from yellow pine—
And plant the sign
In soil that does not yet refuse
Its usual Jews

their first asylum. But the white, dwarfed star—
This dead white star—
Hides nothing, pays for nothing; smoke
Fouls it, a yellow joke,

The needles of the wreath are chalked with ash,
A filmy trash
Litters the black woods with the death
Of men; and one last breath

Curls from the monstrous chimney. . . . I laugh aloud
Again and again;
The star laughs from its rotting shroud
Of flesh. O star of men!

Lisa Ress

## U.S. Army Holds Dance for Camp Survivors. Germany, 1945

We recognize each other, neighbors before the war,
schoolmates until the schools shut against us.
Our families hid past the coalbins,
the children's mouths taped, our heads swollen with sound.
You kept on with your piano lessons,
the silence of the Czerny exercises eroding
the black- and white-painted board.
G.I.'s broke us from the camps.
Now we hold together, circling in time,
not the dead for whom we long, but like them.
Cracked open behind us, our cellars glow with our youth.


Bernard S. Mikofsky

## Mame-Loshen, Yiddish

Long ago
We spoke a mother tongue;
Now its words, its warm words
Have grown cold
And trailed away
Into silence . . .

Those ancient sounds
From childhood's love—
They are dreams,
They are nightmares,
They laughed,

They cried,
They whispered then a while—
And they were gone.

They are wraiths,
They are ghosts,
Once warm and loving syllables:
smoke . . .

Irena Klepfisz

## *Di Rayze Aheym* / The Journey Home

     1. Der fenster / *The window*
She looks out the window.
All is present.
The shadows of the past
fall elsewhere.

This is the wilderness
she thinks.

And our tongues have become
dry  the wilderness has
dried out our tongues  and
we have forgotten speech.

She looks out the window.
All is present.

     2. Vider a mol / *Once again*
*Vider a mol*
she tries
to rise above circumstances.

Too much is at stake
this morning

*yedn frimorgn*
>                every morning
to see what can be wrenched
from the unconscious
crowded darkness
*fun ir zikorn*
>           of her memory.

It is there
*di gantse geshikhte*
*fun folk*
>           the entire history
of the people.

*Vider a mol*
>                she reaches out
and tries to hold on
clinging
>           like a drowning
person
>           to a flimsy plank.

*Ober der yam iz groys*
but the sea is vast
*un di velt*
>                and the world
*afile greser*
>           even larger
>                     *afile greser.*

>           3.  Zi flit / *She flies*
*Zi flit*
*vi a foygl*
>           like a bird
*Zi flit*
*ibern yam*
>                over the sea
*iber di berg*
>           over the mountains.

*Tsurik*
>*tsurik* back
>>back

*zi flit*
>and settles
*oyf a boym*
>>on a tree
*lebn a moyer*
>>near a wall

*a moyer*
*fun a beys-oylem*
>>a wall
>>of a cemetery.

>>4. A beys-oylem / *A cemetery*
*Der moyer*                  the wall
*oyf der zayt*
>>on this side

*un oyf der zayt*
>>and on this side.

*Oyf beyde zaytn*      on both sides.

*Oyf der zayt*
*a keyver*
a grave                  on this side
>>*oyf der zayt*
>>*a vistenish*

on this side
>>a wasteland.

*Der moyer*
*a beys-oylem*
*oyf der zayt*
>>*un oyf der zayt.*

5. Kashes / *Questions*

*In velkhn yor?*

    in what year?

*Mit vemen?*

    with whom?

*Di sibes?*

    the causes?

*Der rezultat?*

    the outcome?


*di geshikhte*

    the history

*fun der milkhome*

    of the war

*fun dem sholem*

    of the peace

*fun di lebn geblibene*

    of the survivors


*tsvishn fremde*

    among strangers

*oyf der zayt*

    on this side
    *tsvishn meysim*

among ghosts

    *oyf der zayt*

on this side.


6. Zi shemt zikh / *She is ashamed*

*Zi shemt zikh.*

    She has forgotten
    *alts fargesn*

forgotten it all.


    Whom can I speak to?
    she wonders.


    *di mame*    the mother
    *der tate*    the father

*di bobe*    the grandmother
*der zeyde*    the grandfather

*di oves*    the ancestors

*alts*
*alts fargesn*
forgotten it all

    *di gantse mishpokhe*
    the entire family

*dos folk*
the people

    *Mit vemen*
    *ken ikh redn?*
    Whom can I speak to?

*di meysim farshteyen*
*mir afile nit*
    even the ghosts
    do not understand me.

    7. In der fremd / *Among strangers*
*Vi azoy?*    how
    she wonders
    should I speak?

    *Velkhe verter*
which words
should I use
*in der fremd*
    among strangers?

*Red*
*bloyz dem emes*
    speak
    only the truth
*kayn lign nit*
    no lies.

*Zi gedenkt*
she remembers
*di lektsies*

      the lessons
*di printsipn*

      the principles


     *un zi shvaygt*

and she remains

     silent.

    8. Di tsung / *The tongue*
*Zi shvaygt.*

*Di verter feln ir*
she  lacks the words
and all that she can force

is sound
unformed sound:

*a*
*der klang*

     the sound
*o*
*dos vort*

     the word
*u*
*di tsung*

     the tongue
*o*
*dos loshn*

     the language
*e*
*di trern*

     the tears.

9.  Di rayze aheym / *The journey home*

*Zi flit*
> she flies

*vi a foygl*
>> like a bird

*vi a mes*
>> like a ghost.


*Zi flit*
*iber di berg*
>>> over the mountains

*ibern yam*
>>> over the sea.


*Tsurik*
>> *tsurik* back
>>>> back


*In der fremd*
>>> among strangers

*iz ir heym*
>>> is her home.


>> *Do*

here
*ot do*
>> right here

*muz zi lebn*
>> she must live.


*Ire zikhroynes*
>> her memories
>> will become monuments

*ire zikhroynes*
will cast shadows.

Abraham Linik

## The Thief

In the foggy distance
I see the pack on his back
In it are my years
Wrapped in a yellow Star of David
Tied up
With rusty chains—
Bracelets of my youth
And my
Dreams.

Owen Dodson

## Jonathan's Song

A Negro Saw the Jewish Pageant, "We Will Never Die"
(for Sol Gordon)

I am part of this:
Four million starving
And six million dead:
I am flesh and bone of this.

I have starved
In the secret alleys of my heart
And died in my soul
Like Ahab at the white whale's mouth.

The twisted cross desire
For final annihilation
Of my race of sufferers:
I am Abel, too.

Because my flesh is whole
Do not think that it signifies life.
I am the husk, believe me.
The rest is dead, remember.

I am a part of this
Memorial to suffering,
Militant strength:
I am a Jew.

Jew is not a race
Any longer—but a condition.
All the desert flowers have thorns;
I am bleeding in the sand.

Take me for your own David:
My father was not cruel,
I will sing your psalms,
I have learned them by heart.

I have loved you as a child,
We pledged in blood together.
The union is not strange,
My brother and my lover.

There was a great scent of death
In the garden when I was born.
Now it is certain:
Love me while you can.

The wedding is powerful as battle,
Singular, dread, passionate, loud,
Ahab screaming and the screaming whale
And the destination among thorns.

Love is a triple desire:
Flesh, freedom, hope:
No wanton thing is allowed.
I will sing thy psalms, all thy psalms,
Take me while you can.

Thomas A. Goldman

## Rotterdam—1946
### the Pre-War Visa Files

In this grey vault
they lie preserved
in steel-walled tombs
against the years,
pressed tightly
one against another.
They are forgotten,
yet the names are here—
Tabakblad, Ferreira, Cohen, Frank—
name, address, occupation,
date and place of birth,
all details documented,
certified and sealed,
and here interred
in pale manila coffins.
Sad faces stare (in duplicate,
two inches square precisely)
from eyes the darkness
long since closed.
This room was but a station
on the bitter road.
We buried here one vital
organ, hope.
The numbed flesh that was left
went to the flames.

Edward Hirsch

## Paul Celan: A Grave and Mysterious Sentence

(Paris, 1948)

It's daybreak and I wish I could believe
In a rain that will wash away the morning
That is just about to rise behind the smokestacks
On the other side of the river, other side
Of nightfall.  I wish I could forget the slab
Of darkness that always fails, the memories
That flood through the window in a murky light.

But now it is too late.  Already the day
Is a bowl of thick smoke filling up the sky
And swallowing the river, covering the buildings
With a sickly, yellow film of sperm and milk.
Soon the streets will be awash with little bright
Patches of oblivion on their way to school,
Dark briefcases of oblivion on their way to work.

Soon my small apartment will be white and solemn
Like a blank page held up to a blank wall,
A secret whispered into a vacant closet.  But
This is a secret which no one else remembers
Because it is stark and German, like the silence,
Like the white fire of daybreak that is burning
Inside my throat.  If only I could stamp it out!

But think of smoke and ashes.  An ominous string
Of railway cars scrawled with a dull pencil
across the horizon at dawn.  A girl in pigtails
Saying, "Soon you are going to be erased."
Imagine thrusting your head into a well
And crying for help in the wrong language,
Or a deaf mute shouting into an empty field.

So don't talk to me about flowers, those blind
Faces of the dead thrust up out of the ground
In bright purples and blues, oranges and reds.
And don't talk to me about the gold leaves
Which the trees are shedding like an extra skin:
They are handkerchiefs pressed over the mouths
Of the dead to keep them quiet.  It's true:

Once I believed in a house asleep, a childhood
Asleep.  Once I believed in a mother dreaming
About a pair of giant iron wings growing
Painfully out of the shoulders of the roof
And lifting us into away-from-here-and-beyond.
Once I even believed in a father calling out
Names in the dark, restless and untransfigured.

But what did we know then about the smoke
That was already beginning to pulse from trains,
To char our foreheads, to transform their bodies
Into two ghosts billowing from a huge oven?
What did we know about a single gray strand
Of barbed wire knotted slowly and tightly
Around their necks?  We didn't know anything then.

And now here is a grave and mysterious sentence
Finally written down, carried out long ago:
At last I have discovered that the darkness
Is a solitary night train carrying my parents
Across a field of dead stumps and wild flowers
Before disappearing on the far horizon,
Leaving nothing much in its earthly wake

But a stranger standing at the window
Suddenly trying to forget his childhood,
To forget a milky black trail of smoke
Slowly unravelling in the distance
Like the victory-flag of death, to forget
The slate clarity of another day
Forever breaking behind the smokestacks.

Barbara Goldberg

## Survivor

for Blanka

They say I should feed you,
child with the gift of tongues.
But darting through woods of dark pine
hounds chase the scent of sandals.

Days spent under cover
in a field of eiderdown,
my fingers search for traces
of my own lost mother.

At night, when the bulb shines through
the parchment, and I scrub
my body down with soap,
I think of her parting lace curtains
looking for Father to round the corner.

A small patch of pine presses against the North
side of this house. Here, by Union Turnpike,
a car is parked in the driveway.
We'd all fit in, all, if we had
to make a quick journey.
I keep a bar of gold under my pillow.

They bring you to me, my locket
clasped in your fist. I want
to feed you.

It's those spiked needles that scrape
against the glass, those shadows
that won't sleep behind the drapes.
It's that woodsman walking
through this forest
swinging his ax.

Ruth Feldman

## Survivor

for Giorgio Bassani

They would have mourned him, dead,
but could not quite forgive
his resurrection when the rest
had lain down quietly
under the marble plaque
on which their names were cut.

This numbered Lazarus whose blue tattoo
the gaping sleeve exposed indecently,
this gadfly with his flesh
hung on a scarecrow frame,
stung alive memories better left interred,
refused to love his enemies
or turn his cheek to one more blow.

The ones on whom his stubborn shadow fell,
heartily wished him dead and safe in hell.

M. Truman Cooper

## At a Mass Grave

We should try not to look away.
Pretend that someone you know
is missing and might be here, or
imagine that these people were like us,
holding, to the last, some wild notion
that human disasters need to be earned.
This could be a pile of lovers
who finally found time and courage
for one another. Now, they're resting.

While they drowse, naked to the sun,
we can wonder what would happen
if they awakened, suddenly whole again.
It seems almost possible. The open
mouths of some sleepers might be snoring.
A man's hand actually does cup
a small breast, here and there, unknowing.
Would he blink, ask the time, dress
and rush back to his old business?

We can guess how they would part
if they could stir or yawn or give
a dreamy head the lap's warmth until
all nightmares have spent themselves.
Stand on the brown waves of dirt
which bulldozers have readied like a tide.
Think of bodies rising to the pit's rim,
reaching up. Whether we grasp
their hands or not, we will feel
their fingers wedged between our own.

Marie Syrkin

# Niemand*

You with the cross and you without the cross,
Come quietly.
We go to Maidanek; all roads lead there
And every sea.
The summons is for all; the pilgrims wait.
It is not far.
You will find stations: shelter in Zbonzyn,
A bed in Babi Yar.

*Niemand* will greet you; *Niemand* knows the way
From ditch to doom.
(Hear the Annunciation: cursed art thou,

And cursed thy womb.)
A little child shall lead you—it is he,
No one, my son.
No one, Nobody, Nothing—now he calls
On everyone.
The house of death is big; its walls will hold
A multitude;
And of this sacrament you must partake,
Body and blood.

You with the cross and you without the cross,
On each the sin.
Seek absolution in no other place.
Come, enter in.

---

*In 1938 a Jewish woman driven out of the Sudeten area gave birth to her son in a ditch. She named him *Niemand,* Nobody.

Nicholas Rinaldi

## Auschwitz

Lucky the ones who were sick and in pain,
they would soon be out of their misery. The ones
who were deaf, there was nothing beautiful
for them to listen to. The ones who had no gold teeth,
they would not be robbed when they died.

The ones who still had warm breath
to blow on their fingers,
trying to keep warm. They could blow on their fingers,
try to keep warm. The ones who could dream,
imagining they were flowers

on the banks of the Nile. They could imagine
they were birds over Egypt, flying,
soaring, lost in the irreverent sky.

The ones who were hungry and dying,
and the ones past hunger, beyond the need to eat.
They remembered nothing, their feet were roots
in the hard ground: they were ruined trees,
numb to the weather,
unmindful of the tedious rain.

The ones who were old and senile,
humming to themselves, thinking the guards
were angels from heaven
come to avenge them. Lucky the ones
who were so lucky, the ones under whose feet
the ground opened up: they could fall and fall
and never be found.

Harvey Shapiro

## Ditty

Where did the Jewish god go?
Up the chimney flues.
Who saw him go?
Six million souls.
How did he go?
All so still
As dew from the grass.

Jacob Glatstein

## Without Jews

Without Jews there is no Jewish God.
If we leave this world
The light will go out in your tent.
Since Abraham knew you in a cloud,
You have burned in every Jewish face,
You have glowed in every Jewish eye,
And we made you in our image.
In each city, each land,
The Jewish God
Was also a stranger.
A broken Jewish head
Is a fragment of divinity.
We, your radiant vessel,
A palpable sign of your miracle.

Now the lifeless skulls
Add up to millions.
The stars are going out around you.
The memory of you is dimming,
Your kingdom will soon be over.
Jewish seed and flower
Are embers.
The dew cries in the dead grass!

The Jewish dream and reality are ravished,
They die together.
Your witnesses are sleeping:
Infants, women,
Young men, old.
Even the Thirty-six,
Your saints, Pillars of your World,
Have fallen into a dead, an everlasting sleep.

Who will dream you?
Who will remember you?
Who deny you?

Who yearn for you?
Who, on a lonely bridge,
Will leave you—in order to return?

The night is endless when a race is dead.
Earth and heaven are wiped bare.
The light is fading in your shabby tent.
The Jewish hour is guttering.
Jewish God!
You are almost gone.

---

Translated from the Yiddish by Nathan Halper

Florence W. Freed

## God's Death

during the Holocaust
along with the six million
God is slowly dying

golden glares of
Stars of David
blind Him

shattered glass
from Kristallnacht
cuts Him

devilish plans
in Hitler's ravings
deafen Him

Emanuel Ringelblum's pen
scratching his ghetto diary
crazes Him

shrieks of Jews
tortured in experiments
pierce Him

blood of victims
shot naked into pits
drowns Him

Zyklon B gas
shaken into "showers"
poisons Him

stench of smoke
rising from ovens
suffocates Him

even God almighty
can not go on
can not survive

closing Anne Frank's
innocent eyes
in Bergen-Belsen

God flings
Himself
to the four winds

hurls
Himself
beyond the Heavens

banishes
Himself
from the Universe

forever
I say
forever

Carol Adler

## We Are the Echoes

find another place for them
another time
put them back in their boxes
bury them
or carry them so high
we will never hear them
even when they fall

they fall from us
still-born
they rise before us
standing on the mountains
like statues

standing on the mountains
and calling

we are the echoes
the refugees of echoes

gingerly we pick among the shards
pretending to search

searching for what
for we are fooling no one

there is no one to fool

even the ghetto is a hideous dream
and the nation so long
we have longed for
is finally a young heifer
growing into its own

yet where have we gone
and what is our promise

we who sit here praying not for prayers
but for miracles

we who call to the Unknown
only to mock It when It comes

or is the mockery only despair
the shawl we wrap around us
because we must

take away your echoes
we say
talking to you as if you were listening


Julius Balbin

## Lament for the Gypsies

Their home was the endless
                    plains of Eurasia.
Their roof was the starlit sky
                    under which they slept in tribal embrace.
Like butterflies they would never settle
                    for the taste of one flower
but move on to the light
                    of ever new gardens.
They did not want to give up
                    their freedom to roam the continent
for the price of a homeland.
                    To rove without hindrance
from land to land
                    was as precious to them
as life itself.
                    They spoke a strange tongue

scholars count among the oldest
>but they left no writings.
That they dared to be so different from others
>remains their chief heritage.
Yet their love of music was as boundless
>as their love of freedom.
The vibrant and melancholy tunes they fiddled and danced
>as they wandered from country to country
found their way into notebooks
>of many a famous composer.
Their nomadic ways aroused suspicion
>and often they were persecuted.
Although innocent of any idolatry
>many were forced to adopt alien creeds.
Their women possessed the art
>of foretelling the future of others
yet had no foreboding of what
>was in store for their own people.
Before they were consumed by crematoria
>they bequeathed to us
a unique legacy:
>that of a people
who practiced without preaching
>what they believed—
that peoples should not be divided by frontiers.

———

Translated from the Esperanto by Charlz Rizzuto

David McKain

## For the Children

In a painting by Brueghel
a hunter sights the hart
then strings his gut.

I would put him on a rooftop
as the king rides by—or, better,
near the Führerbunker:
Hitler loved the old masters,
hanging his favorites on the wall.

Did he see
the Brueghel of the hunters on the hill,
the children in the village?

He might have seen the red angle of their caps
and the cold blood deer hanging from a pole.

But in his final days
he'd stand at the window and gaze,
the winter woods a print
bled to the sash of their border.

His back to the Brueghel
the hunters could escape—
they could roast their venison under a hemlock,
scratch a plan in the snow with a stick.

Later they could slip back in
to do their work—
to parade the Führer
through the village,
slung on a pole like a deer,
upside down in the cold winter light
for all the children to see.

Ginger Porter

# I Am Babi Yar

My gold six-pointed star
is underground, bloodstained.
The sides of the pit are steep,
they reach to the
endless expanse of steely-blue sky.

The swastikas are gone—
they were washed away
by the tears of mourning.
The mad Führer is dead,
but his legacy lives;
my brethren all died with him.
I am alone here among ghosts.

Machine-gun fire echoes in my head.
My efforts to climb up are useless.
I feel the greasy dust of the dead around me.
I can taste the blood-soaked earth,
but I cannot feel it.

Here is where I will remain.
I can never die;
my soul cannot be at rest.
I am a memory, a message to posterity,
damned to haunt this pit
in the heart of Russia forever,
a sorrowful spirit,
a testimonial.
I am Babi Yar.

Gloria Glickstein

## Diary of a Tashkent Jew

In white Siberia where the fallen have risen
little bees come sting me
from under the snow like a miracle.
They come to wake and warn me of death.
They come to tell time
with tiny voices and slender stingers
they gently insert into my palms.
They have no real news to bring me
but ariose songs to sing: death, death,
threnodies of despair.
There is no hope to dress and warm me
but the sound of blanketing snow.
The war is over.  Far from its borders
boots march above its debris.

We who were murdered lie eternally awake
stirring the ashes.

Philip Levine

## In Saxony

A little girl with blond braids
waved from behind the barricade.
I answered.  We were smiling.

The only noise was the train
slipping on oiled rails, and the sun
snapping through the poplar boughs.

We were going.  No burned-out cars,
no tumbled field of oil drums
at the town's end, only a man

in a peaked grey cap, waving.
When he lit a cigarette
with a square, stainless lighter

I could see the egg of flame
in the still air, I could feel
it burning through the last wall

into my mind, I could smell
my own mind like singed hair.
How could it happen here?


Maxine Kumin

## The Amsterdam Poem

I
All-Beethoven night at the Concertgebouw
is unashamedly schmaltz.
The audience melts into the Eroica
and we too, we the Americans
in our on-stage seats directly behind
five bass viols whose plucked strings set
the floorboards trembling, we sway
with mijnheer and mevrouw

The conductor is Japanese.
When the firebombs fell on Tokyo
he was ten years old. Screaming.
Surely his hair, superfine, black,

grew forward then from the delicate crown.
His baton writes on air.
He conducts from the groin.
What his hips say, the violins seize:
*Ars longa,* my life is but a leaf.

In the morning we go to the gallery.
The exhibit is called *Bittere Jaren,*
1935 to 1941.
We who grew up in a safe place
expect the iron cross, the sealed boxcars
but the bitter years turn out to be
a rerun of the dustbowl by
Steichen, Walker Evans, Ben Shahn.

Remember the slogan, The American Way?
Here is the poster plastered on billboards,
the family of four in its brand new car
smiling their toothpaste smiles
while a sharecropper across the hall
in a lovely grainy enlargement starves.
Here are the bloated babies
and the farms whipped into sand.
We two Americans, we two fools
taking in the town on our five-day week
hunch like turkey buzzards and
cannot lift our eyes and
do not speak.

II
Later, a pilgrimage
to Anne,
Anne Frank who was almost my age.
We go behind
the fake bookcase, climb
stairs that pitch
up to the little judas rooms
in which
they hid: Mother, sister,
the dentist, Peter,

and Papa who brought them to safety
from Frankfurt in '33
never dreaming of here,
never dreaming at all
of the makeshift kitchen, three
stools, a ladder
up to where Peter, "that boy,"
slept. I peer
at the w.c., its bowl
of blue-sprigged delft a beautiful
improbable toy.
In '33 I was eight years old,
soon to begin the Nazi nightmares
a hundred cold
wakings upstairs
in a warm bed in Germantown,
Pennsylvania.

We come down
into sunlight. There must have been
a few good years for Anne,
years of being a healthy animal
mooning along the estuaries,
skating on the canal
and eating cherries
in the Vondelpark
before, before
they went up in the dark.
I think of her
coming out, a prisoner,
a paradox
from behind the books
with the SS at her back . . .

III
Along the canal that she could sometimes see
from Peter's window, a crowd has gathered.
The police arrive in a Volkswagen. A pigeon
has somehow blundered into the water. It floats
downstream, dumbly preparing to drown

but a girl guide fluent in five languages
dives in and bears it aloft like a pastry.
Everyone cheers.

In 1941, there wasn't a pigeon here
and the Dutch had begun to eat rats.
What can't I forgive?  The rebirth of pigeons?
Of caring?  Of live and let live?  The carillons
in the Westerkirk on the corner ring out.
An old woman hawks eels from a pushcart.
For suffering there is no quantum.  What heals
the city, its citizens, I know nothing about.

Tomorrow KLM can fly us out.

Aaron Kramer

# Westminster Synagogue

Ears afire, I knock at Kent House door.
My hands could not protect them if I tried
except from the drone of Heathrow jets, the roar
of a bus marked "Kensington." Too deep inside,
the tick of an Irish bomb at Harrod's store,
the swords forever committing chivalricide
athwart Knightsbridge, the million-footed squall
from Victoria's trains to Exhibition Hall.

The door shuts out those ghosts storming the Park
across the way; the dignity and calm
of my friend Rabbi uncurtaining his Ark
halts the old swords, defuses the young bomb.
But smilingly he chooses to remark
that where the Torah blazes now, Madame
de St. Laurent enjoyed her fireplace,
herself enjoyed through long years by His Grace

the Duke of Kent.  At once his royal groans
roll 'round the room, her murmured syllables
mock what the cantor loftily intones.
But now a door is opened; silence drills
my skull; it fills my rib-cage, chills my bones.
With dignity, with calm the Rabbi tells
that in this room heal fifteen hundred holy
scrolls a scribe has been repairing slowly,

and as each wraith-loved Torah is repaired,
some living congregation takes it in.
—Not for such future were these writings spared,
the Rabbi makes me understand: Berlin
had a museum in mind; these would be aired
as trophies of a tribe that once had been.
I ask: Might one be opened?—but at once
desist . . . No need!  Madame de St. Laurent's

syllables, and the groans of her high lover,
are hammered into dust by the dear notes
that—scroll by scroll, rack under rack—recover
their Sabbath force.  Seventy thousand throats
flame in my ears.  The interview is over;
I'm at the bus stop; but around me floats
a choral fire from every synagogue
of Brno, Pilsen, Bratislava, Prague.


## Zudioska

Smug in her Adriatic noon, Dubrovnik beams.
Within her walls, unconquered and intact,
was much to save—with guns or cunning.
It is all on file in the Rector's Palace.

The streets, in conscious harmony,
flow down from her twin hills
to merge in the Placa, where tourists go

marveling, that after a thousand years
in this world of wounded columns, ravished mausoleums,
no stone is vexed.

Here stands Zudioska, street of the Spanish Jews.
(Dubrovnik took in their banished scrolls;
not often made them wear the yellow badge,
pay special fees, stand trial for ritual murder.)

Ask no question of the stones.  Go past.
You will find nothing peculiar on Zudioska.
Women dry their wash.
Children throw their ball.
A cartload rumbles down the narrow steps.
No room is vacant.
There are customers enough in the cafe.

Across from the cafe a door is open.
At the first landing the rabbi awaits you.
On the second landing is the synagogue—
six hundred eighteen years old.
The worshippers await you, though one cannot see them.

Ask no question of the stones.
The Jews had names, but what's the difference?
had women, children, trades—but what's the difference?
It is all on file, no doubt, in the Rector's Palace.
The rabbi could tell you:
      two hundred Jews dwelled on this street.
      The Italians came, and put us on Rab.
      The Germans came, and took us to Auschwitz.
      Seventeen crawled home, and not one child.

      We sweep the floor of the synagogue each day.
      We hold our service without a minyan.
      Soon the synagogue will be perfectly silent,

as silent as the perfect stones of the city,
a museum with a guard collecting fees.

God saved us from the quake of 1667.
Nobody saved us in 1943.
And you, if you were Dubrovnik, would you have cried
    *Shame!*
as they checked off each name and shoved us into
        the boat?

Zudioska drowns in shadow.
The Placa runs in light.
Shield your eyes when you come back into the light
or the beaming stones will burn them as if you are crying.

Willis Barnstone

## The Rose of Blue Flesh

1
Facing a long Byzantine city wall,
the synagogue in Ioannina is white and bold
with Hebrew script over the portal.
Beyond the city,
the mountains lean like awkward ghosts,
ghost after ghost blurring into Albania
with its unmapped capital called Tirana.

2
The gatekeeper of the synagogue (a Greek word)
        is old, short,
a typical Epirote face.
I see his number tattooed on his left arm

which I lift to examine.
The ink is as fresh as the day of tattooing
in 1943.

"They shot my son in front of me.
A thousand of us were carried off.
Who are you?" he says, menacingly.
"I'm a Jew."


3
Paul came here.  He proselytized in synagogues
in Corinth and nearby Thessaloniki,
speaking Aramaic and Greek to kinsmen of the first diaspora.
Only these Jews from Ioannina never spoke Ladino,
were never Sephardized when ships from Spain
poured into Greece after terrible 1492.
            Ladino
(there are four alive from 1,000).
A loudspeaker from a cafe is singing *agonia, agonia,*
            *agonia.*


"They put their pigs in the synagogue."
"How did you survive?"
"God wished it so."


4
The mountains are gray ghosts upon blue ghosts
over hunters' game and green tomato valleys.
The crooked fir and granite ghosts blur into
            Albania the Obscure,
whose unmapped capital is Tirana.
On the Greek side a trembling *tsamiko* flute
balloons wildly into the clouds.
White happiness tinkles down from the summit village wedding.

5

We say goodbye.
The little man picks up his cane and wobbles away
             behind the Byzantine wall.
The horror flower of tyranny,
the blue rose of the tattoo on the forearm
stays fresh and alive in 1986.

I wonder about forgetting at last.
Like the blue milk of morning and the black milk
             of night,
each number keeps its florid memory till death.

"Next year in Jerusalem!"
*agonia, agonia, agonia!*

Everyone is born with a blue rose number on the flesh.

Yaacov Luria

## There Is One Synagogue Extant in Kiev

They do not talk of loss at Babi Yar.
These aged men who blink into the sun
On benches in the courtyard of the *shul*
Have no more words or tears.  *What's done is done.*

Their faces speak, each furrow slaughter-etched.
They sense the stranger's grief, yet know the cost
Of grief is small to him who merely sees,
Then journeys on his way.  *What's lost stays lost.*

Their ninth of Ab came early and stayed on.
There were forty temples once.  Now one is all
That stands in Kiev, their Jerusalem,
A crumbling, wordless, tearless Western Wall.

So long ago their Queen of Sabbath fled,
All that's left is *kaddish* for the dead.


Marilynn Talal

## For Our Dead

1
The air where their ashes have gone
is a mirror against our faces.
Each breath carries mute pleading, hear it, hear
this pathetic rebuke to inadequacy
and constant failure.

These ashes stop our mouths.
The dead lay claim to us
who must not let go the millions of destroyed worlds
that, unredeemed, call and call.
There is no answer.

How can we say Kaddish? praise God?
The bitterness breaks our teeth.

Torn from this life, the ties
to this world not tenderly laid aside,
these ghosts hover over the surface of the earth
tethered to the fragrance of a pot of soup
steaming on the stove,

the horse's harness on a nail to be mended,
the severed rope of a toy pullwagon
wheels spinning on finger-sized axles.

They died many deaths at each
hopeless point: roundup, the clanging doors,
whips and loud, rude calls: "Herraus!" "Herraus!"
Slowly their suffering reshapes our being
and we are helpless children
in a world without guidance.

2
O, our loved ones, the places shorn of you
cry out.  They are not vacant but burn
as witnesses of torment.
The very stones tremble with damnation.

Our lives will always be in disarray
around this great wound.  Particles
in the mass, we make small
arrangements at the edges.
Evil has become too large.

The Kaddish is supposed to comfort, to begin
to mend the tear.  What blood song
can redeem this blood lesson?

Ripped out of lives in midstep,
that hole in the air hangs, shaping itself
into a mouth silently screaming.

Miriam Kessler

## Yahrzeit

Your memory is leashed into my life,
lashed about me.
It strangles
like a morning-glory vine.
Six million muffled cries
smothered in the hiss of Zyklon-B.

Today I will be joyful
for no good reason,
only because you were denied joy.
I live what you had a right to.
My presumption is your gift,
my debt inexhaustible,
though you were not.
My candle is not *Yahrzeit* enough.
I burn it anyway.

When day blinks down through grey shutters
and cardinals begin their red cantata;
when leaves curl away from rain,
you will not know it.
My voice,
my sobbing
will not shake you
from your Six Million sleeps.

Peretz Kaminsky

## Identifications

From shadows such as these I shape my songs:
"My hand wrote the message on Belshazzar's wall";
"The pen I use for poetry wrote psalms";
"My signet reads, 'Lord, from the depths I call' ";

"My belt is braided from blind Samson's hair";
"I crawl up Jacob's ladder rung by rung";
"My sandals, made from scraps of parchment scrolls,
    use broken strings from David's harp for thongs."

I bless the Sabbath's end in candlelight
    and dip my pen into the kiddush cup.
The festive candles flicker as I write.
My written words are prayer, and wine, and bread.
They sound like looming thunder in my head,
    whispering the names of our sixmillion dead.


## Bramble

I add my silence
to the spent years of my life.
I add my silence
to all the silences I have known.
I add my silence
to the ending of prayers I cannot say.
I add my silence
to the silence that speaks from unnamed graves.
I add my silence
to the unheard voices in gas chambers.
I add my silence
to the silence that weeps from crematoriums.

Memory makes a noise in my head
and words gather strength in my lungs
and sounds flood into my throat
and a wailing flows from my mouth
and my silence will not be silent
and I argue with God who is silent within me.

I light a bramble bush.
No voice speaks from its silence.
The fires of Auschwitz rise from the thorns.

Bradley R. Strahan

# Yom Kippur

In this great Synagogue
on this great Sabbath
of the year,
the altar is spread
with flowers.

Not white alone
that mourns endless martyrs
but blues and yellows,
orange and purple,
litany of a people
various as these blossoms,
picked over by some
merciless angel.

Here I count my sins
in silence, like cut flowers.
Walking slowly,
I measure my distance
from the stench
of Auschwitz
by the sweet purity
of this day.

Early fallen leaves
litter the path,
abandoned follies
of summer.
Still clinging
to this great tree,
I feel the surge
that year by year
pushes heavenward
in scorn of ax and saw.

AMERICAN POETS ON THE HOLOCAUST

Martin Robbins

## A Cantor's Dream before "The Days of Awe"

In white robes I'm joined by a
Buchenwald survivor who
sways with a tune he can't sing.

Blood-red twilight selects, one
by one, "who shall die by fire . . .
and who by beasts." Yom Kippur

is ending and I try to sing
"Return, my heart, as in days
of old"; but the Torah burns,
the ark is a boxcar's mouth.

"Hurry, the gates, *bim-bom,*
the gates are closing, *bim-bom.*"
Shadows mock my prayerbook's words:

"You are inscribed in the Book
of Life?" A guard grabs my mike:
"In Auschwitz, there is no why."

The dream sun explodes,
collapsing in the unwavering
blast of the Shofar's one call.

Laurence Josephs

## Passover at Auschwitz

Possibly they thought of it,
Remembering the old days; possibly
They could savor, still, the memory

162

Of spices, the clean bone, the glass
Of quiet wine left in the cool
Opacity of symbol, for the Guest.

Here were no calendars: perhaps
A knotted cord: more likely
That the stars alone beat time, aware and distant,
Or that clouds, like immaculate grandfathers,
Lay against the void of memory.
Here it was Passover all year long! What ghosts

Flamed in their blood, their terrible dreams!
The plague: life! The sea: tears! The serpent:
Hope! For in the dying
Center of history newer than theirs,
The world, like a wingéd horse, flew upside down.
They, then, firstborn, were prey of angels,

Where in an endless, idiot night
They waited for a sound of wings or feet.
Pass over! or Come down! they must have cried.
Or from their myth of sleep, reached out
To the angel death who once, in old bondage,
Did not forget, but held them more than dear.

Bert Meyers

## Pigeons

Wherever I go to find
peace or an island
under palms in the afternoon

at midnight to pity my neighborhood
at dawn in the shrubs
to look for a child

I hear them
they fly by
applauding themselves
I see them
they pray as they walk
their eyes are halos
around a pit
they look amazed

who are these that come
as a cloud to our windows
who rush up like smoke
before the town burns

You will find one
on a mountain
in a carpenter's shop
at home on the lawn
of an old estate
at the library
in the forehead of paradise

Whoever is mad
can accuse them
thousands were killed in a day

What happens to them
happens to me
when I can't sleep
they moan and I'm there
and it's still like that

Gloria Glickstein

## The Ghetto

Still I see them.  Infirm, creeping
under the light of day,
some sorting buttons, some stitching
sleeves, stifling the nightmares
and making a living.

Along Broadway they still seek survivors,
someone who knew someone who knew. . . .
Along Rue de Belleville and Rehov Yehuda.
Where did the ghosts disappear?
Irkutsk?  Kazakhstan?

Shadows bend in Siberian cornfields,
shadows loot the Warsaw pickle factory,
shadows remain unforgiving.

I see their dybbuks: bunk to bunk,
scalps itching, brains burning,
jammed like toes in tight shoes.
My mother's mother, my father's father
an integrated pile of ash.

Lois Mathieu

## Counting Sheep by Night

They walk among us in the cold
abstraction of reality,
tied to a motherless life

by death's tattoo.
Still raw to the bone,
they walk down Main Street,
haunted by images.

They walk through streets
of daylight, camouflaging
countless skeletons
until the night time comes
to count them up. One by one,
they writhe, as one by one
their flock jumps from the blue sky
into the darkest pits of conscience.

Julius Balbin

## Tonight

Tonight
    the silence of my room
weighs
on my chest

As I shudder
    the silence of my room
enshrouds millions
    the womb
of the aborted
world

    The silence of my room
is the coffin
of my martyred mother

The silence of my room
has swallowed
the cries
of my past

The silence of my room
is pregnant
with the sound
of your voice
that rings
with the screams
of that day
we parted

The silence of my room
is waiting patiently
yet you
are not
going
to call me
tonight

The silence of my room
is like the silence
of God

The silence
of my room
suddenly
starts
shrieking
from the womb
of despair
tonight

———

Translated from the Esperanto by Charlz Rizzuto

Jacob Glatstein

# Nightsong

Strangers' eyes don't see
how in my small room I open a door
and begin my nightly stroll among the graves.
(How much earth—if you can call it earth—does it take to bury smoke?)
There are valleys and hills
and hidden twisted paths,
enough to last a whole night's journey.
In the dark I see shining towards me
faces of epitaphs
wailing their song.
Graves of the whole
vanished Jewish world
blossom in my one-man tent.
And I pray:
Be a father, a mother to me,
a sister, a brother,
my own children, body-kin,
real as pain,
from my own blood and skin,
be my own dead,
let me grasp and take in
these destroyed millions.

At dawn I shut the door
to my people's house of death.
I sit at the table and doze off,
humming a tune.
The enemy had no dominion over them.
Fathers, mothers, children from their cradles
ringed around death and overcame him.
All the children, astonished,
ran to meet the fear of death

without tears, like little Jewish bedtime stories.
And soon they flickered into flames
like small namesakes of God.

Who else, like me, has
his own nighttime
dead garden?
Who is destined for this, as I am?
Who has so much dead earth waiting for him, as for me?
And when I die
who will inherit my small house of death
and that shining gift, an eternal deathday light
forever flickering?

———

Translated from the Yiddish by Ruth Whitman

## I'll Find My Self-Belief

I'll find my self-belief in a dustpuff of wonder
flecking my view back
as far as dim sight
can imagine, can see.
In the bobbing
kindled dark
there rises up
a salvaged half-star
that managed not to be killed.
A chunk of exploded planet
that once had life,
green abundance, grazing luxury.
Witnesses: my tearfilled eyes,
the distant flora, grapestained with blood,
under a sky eternally sinking;
leaves rocking like bells

deafened, soundless,
on unlooked-at-trees
in an empty world.

I'll be stubborn,
plant myself
in my own intimate night
which I've entirely invented
and admired from all sides.
I'll find my place in space
as big as a fly,
and for all time
compel a cradle to stand there,
and a child
into whom I'll sing the voice
of a father drowsing,
with a face in the voice,
with love in the voice,
with hazy eyes
that swim in the child's sleepy eyes
like warm moons.
And I'll build around this cradle a Jewish city
with a *shul,* with a God who never sleeps,
who watches over the poor shops,
over Jewish fear
over the cemetery
that's lively all night
with worried corpses.

And I'll buckle myself up with my last days
and, for spite, count them in you, my frozen past
who mocked me,
who invented my living, garrulous
Jewish world.
You silenced it
and in Maidanek woods
finished it off with a few shots.

———

Translated from the Yiddish by Ruth Whitman

## Dead Men Don't Praise God

We received the Torah on Sinai
and in Lublin we gave it back.
Dead men don't praise God,
the Torah was given to the living.
And just as we all stood together
at the giving of the Torah,
so did we all die together at Lublin.

I'll translate the tousled head, the pure eyes,
the tremulous mouth of a Jewish child
into this frightful fairy tale.
I'll fill the sky with stars
and I'll tell him:
our people is a fiery sun
from beginning to beginning to beginning.
Learn this, my little one,
from beginning to beginning to beginning.

Our whole imagined people
stood at Mount Sinai
and received the Torah.
The dead, the living, the unborn,
every soul among us answered:
we will obey and hear.
You, the saddest boy of all generations,
you also stood on Mount Sinai.
Your nostrils caught the raisin-almond fragrance of each
                    word of the Torah.
It was Shavuoth, the green holiday.
You sang with them like a songbird:
I will hear and obey, obey and hear
from beginning to beginning to beginning.

Little one, your life is carved
in the constellations of our sky,
you were never absent,

you could never be missing.
When we were, you were.
And when we vanished,
you vanished with us.

And just as we all stood together
at the giving of the Torah,
so did we all die together in Lublin.
From all sides the souls came flocking,
The souls of those who had lived out their lives, of those
        who had died young,
of those who were tortured, tested in every fire,
of those who were not yet born,
and of all the dead Jews from great-grandfather Abraham down,
they all came to Lublin for the great slaughter.
All those who stood at Mount Sinai
and received the Torah
took these holy deaths upon themselves.
"We want to perish with our whole people,
we want to be dead again,"
the ancient souls cried out.
Mama Sara, Mother Rachel,
Miriam and Deborah the prophetess
went down singing prayers and songs,
and even Moses, who so much didn't want to die
when his time came,
now died again.
And his brother, Aaron,
and King David
and the Rambam, the Vilna Gaon,
and Mahram and Marshal
the Seer and Abraham Geiger.
And with every holy soul
that perished in torture
hundreds of souls
of Jews long dead died with them.

And you, beloved boy, you too were there.
You, carved against the constellated sky,
you were there, and you died there.

Sweet as a dove you stretched out your neck
and sang together with the fathers and mothers.
From beginning to beginning to beginning.
Shut your eyes, Jewish child,
and remember how the Baal Shem rocked you
in his arms
when your whole imagined people
vanished in the gas chambers of Lublin.

And above the gas chambers
and the holy dead souls,
a forsaken abandoned Mountain Sinai veiled itself in smoke.
Little boy with the tousled head, pure eyes, tremulous mouth,
that was you, then,—the quiet, tiny, forlorn
given-back Torah.
You stood on top of Mount Sinai and cried,
you cried your cry to a dead world.
From beginning to beginning to beginning.

And this was your cry:
we received the Torah on Sinai
and in Lublin we gave it back.
Dead men don't praise God.
The Torah was given to the living.

———————

Translated from the Yiddish by Ruth Whitman

Gerald Stern

## Soap

Here is a green Jew
with thin black lips.
I stole him from the men's room
of the Amelia Earhart and wrapped him in toilet paper.
Up the street in *Parfumes*
are Austrian Jews and Hungarian,

without memories really,
holding their noses in the midst of that
paradise of theirs.
There is a woman outside
who hesitates because it is almost Christmas.
"I think I'll go in and buy a Jew," she says.
"I mean some soap, some nice new lilac or lily
to soothe me over the hard parts,
some Zest, some Fleur de Loo, some Wild Gardenia."

And here is a blue Jew.
It is his color, you know,
and he feels better buried in it, imprisoned
in all that sky, the land of death and plenty.
If he is an old one he dances,
or he sits stiffly,
listening to the meek words and admiring the vile actions
of first the Goths and then the Ostrogoths.
Inside is a lovely young girl,
a Dane, who gave good comfort
and sad support to soap of all kinds and sorts
during the war and during the occupation.
She touches my hand with unguents and salves.
She puts one under my nose all wrapped in tissue,
and squeezes his cheeks.

I buy a black Rumanian for my shelf.
I use him for hair and beard,
and even for teeth when things get bitter and sad.
He had one dream, this piece of soap,
if I'm getting it right,
he wanted to live in Wien
and sit behind a hedge on Sunday afternoon
listening to music and eating a tender schnitzel.
That was delirium. Other than that he'd dréam
of America sometimes, but he was a kind of cynic,
and kind of lazy—conservative—even in his dream,

and for this he would pay, he paid for his lack of dream.
The Germans killed him because he didn't dream
enough, because he had no vision.

I buy a brush for my back, a simple plastic
handle with gentle bristles. I buy some dust
to sweeten my body. I buy a yellow cream
for my hairy face. From time to time I meet
a piece of soap on Broadway, a sliver really,
without much on him, sometimes I meet two friends
stuck together the way those slivers get
and bow a little, I bow to hide my horror,
my grief, sometimes the soap is so thin
the light goes through it, these are the thin old men
and thin old women the light goes through, these are
the Jews who were born in 1865
or 1870, for them I cringe, for them
I whimper a little, they are the ones who remember
the eighteenth century, they are the ones who listened
to heavenly voices, they were lied to and cheated.

My counterpart was born in 1925
in a city in Poland—I don't like to see him born
in a little village fifty miles from Kiev
and have to fight so wildly just for access
to books, I don't want to see him struggle
half his life to see a painting or just to
sit in one of the plush chairs listening to music.
He was dragged away in 1940
and turned to some use in 1941,
although he may have fought a little, piled
some bricks up or poured some dirty gasoline
over a German truck. His color was rose
and he floated for me for days and days; I love
the way he smelled the air, I love how he looked,
how his eyes lighted up, how his cheeks were almost pink
when he was happy. I loved how he dreamed, how he almost
disappeared when he was in thought. For him
I write this poem, for my little brother, if I
should call him that—maybe he is the ghost

that lives in the place I have forgotten, that dear one
that died instead of me—oh ghost, forgive me!—
Maybe he stayed so I could leave, the *older* one
who stayed so I could leave—oh live forever!
forever!—Maybe he is a Being from the other
world, his left arm agate, his left eye crystal,
and he has come back again for the twentieth time,
this time to Poland, to Warsaw or Bialystok,
to see what hell is like. I think it's that,
he has come back to live in our hell, if he could
even prick his agate arm or even weep
with those crystal eyes—oh weep with your crystal eyes,
dear helpless Being, dear helpless Being. I'm writing this
in Iowa and Pennsylvania and New York City,
in time for Christmas, 1982,
the odor of Irish Spring, the stench of Ivory.


Irving Feldman

## The Pripet Marshes

Often I think of my Jewish friends and seize them as they are and
    transport them in my mind to the *shtetlach* and ghettos,

And set them walking the streets, visiting, praying in *shul,* feasting and
    dancing. The men I set to arguing, because I love dialectic and
    song—my ears tingle when I hear their voices—and the girls and

women I set to promenading or to cooking in the kitchens, for the sake of their tiny feet and clever hands.

And put kerchiefs and long dresses on them, and some of the men I dress in black and reward with beards. And all of them I set among the mists of the Pripet Marshes, which I have never seen, among wooden buildings that loom up suddenly one at a time, because I have only heard of them in stories, and that long ago.

It is the moment before the Germans will arrive.

Maury is there, uncomfortable, and pigeon-toed, his voice is rapid and slurred, and he is brilliant;

And Frank who is goodhearted and has the hair and yellow skin of a Tartar and is like a flame turned low;

And blond Lottie who is coarse and miserable, her full mouth is turning down with a self-contempt she can never hide, while the steamroller of her voice flattens every delicacy;

And Marian, her long body, her face pale under her bewildered black hair and of the purest oval of those Greek signets she loves; her head tilts now like the heads of the birds she draws;

And Adele who is sullen and an orphan and so like a beaten creature she trusts no one, and who doesn't know what to do with herself, lurching with her magnificent body like a despoiled tigress;

And Munji, moping melancholy clown, arms too short for his barrel chest, his penny-whistle nose, and mocking nearsighted eyes that want to be straightforward and good;

And Abbie who, when I listen closely is speaking to me, beautiful with her large nose and witty mouth, her coloring that always wants lavender, her vitality that body and mind can't quite master;

And my mother whose gray eyes are touched with yellow, and who is as merry as a young girl;

And my brown-eyed son who is glowing like a messenger impatient to be

gone and who may stand for me.
I cannot breathe when I think of him there.
And my red-haired sisters, and all my family, our embarrassed love
bantering our tenderness away.

Others, others, in crowds filling the town on a day I have made sunny for
them; the streets are warm and they are at their ease.

How clearly I see them all now, how miraculously we are linked! And
sometimes I make them speak Yiddish in timbres whose unfamiliarity
thrills me.

But in a moment the Germans will come.

What, will Maury die? Will Marian die?

Not a one of them who is not transfigured then!

The brilliant in mind have bodies that glimmer with a total dialectic;
The stupid suffer an inward illumination; their stupidity is a subtle
tenderness that glows in and around them;
The sullen are surrounded with great tortured shadows raging with pain,
against whom they struggle like Titans;
In Frank's low flame I discover an enormous perspectiveless depth;
The gray of my mother's eyes dazzles me with our love;
No one is more beautiful than my red-haired sisters.
And always I imagine the least among them last, one I did not love, who
was almost a stranger to me.
I can barely see her blond hair under the kerchief; her cheeks are large and
faintly pitted, her raucous laugh is tinged with shame as it subsides; her
bravado forces her into still another lie;
But her vulgarity is touched with a humanity I cannot exhaust, her
wretched self-hatred is as radiant as the faith of Abraham, or

indistinguishable from that faith.
I can never believe my eyes when this happens, and I want to kiss her
    hand, to exchange a blessing

In the moment when the Germans are beginning to enter the town.

But there isn't a second to lose, I snatch them all back,
For, when I want to, I can be a God.
No, the Germans won't have one of them!
This is my people, they are mine!

And I flee with them, crowd out with them: I hide myself in a pillowcase
    stuffed with clothing, in a woman's knotted handkerchief, in a
    shoebox.
And one by one I cover them in mist, I take them out.
The German motorcycles zoom through the town,
They break their fists on the hollow doors.
But I can't hold out any longer.  My mind clouds over.
I sink down as though drugged or beaten.

Louis Simpson

## A Story about Chicken Soup

In my grandmother's house there was always chicken soup
And talk of the old country—mud and boards,
Poverty,
The snow falling down the necks of lovers.

Now and then, out of her savings
She sent them a dowry.  Imagine
The rice-powdered faces!
And the smell of the bride, like chicken soup.

But the Germans killed them.
I know it's in bad taste to say it,
But it's true.  The Germans killed them all.

*

In the ruins of Berchtesgaden
A child with yellow hair
Ran out of a doorway.

A German girl-child—
Cuckoo, all skin and bones—
Not even enough to make chicken soup.
She sat by the stream and smiled.

Then as we splashed in the sun
She laughed at us.
We had killed her mechanical brothers,
So we forgave her.

*

The sun is shining.
The shadows of the lovers have disappeared.
They are all eyes; they have some demand on me—
They want me to be more serious than I want to be.

They want me to stick in their mudhole
Where no one is elegant.
They want me to wear old clothes,
They want me to be poor, to sleep in a room with many others—

Not to walk in the painted sunshine
To a summer house,
But to live in the tragic world forever.

Charles Fishman

# The Death Mazurka

It was late—late in the silence—
yet a mangled tune still rose
as if from a needle trapped
in a warped and spinning groove:
an inarticulate moan
fragmented out of sense
but insistent it be known.

Footfalls turned me around:
a troupe of dancers spun
and kicked and dipped as one—
three score minus one,
and that *one* danced alone.
I watched them skip and prance
but followed only her.

And yes, the drum was swift
and kept a lively beat,
and violins sang sweet
then stridently miaoued—
a mocking sliding note.
She alone danced on
uncoupled, incomplete.

But the trumpets shrilled their tongues
and the saxophones crooned deep
and cymbals scoured the night
to a clashing brassy gleam.
How the women's earrings shined!
like sparks from a whirling fire
that never would be ash.

Then the men whisked off their hats
and bowed to the slide trombone
as though it sat enshrined.
But still *she* danced alone

at the edge of the wheeling ring:
I could feel the horizon tilt
when she veered close to me.

Then she turned   then I   then the night
blew back forty years:
I stood in a desolate place,
a reservoir of death
—I could kneel anywhere and drink!
Yes, here was the shul in its bones
and here *Judenrein Square*

and here a few scorched teeth
from some martyred, unknown saint.
The sky was a scroll of pain
—each star a sacred name!
I saw through time in that light.
But I turned and blood rained down
and I turned and dipped and drank

and could not take my fill:
I yearned to find *her* there.
And I turned toward darkness again
where dancers in masks like skulls
twirled in smoke and fire,
whirled in fire and smoke.
*Now!* screamed the violins.

And she was near as my heart
as we clasped each other and turned.
And *Now!* they shrieked.  And *Now!*

William Pillin

## Miserere

I will not endow you with a false glow
ghetto
or say that only poets and seers
died in your ashes.
Many mourn the scholars and dreamers,
the beautiful innocent talented victims.
I will spare my tears for the
loudmouthed unhappy conniving
jews
the usurious lenders,

tuberculous hunchbacked
scum of the ghettos (the sweepings of Europe).
For them I will weep,
                for the whores
pale in doorways, for the spiderous tradesmen
with their false measures
                and for all the grey sparrows
hopping about the winters of Poland
                the grief of whose eyes
went up in thin smoke like a final prayer.
For them I will weep, I want them returned,
the dwellers of dives, brothels and taverns.
I want them
back as they were, piteous, ignoble,
instead of this white ash
that like a winding sheet settles on shivering Europe.

## The Ascensions

You, Marc Chagall, should be able to tell us
what was cremated in Thor's ovens,
you who were always painting ascensions.

The ascension of priestly violinists,
the ascension of white-gowned brides,
the ascension of purple donkeys,
of lovers, of bouquets, of golden cockerels,
ascension into the clair-de-lune.

O this soaring
out of shanties and cellars!
the folk spirit ascending
through enchanted alphabets,
through magical numbers,
to a wandering in the bluest realm.

The ascension
(from sewers, dives, back-alleys)
of folk-songs to the new moon,
to the feast of lights,
to the silences of Friday evening . . .

. . . and suddenly
in the quietude of steppes
a thin column of smoke ascending
and after that
no more ascensions.

*

No more ascensions!

Only stone chimneys
heavily clinging
to the earth of Poland.
Not even a marker saying:
here the kikes
en-masse ascended.

## Farewell to Europe

We, the captives of a thousand skies,
sang the airs of many peoples,
tango, waltz and leaping czardash;

but the waltz stumbles, the oboe
is poised on the point of a scream.

We whispered madrigals of woe
in sewers and cellars.
We learned sparrow wit, hangman humor,
at the bottom of scaffolds,
at the gates of stone chimneys.

Europe, the odor of your guilt
lingers in our nostrils.
You are a perspective of walls
diminishing in cold moonlight.

Vanish from our songs!

*

Will your pianos haunt us to the end?
The stars in your snows, O steppes?
the sunlight bleeding gold
on the rim of a snow-foaming mountain?

Facade of roses and wings,
shall we cloak our memories in blue
because your gardens sang to the sun?

The kaftaned companions of the Presence
are swept from the streets of your cities.
Our migrants kiss a new wind
scented with ancient cedars.

Farewell, the Vienna woods are no longer calling,
or the grimacing spires of Cologne,
or your gleaming cupolas, Kiev.

Your temples are Gothic stalactites,
frozen tears of eternity;
your gardens are lavender clouds;
your streetlamps shimmering buoys
of musical boulevards.

But you were never our motherland.
We were born
not on the Rhine or the Vistula
but in Abraham's tent
on a journey from Ur to Judea.

This you never ceased to remind us;
that we were alien,
remote from you, the light of a dead star
that faintly lingers upon this planet.

*

We are leaving.  We take little with us;
some music, a few poems.

It is well that we stand under new arches
bequeathing to our children
our praises, our celebrations.

Our Einstein will toughen the mental sinews
        of other continents.
Our Freud will plumb the dark soul of Asia.
Our Marx will rally the cadres of jungles
        and savannahs.

*

We are leaving.  No longer will you have to cross
        yourself, people with pitchforks and cudgels,
        as our huddled remnants trudge over your meadows.

O mother of white nights, after a millennium on
        your steppes your hostages are pleading: let
        us depart!

## WITHOUT JEWS

We are leaving our ancestral tombs, our shrines,
        our wealth endlessly plundered by the card-
        playing nobles.

We are leaving you forever, belching Siegfried,
        Vladimir red-eyed from distilled potatoes!

\*

Europe, you realm of carnivorous blonds!
Your grand canals are clogged by chemical silt.
The sculptures of your saints are eroded by
        pigeon droppings.
Smokestacks spew their spittle on the
        vineyards of Chateau de Rothschild.

Elegant bushmen celebrate your Requiem Mass
        with tom-toms and banjos.

Even as you revel in your utopia of pig-fat,
        blood-sausage and Pilsen
you look nervously over your shoulder
at the lean wolves of the east.

They will strip your flesh leaving
the bare bones of cathedrals.
What the wolves will not eat—
monuments, fountains, castles—
will be shipped stone by antique stone
to the Disneylands of America.

\*

Basta! Genug! Assez! Dostatochno!

Farewell, blue-eyed maiden. You need no
        longer exclaim on seeing the mark of our
       ancient covenant: "You cheated me! You
       never told me!"

Farewell, priests whose blood mysteries at Lent
      goaded the tavern heroes to wield their
      axes among us.

Zbignew, whom will your children curse?
Zoltan, astride a stallion, at whom will you
      lash out galloping by?

You have no one to bludgeon but each other!


## The Requirement

Having avoided fatal accidents,
having somehow survived
wars, illnesses and sundry disasters,
having passed unscathed
through the thick black smoke
from the blood of my burning cousins,
I can say this now, I can say it quietly:
to go on is the only requirement.

To love you, to eat my meals with you,
to sip my brandy,
to cut the grass on the front lawn,
to say "hello" and "how are you."

To attend to matters that need attending;
to kindle the candles on festival evenings;
to conciliate powers superior to mine:
the eye of Medusa, the kiss of the white-faced vixen.
To go on
through the butchered air between the alarms;
to feel in the brutal darkness
the touch of your hand, my companion.

To go on and on as the winds blow
through the night of stars and storms,

188

to endure
the great cold constellations,
to go on
on the boulevards increasingly silent and bare,
to persist
until nothing is left,
not the trees, not the house,
not the winds,
not even you, not even you!


Linda Pastan

# Rachel (rā'chal), a Ewe

We named you
for the sake
of the syllables
and for the small boat
that followed the Pequod,
gathering lost children
of the sea.

We named you
for the dark-eyed girl
who waited at the well
while her lover
worked seven years
and again
seven.

We named you
for the small daughters
of the Holocaust
who followed their six-pointed stars
to death
and were all of them
known as
Rachel.

Deborah S. Snyder

## Carolyn's Neighbor

Rhoda Bok
who survived Treblinka, said to us
that to this day she lives

for the comfort of the smallest things—a book; wool
coverlets; the flannel robe she wraps
closely around her;
the hot
glass of tea she takes with supper.

Of it, she mentioned
being cold.
She would speak
only of the cold; of always,
always

still shaking with it.

Mike Frenkel

## Quiet Desperation

my parents endured
the Nazi death blitz—
but barely.
my mother cushioned
the fatal tremors
of her mother,
her father,
her younger brother;
then on stick legs
exorcized the typhoid
from her own body.
my father

rested in a 3 month coma,
eaten by bed sores and fever.
when he awoke,
he quietly longed for
that unconscious sanity.

their hands were mangled—
fingers un-
hinged and re-sewn.
to this day,
they are unable to
make a fist.
my mother,
who was a prodigy
and hammered out
sonatas—
*allegro di bravura*—
on a simple piano
long since looted
and burned,
now plays an occasional
listless bagatelle.

Theodore Deppe

## School of Music

for Zhanna Dawson

My first lesson: you won't even let me touch
the keyboard. You have me drum my fingers
against a table to work the stone from my wrists.

We all start with stone. For you
it was the laughter of Germans as the rabbi
danced. When the rope stopped red bullwhips cracked

and the rabbi danced again, briefly resurrected
in the sleet-backed wind of your childhood.
Or, say the stone *is* the wind

and the wind is the crying of children
loaded in open trucks.  Even today you hate
wind.  You are so still, sit such a long time

preparing to play.  Your gold watch waits
silent as a heron over white keys.
You were one of thirteen thousand

marched out of Kharkov into the storm.
You wear the watch now to remind you of the one
your father gave a guard: barter for your life.

Almost imperceptibly it rises alone
over winter fields, and the music starts—
your fingers striking out

over unmarked graves, playing
for the demanding ears of your father
music that is first of all survival.


Florence Weinberger

## Survivor

for Ted

He knows the depths of smokestacks,
from their bleak rims down
their spattered walls, from their ash cones
to the bone-bottom ground.
Once he could see under skin,
inside the body, where deprivation
thins the blood of all desire

except hunger.
For years he wanted to forget
everything.  He knows it is possible
to live only at the surface,
it is possible to work,
to marry and have daughters.
But his daughters
look like people he once knew,
and he dreams them.
He dreams them opening doors,
sending letters.  When he wakes,
he knows he has been dreaming.
This year, he will show his daughters
where he was born.  He will show them
the chimney, the iron gate,
the deep oven where his mother baked bread.


Rosa Felsenburg Kaplan

## Kol Nidre

(For an adolescent during the Holocaust)

All the vows
And all the promises not kept
Because life was too short
Or too difficult,
Or we were too young,
Not wise enough, or too weak—
Let them be cancelled!

I remember being glad
To leave behind my friend and Europe.
When she told me how life was started,

She had sworn me to secrecy.
Now she would not have to know
That I had told our secret.

The choking void of unsaid farewells
Because we did not know
We were together for the last time—
Let it be closed!

Alice and Malka, twin cousins with whom I played,
And who I wished I looked like,
And whose parents, I thought,
Must love them more than mine loved me—
"One time," said their mother. "They mostly took
        young girls. . . ."

For the sins committed on them
Forgive us: *S'lach lanu, m'chal lanu, kaper lanu!*

The unsaid thanks
To those who gave to us,
Life, sometimes,
But to whom we could not give—
Let thanks be understood!

Twice I took another's name
To cross a border
What happened to my namesakes?

And to Onkel Michel,
And Tante Esti
And Kati Neni—
Who took me in, housed me and fed me,

And whom I loathed and made fun of
Because they were not my parents,
Nor like them. . . ?

The tears unshed
Because we were too busy living
To mourn—
Let them now flow!

Trying to finish high school
And enter college,
Becoming American—
I shut my eyes to my parents' fears,
My heart to their losses as well as to my own . . .

To those of us who live,
To our families and friends,
And all of those whom we're supposed to love—
Father of mercy,
Give them life
And us, time enough
To make peace,
Perhaps even to love them.

Kinereth Gensler

## For Nelly Sachs

Every morning I took a shower
Every morning under the hot spray
tuned by my hand
I saw the valves
streaming gas

from the walls and ceilings
of rooms marked "BATH"
in Buchenwald   Bergen-Belsen

As if I'd been there
As if it were required of me
As if all Jews
were forced to start each day
stripped in a locked room
remembering in their skins
unable to stop it
just as one by one women
like me had stood
packed in a locked room
under the streaming gas

> Give us this day
> the grace
> of showers

I can't remember when it stopped
in the crush of body-counts
in the years of drought & floods
& saturation bombing
I lost them all
they went up
in numbers

O the showers Nelly
the showers
where I stand alone graceless

This numbness
like the end of all desire
the terrible forgetting in my body

William Pitt Root

## Late Twentieth Century Pastoral

Not far from Belsen the countryside
is forgetful and kind,
senile and green.

The air is clear as a natural's conscience.

Pastures are plotted out
like stamps in an old album so vast
only a pilot inclined to glance down
might appreciate its pattern.

Those on the ground require
sealed boots to inspect
fields in the flood plains.

Viewing them through binoculars
you might startle a moment
at the sight of farmers walking on water,
plodding like cattle.

The cattle graze unattended
—munching the tallest stalks,
sloshing about,
swishing their tails and swinging
their spiritual heads to and fro,

mooing as if they bore
the griefs of the world on their bones,
their eyes a constant reference
to those sufferings
none can name.

The river that meanders there,
flushed back and forth
by floods from north and south,

gathers up flotsam and jetsam
—weeds here, sheafs of bark there—
hanging it up on barbed wire.

When eventually it cures
it is natural paper,
crude imperfect parchment,
sunbleached and rainbeaten,
where certain indigestible
fragments stubbornly
scrawl out the random glyphs
and tentative ciphers
cattle come upon in
their harmless ritual
testing of the fences.

They do this year after year,
flood after flood,
each ripening herd
bunched and huddled against
new rainfall, nibbling
a passage from
one text or another, lifting
the drooling magnificence
of heads stuffed
with scriptures assembled
by the flood.

And how inscrutably
they low
before the rainbow,
that tireless witness
their masters more knowingly
dismiss, one foot
in a pot of gold,
the other god knows where.

Marilynn Talal

## Being Children

That year each day's paper
brought more stories.
People with blue numbers
on their bare arms began to ride
the rattling subway
and we would look up, hypnotized, among
the white enamelled straps for those tattoos.

Summer days, we sat, Ruthann,
on your pink stoop with Barbara and Vita,
not always dressing our stories
in our mothers' clothes or giggling about boys.
Our fantasies were often women humiliated by men,
made to walk like dogs on a leash.
Or displayed naked in cases, row on row.
The men were dressed in uniforms with boots.
They carried whips.

How could we name our fears,
talk to fathers
grown distant?
In some animal way we dreamed
the small swellings on our ribs
turned them away.

Norah Reap

## Numbers

I met you as a child
  and the world I knew then was a glare of color and sound
  an overexposed world of too much sunlight and garbled
  noise.
And you took me into your cool dark world

199

and gradually my eyes adjusted to a more kindly light
and a quieter voice soothed my ears, battered
by the shrillness of my family's rancor
and the muffled sobs of my own mourning.

You spoke to me
    in a language I couldn't comprehend
    but that I understood,
    like a caress from a stranger who is not really unknown.
In my pain, which I only dimly understood,
    I could freely take the love you gave,
    though I could not know why you wept a little
    as you stroked my pale hair
    or, wiping away your tears, gruffly pushed me on my way.
You knew why I came to this refuge.
I knew that the soft growl of the language
    spoke of loss beyond my own,
    of worlds neither of us could reclaim.

But when you stretched out your arms,
    I saw the purple numbers
    and felt the cruelty and fear of the moment
    and the mottled pink innocence outraged.
I could not ask what they meant, but I knew
    as I looked into your sad eyes
A nightmare vision of horror I would never know.

And so daily I came to you, a silent unanswerable question
        on my lips,
    braving traffic and the forbidden street crossings
    to stand in the cool darkness of your little store
    amid the pickles, amid the love neither of us questioned,
    though we knew little of the journeys that brought us
        together.

Gregg Shapiro

## Tattoo

My father won't talk about the numbers
3-7-8-2-5 between the wrist and elbow
blue as blood on his left forearm
Instead, he spreads himself over me
spilling his protection, like acid, until it burns
I wear him like a cloak, sweat under the weight

There were stories in the lines on his face
the nervous blue flash in his eyes
his bone-crushing hugs
I am drowning in his silence
trying to stay afloat on curiosity
Questions choke me and I swallow hard

We don't breathe the same air
speak the same language
live in the same universe
We are continents, worlds apart
I am sorry my life has remained unscathed
His scars still bleed, his bruises don't fade

If I could trade places with him
I would pad the rest of his days
wrap him in gauze and velvet
absorb the shocks and treat his wounds
I would scrub the numbers from his flesh
extinguish the fire and give him back his life

Sari Friedman

# Skin

I
Mother, they say we never really leave you.
At the moment our bodies part
a new mutual dependence arises.

But from the look of you,
the limp color and dissonant rattling,
angers inflaming you for brief wild moments
from inside,
it seems impossible that I ever started
from one as you, or existed alongside.

II
I wasn't meant to see
that time you tried to kill yourself,
but I did, and that small thing
saved you.
I dragged you back
like picking through garbage.
What was left of you
didn't want to exist.

III
When you fled from the Germans,
and the gooseflesh fear,
their teeth sinking through your creamy layers,
you even escaped from yourself, and arrived,
still burning inside like the ovens.

And you changed your name to Mary;
almost happy in a swirl of houses, clothes,
freckles, and a child . . .
the silly wet sponge, always crying.

IV

You tried to be a good mother,
but like everything else in your life
it went wrong.
Breakfast after breakfast you piled
all the emptied eggshells back
into their original cartons,
and burnt all the eggs,
and became confused by our eyes.

If you were to read these words . . .
Would you understand?  Would you see?
Would you collapse sobbing?
Freed?

V

Hey Ma, does it hurt much?
You push back your hair,
palm up, a girlish gesture;
and I feel for the broken crunch of you,
the hurt of you,
my love a salve or a stab,
washes over, relentless.
What is left of you?

VI

I cannot know.
I am not you.
I am your American child,
and I want my mother.
I still look for your face,
that skin I know so well,
love, even if I love alone.
In one face, the shadows of another.
In swells and hollows,
hope.

Dori Katz

## Line-up

after viewing Andrzei Munk's film, *The Passenger*

All this is history, the still disputed fate
of those who lived, then were deported, died.
Our meeting was accidental. Were you the third man
from the left, staring out of an old newsreel,
his long thin hands against the fence?
No, I said, but the face held me.
                                    Remember,
behind you stood the crematory buildings,
smoke rising from their stacks
like unrelenting ghosts against the wind
forming and dispersing the same question
until I wanted to dig my hands into the ground,
hoping to unearth you still
breathing from a common grave, o frozen Auschwitz.

So many times since then
I have gone back into that film,
trying to place you somewhere else,
perhaps with drivers of the Red-Cross vans,
perhaps behind the calm and ancient trees
that stand evoked, fictitious, out of reach.
Each time, the same men carrying their clothes
line up before a smoking building.
Absorbed, an inmate string quartet
plays Bach so lovingly
you would not notice all the guards,
the straining dogs baring their teeth,
were it not for that man staring out,
his hands grotesque against the fence,
his mouth an open grave waiting to be filled.

Father, the distance is so great between us;
light-years from now, you'll still be standing
by that fence, I on the other side. Forgive me
if to release myself, I say it wasn't you
speaking to me with broken hands.

## The Return

The light I turn on to remember you these days
is small and distant in the dark.
I go back very deeply for you, and very carefully.
One false move and I fall off your shoulder
where I placed myself at three to be carried across
rain puddles; one inadvertent slip and you are gone
while I wait for you, once again, by the kitchen window,
angry because you promised to be right back
and I never saw you again.
No time to say goodbye when they arrested you.
No time to send messages when they took you to Malines
and made you climb into a boxcar with the others.
The doors are shut. I squat in a corner crying for you.

Years pass. Your wife survives. Converted,
your daughter goes from house to home,
a different child now, quiet, tamed,
but at night she walks in her sleep
opening door after door to find you;
you are not there for you're living in Auschwitz now.
Your head is shaved, your hands swollen;
soon they will amputate a leg. You are 177679,
not Moishe Chaim anymore, not anyone.
                                        I waited for you.
I used to think of accidents, cured amnesia,
a hospital file that would turn up your name,
or that you had married again, forgotten me.
I pictured running into you on a deserted street;
you'd be dragging your bad leg behind you against the wind.
You'd recognize me and the dark years would disappear
like rain drying up, or clouds pushed away by strong gusts.
Other times, I saw you as a one-legged man hopping
around the house outside, pressing his face
against the window, against my new life all patched up.

And so I carried you for years, like salt upon the tongue,
a bitter taste always dissolving, always there;
I was afraid that you were lost, afraid you'd return,

old, crippled, gray, and we'd be singled out again.
Today, it doesn't matter what I want; you have been dead
so long there's nothing left that could come back:
you are not flesh, not bone, not even dust of dust;
you are a light behind that kitchen window now,
behind that glass—a light that comes and disappears.

Amos Neufeld

## In the Heaven of Night

Chagall's villages float across the room,
curl into yesterday's clouds
and join the world destroyed
floating in the heaven of night.

The displaced figures and the silence of fiddles
join orphans and angels and sparks belched into the sky,
join a generation of capsized hearts, upturned towns
and inverted hopes, and mix with remnants
of memory, clouds and a sea breeze.
And all, all are rejoined
as dust and smoke
whirling silent in the heaven of night.

And we, the orphaned remnant, abandoned
to chambers of air, leaking memory,
lonely, beyond the frame of night still burning,
exiled to towns beyond our home,
beyond the capsized ghetto and shtetl uprooted,
we, who like a generation of smoke
have risen out of night's chamber furnace,
brother and sister to mounds
of heaving grass, tree and stone,
children of dust and stars, cannot believe
that we are part of this underworld,
this earth that would not have us,

that drove us out in chains of smoke,
and not part of the world destroyed,
that floats across the room
and curls in the heaven of night.

## A Shade of Night

I am a shade,
a remnant,
here to recall
not explain.
The light is cast on others,
those responsible
for the darkness
and the pain
of the shadows
I try to recall.

I am a shade
cast
by the lost light
of my family,
a son
of ashes and memory
risen to fall
on the side of pain
and innocence;
not to forgive or forget
those
who created
the darkness and pain
in their image
over the mass graves
and under
the indifferent
silence:
only a shade,

the lost light
of that other world,
a blade of sadness,
fallen
on the side of the living.

Menachem Z. Rosensaft

## The Second Generation

true, we are the children
of a nocturnal twilight
the heirs of Auschwitz and Ponar
but ours is also the rainbow:
in us the storm meets sunlight
to create new colors
as we add defiant sparks
to an eternal fire

Lora Berg

## Maschlacki

The boys in Bellingham like picking raspberries best.
They bob down among the bush rows, then pop up
To scare the girls. I tell what my father Alec tells,
How, out picking as a boy in the Tatras, he circled
The stout bushes with many uncles. Each uncle, a tooth-
Pick stuck between his teeth, would jauntily close in
On a berry, pick it, probe, flick the green worm out,
Pop the berry into his mouth. This story makes me laugh.
The boys here think it's just some crazy Polish joke,
But it's true, and none of those uncles are left.

When I go biking in the fall to harvest wild fruit,
I imagine myself a Great Uncle Jerzy, from Warsaw.
He is wise about things that grow.  Maple leaves
Stick like starfish to his sleeves and fingertips;
In a basket we gather tart grapes for winter jam.
Bushels fall, tight as beads.  At night, we boil
The glass, melt paraffin, squeeze the sour clusters
Through cloth until the whole kitchen turns purple!
As I soften the jam with caramel, I dream up cousins'
Names to print on the labels of the still steaming jars.

Or Jerzy and I, on our knees, quietly hunt mushrooms.
He uncovers a circle of maschlacki, a grey, dainty family
That must be harvested swiftly, before they melt back
Into the carpet of pine.  In brine, their texture
Becomes like schleemak, the shy snails that emerge
After rain, inhabitants of water and dark, with no final
Texture of animal or plant.  Then, Jerzy talks of evolution:
How it is a way of saying all life descends from one Adam.
But what was he?  Tell, Jerzy, how life in this new place
Corresponds to us, tell again what happened to my family.

Morrie Warshawski

## Sonia at 32

The lady never shakes free the ashes
of the dead. Dark clouds.
Dark cauliflower fists.
A birdbath full of urine.  The fish

bladder that bubbles up and
bounces in the sink.  I climb
the cherry tree for her this year,
watch the large rats dart

into the basement below, and
carry 5-gallon jars of fresh
clover honey up rickety
back stairs.  This lady is

the witness who never forgets.
She hangs wet wash on the
line in a stiff wind against
a background of dust.  She yells

at the dog catcher and cuts
chicken to the bone.  She cries
long distance about this and
that.  About the little man

who is her son.  The little
son who is her husband.  Over
and over she sings the song
her dead brother hummed hiding

behind their house, and holds
each breath as if to say, "Don't Shoot!"

Cecile Hamermesh

# Trilogy

My grandmother is an ivory chord
with the breath of Mt. Sinai
blown into her.

When wisdom rushed down the hill
to crouch into tablets,
my people flamed into orange prayers,

settled deep into the ground
to join hands with hope.

My mother is from that Judaic boulder
with her own natural curves.
She is a prayer shawl
silky with resolve
whirling in her own wind.

My momma sews quietly
the ends of my beginnings
and
embroiders timelessness.

Grandmother rises at night
from dreamyard cemeteries
to cry when innocence
was marched, single file,
to the *Umschlagplatz*
to be carried away in sidecars
of Wagnerian darkness.

Grandmother and mother
were both charms
hung on Teutonic medals.

They made a piece of bread
a story,
feeding themselves with
crusts of gentility.

Momma's laughs are handbrakes.

She makes slipcovers for prophecies.

If I could embrace their thin anguish,
I would rock them
beyond
the strokes of movement.

Olga Drucker

## The Brooch

White bone-rose, silver thorns,
piercing my breast,
fastening our past
each to the other
with questions never asked,
answers never given.

Deep in the center
I see you still
Mother
standing bravely
watching me go
on a trainload of children
escaping.

I never saw your tears.

And after I left,
did you turn to your mother,
did she take you in her arms
before she too was dragged away
leaving us
our legacy?

Jacob Glatstein

## Little Boy

Precious Jewish child,
You escaped with your laughter
From all the darkest dangers.
The bullets couldn't overtake your joy
When a stranger held you in his arms

And you both fled from the slaughterer.
Little fugitive of my times,
Radiant orphan of ours,
Truly I should have added you
To our household, serving you,
Every moment at your command,
Teaching you the inexplicable alphabet
And how God, the righteous,
Created the world.
And you would strike my face
With your laughter
From those bloodied paths—
And all would be laughed away, all refuted.

——————

Translated from the Yiddish by Doris Vidaver

Julie N. Heifetz

## The Blue Parakeet

based on the tape of Ann Lenga, sent as a child
by her parents to hide in the Polish countryside

They knew what was coming to Radom, to all the Jews.
My parents paid to send me to a farm in the country
with a Gentile family. They treated me like
I was one of them. I learned to milk a cow
and churn my own butter. In the woods there were
mulberries and sweet clover. In the evening
I went to the edge of the property where Gypsies
played their violins and danced. I never saw
so much jewelry.

Because I talked to trees and said I heard
my Father singing, they called me Dreamer.
I like to play games by myself, the games
I used to play with Papa. Especially the game
we called the Color Game. "I'm thinking of

something blue," I'd say. Papa had to guess
what I was thinking. "Your dress? Your eyes?
The book on the library table?" Until finally
I'd tell him "I'm thinking of the color blue.
Blue as the moonstone on your finger."
All the colors of home came back to me
playing the Color Game. The pale yellow grass
tall enough to hide in, Papa's cotton shirt,
embroidered like a silk bouquet
with every color of the rainbow.

Winter came. I heard Papa tell me, "Look
how the icicles are candles in the starlight.
Think of them as friends. Also,
slap yourself, move around, keep active.
You'll be warmer." With the first snowfall
I thought about my cousin Helga. We visited
winters in Cologne, flirted with boys
at the skating rink in our sophisticated dresses.
Helga was prettier than I was. I hoped
she was still pretty that Winter.

Many nights the same dream came back to me.
I was in the forest, alone. on every tree
a sign with candy-striped colored letters.
LOST. A BLUE PARAKEET !!
I tried to see the treetops, a little spot
of blue in green leaves, but the limbs were
twisted fingers reaching out to grab me.
I ran faster and faster, until I woke up
whimpering, sad for the bird alone
in the world she hadn't been born to,
sad for the child who'd lost her.
Of all the nights I had the dream,
I never saw the bird.

One day some neighbors came. While I was
gathering eggs they saw me. "She has
a Jewish nose. You have Jews hiding here."
After that I hid in the hayloft,

but eventually the Germans found me.
I was sent to Auschwitz, the youngest
in my lager. Some would take bread
from the dead. I could never do this.
There was even cannibalism there. One old woman
tried to protect me. She put her arms around me.
"Cover your eyes. Nothing important is happening."
What I saw I did not see. What I felt
somedays I could not feel. I became like a robot,
empty, except for dreaming of hundreds of faces
streaked with color, melting in the rain.

To keep my spirits up, I started rumors.
"The war is over, someone with a radio told me
the liberators are coming." After a while,
whatever I said, nobody believed.
The Lagerführerin, our camp commander,
had the prettiest hair, hair like cotton candy.
You couldn't paint a doll that beautiful.
She loved to torture. The minute our hair
would grow a quarter of an inch, she'd cut it.
When she walked by, I imagined her bald and naked,
me holding the razor.

In 1945 after the war, I went back to Radom.
Our house was there, the Gentiles gave it back
for me to live in. Someone told me
while I was in the country they saw my Father
on a transport. He was strong.
He was young enough to make it. I knew
where my strength had come from.
Three months I waited. One day I went
to an open window. Down below my Mother was walking.
I must have screamed. She turned around.
I ran to the street where she was waiting.
Her hands were all over me. She was crying,
so much smaller than I remembered.
I thought she was a lie I wanted to believe in.
I held her very gently, the way a child would hold
a tiny bird in her hands.

## The Wheel

based on the tape of Jakob Szapszewicz,
who escaped from his town in Poland and lived
alone in the surrounding woods

I began to think
This is the way you should live.
For me it is normal, completely normal
to walk on these rocks in wooden shoes
not to have a shirt, to be so dirty
always dirty.
To live without food for a week
and don't feel sick, to sleep
outside in cold weather and not get a cold.
In the pine forest what smelled so sweet
in summertime, so peaceful,
maybe in the stone quarries,
in that hole filled with rain,
maybe here in the fog,
I can cover myself with leaves.
When the bullets fall, the dogs won't find me.

At night I feel in my surroundings
nobody could see me.
I walked around, with all those cold stars,
and see houses, a little light, I think
inside it's warm, and people are sitting,
maybe sleeping in a good bed, a clean bed.
And who am I?  Even a murderer
when he escapes has someone,
parents, an uncle, a friend to exchange,
to talk to him before they kill him.

So many days I have not eaten.
I passed a meadow where cows were grazing.
An old stone well rose from the pastureland
like a voice, reminding me the way

we separated milk from cream before we had
machines at home, then set the vials into
cool streams, hot afternoons.

It was exactly like my Mother's voice led me
to that well that day to feel inside
the darkness of the bricks
until my fingers found a string,
lifted bottle after bottle
of fresh cold milk and separated cream from the body of
the earth,
where peasants hid it just for me.
I drank maybe a gallon of that rich cream
beside the well, healthy in my belly,
empty so long. For two whole days
I was content thinking someone watches and
takes care of me.

So hungry for news,
I taught myself to read Gothic
from the Germans' newspapers.
I could sit in the dark on a stone,
my eyes lightening like a wolf's eyes
that light from the inside, and read
the fine print of the German paper.
Sometimes I was laughing to myself,
What am I doing here?
a Jewish boy from a good family,
who studied Torah fourteen years,
reading Gothic by the moon
longing for friends, for somebody else.
That's all I wanted, not to be the only one.

It came to my mind,
my family's mill, the happy occasions
when we were playing by the water wheel,
with children, as children of the mill.
I remembered every patch, every stone,
the key hidden under the stone,

the feel of the best flour.
New Year's Eve, in the dark,
I went back home.
There were Germans burning those bonfires
and skating on the ice of this lake
that belong to us, and singing.
I was lying on top of the hill
looking down, thinking, look those Germans,
dancing and skating, what I used to do sometimes.

Now I lie in this snow
in the dark, a thief who steals flour
from his own mill from a boy
what wouldn't even think to steal a pin.
How the world change.  Sometimes we will be
in the top, like a wheel history turns around.
At the bottom, it's possible to go up.
As long as you live,
anything can happen.

## Harry Lenga

based on the tape of his experiences

i.  Kozienice, Poland 1939
We had a Rabbi which was named the Kozienicer Rabbi.
The Hassidim believed in that Rabbi.  They used to come and . . .
on the holidays, especially the High Holidays,
they used to go and see the Rabbi, the closest man to God.
Such a beautiful thing already
to sit by the table and study the Torah.
First thing, when the Germans came in to Kozienice,
they burned the Synagogue.  They assembled the most honored Jews,
my father included, and told them to bring 20,000 zlotys
for ransom, and assembled them,
and lighted the Synagogue, and told them to take out
all the books.  Before they light the fire,

to take out all the books and throw them in.
Then they told them to take out the Torah scrolls
and they asked for the Rabbi.  He walked over—
and said, "I'm the Rabbi."
"So," they said, "you take the scrolls and throw them in the fire."
The Rabbi took the scrolls and went forward to the fire,
but when he came to the fire, he stopped.
The SS men commanded him "Throw it in . . . throw it in,"
and he didn't do nothing.
So finally they came and hit him over the head
and pushed him into the fire.  The Torah scrolls fell
into the flames, and a few Jews close
grabbed the Rabbi, and took him out of the fire.
Then they lighted up the Synagogue—they throw gasoline—
and they light it, and the fire was burning,
and they told them to dance and sing happy songs.


ii. Departure 1940
My mother she won't leave her mother.
Her sister can't go away and leave the mother with the sister.
My father can't go away and leave his wife with her mother.
That day after the Synagogue was burned
my father took everything together and gave it to us,
tools, watches, rings, you know, whatever he had,
he gave it to my brothers and me.
Without his tools, a watchmaker is nothing.
"I don't need them—you're young, one day
you might have a use for it."
My mother, she smiled. "It's not so bad, don't worry,
tomorrow we'll all probably go on the train
without having to pay for a ticket."
She took a photograph of my Father in his caftan
and her in her new Shabbas dress,
and put it in my shoe, that they should always walk with me.
Then she kissed me goodbye.
It was the second night of Sukkoth.


iii. Auschwitz
Fourteen hours, and suddenly,
the train stopped, and we thought—

we imagined we're already at wherever they're taking us.
Loud voices were talking from far away.
Everybody tried to listen, many people
what understood different languages,
but we couldn't make it out what kind of language it is.
We thought maybe they're taking us to some kind of crazy house.
Somebody what looked out of the one little window
in the dawn—in the morning light—
they told us they could see some Germans . . .
Gestapo coming up . . . Sturmführer, majors, big battalions of SS.
Suddenly the doors opened and they told us to step out . . . and . . .
we stepped out from those cars and they tried to—
with the rifles—whoever got close they hit.
They told us to line up and take everything out . . .
all our belongings—whoever had anything with them . . .

Then I saw from the other wagons, cars,
they started to carry out dead people.
We looked around and saw those high chimneys in the crematoriums—
the fire coming out of the chimney . . .
no matter how high the chimneys were, we saw the fire coming out . . .
spraying from the chimney.
And we thought, maybe we didn't know where we're going . . .
maybe it's our last moment already.
And they told us to undress and give up all the belongings.
Only thing was to keep our shoes.

They gave us soap, each one got a piece of soap,
for the showers. They checked us through,
they looked in our mouths, everyway,
with a flashlight and all the other places,
looked in where anything can be hidden . . .
for diamonds, for gold, for watches, whatever.
They looked in my shoes . . . a Jewish guy . . .
he saw the picture I had hidden,

and took it and threw it away, just like that.
And I asked . . . I said . . . "That's all I have left of my family . . .
Can I keep it?"
And he said, "Be glad they let you keep your shoes."

After the shower, they gave us a package of clothes,
and I dressed and walked outside, looking for my brothers.
The tall one, they gave him a pair of short pants
that reached him to his knees,
the one that was shorter, him they gave a pair of pants
covering his shoes, and I see them, I started laughing and laughing,
and they're looking at me in my big coat and round hat,
and they're laughing. For so long we never stopped laughing.
We see we're alive.

iv. Ebensee, Austria, May, 1945
The ones what gave up—it's like a signal to their bodies.
We made a pact, my brothers, we shave, we look busy, healthy,
even not healthy, be strong and never give up thinking
We have to survive. We have to hold on.
We see a bowl of soup, a crust of bread,
every morning, maybe a butterfly,
we see a sign they cannot kill us.

When the Americans came,
all the people, Russians, Poles, French, Gypsies,
every nationality poured into the yard. They put up a flag,
each country, from nowhere, I don't know how they do this,
they saved a little flag. They waved their flags and each one
sang their national anthem, till one more nation,
the Jews, in such weak voices, skeletons of Jews from everywhere,
singing Hatikvah.

Michael D. Riley

## Hands: Abraham Kunstler

Cursed with a body
Stronger than stone,
I lived on, and on,
And do so still, prisoner
Of some dull will and purpose
Buried under skin.
Starvation
Only hollowed every muscle
Into sharper definition.
Doomed at seventeen
To endure in blood and vein
The powerful shell of man,
I became the stranger
Hidden in each pair of hands,
The stranger in my own.
"Iron Cross" they called me,
Salting praise with irony—
I a Jew in recent flesh
Become the spade of Jews beyond redemption,
My iron arms outstretched
Like the heavy wings of earth,
To gather in the dead.

For twenty-seven months
I lugged the guts of other Jews, Gypsies,
Communists, morons with their cow eyes,
The old, lame, sick, at last
Anyone at all,
In wagons, trucks, wheelbarrows,
Many times by hand,
Their soft parts bouncing on the rutted frost,
In spring carving like colters
Shallow furrows in the mud,
Sliding with odd grace
Until they tumbled, broken, down the sides of pits

And all grace collapsed in heaps.
Legs and arms and backs would snap
Like dead trees in a storm,
And more than once one going down head first
Would break his neck and turn
To fix me with dead eyes.
Women and men tangled
In a parody of love.

So many shades inscribed
The page of flesh:
The bleached chalk of bone,
A gray sky pregnant with snow,
The golden yellow of a finger of wheat.
(Like teeth, one dental student said,
Though only dentists notice.
And only we and lovers, I thought,
While I could think.)
All rolled into my net
Eighteen hours every day—
The flat bellies of starving fish
On a tide that only grew,
As if each body were a cell
And the sea of flesh a cancer.
While I could think,
It seemed a world was dying
But could never quite be done.

By the time the ovens rose
Like churches with small steeples,
The wave had washed away distinction.
Age and disease,
A spirit folded like a letter in a purse
And meant for someone else,
Or signed over like a will
Too soon: these gave way to young women
with bellies still round with hope,
Men heavy with health
As if they still had lives to lead
And somewhere to walk to on strong legs,

Children delicate as orchids
With hands like petals.
I bore them all
As the labor of my hands.

I shoveled till my shovel broke
And dragged until muscles turned to brine,
Turned green and choked
On Zyklon B from going in too soon,
Found lesions bleeding on my hands.
The ovens stripped my eyebrows, arms,
And half my head of hair,
Branded my face with permanent fever
And burned my retina past repair.
Today the world appears to me
A watercolor over gray.
Taste and smell were sanded down the same,
Though nothing but more death
Will unbend and break
The stubborn fingers of my memory.

I pushed in all the other hands I knew
but one pale boy, tiny as a seed,
Not yet fifteen, whose three months' work
Came just before the end
When the Americans arrived
To vomit and to stare,
Who thought perhaps beyond our gates
God left no more for them to see.
They had young hands and faces.
Some no doubt still had souls.

For nearly forty years I kept
With a fine hand all the ledger books
For a small firm on the *Neue Strasse*.
We specialized in art supplies.
Every day I ran my pale blue numbers
As intricate and thin as fingerprints
In perfect order page after columned page
Without error or tedium,

Quite alone.
Retirement merely hollows out my time
Into the palms of my hands,
Becoming one more thing to hold
Without complaint.
With no hint of weakness or disease,
This body bears it much the same.
I busy myself with chores about the house.
In my garden, I tend my crops
In even rows, lush and beautiful.
Flowers I must imagine, though.
Somehow their heavy scent gets through,
Like a finger down my throat.
I remember how the spade shook my hands
When I turned my first crop down,
Crimping their bright heads with the shovel tip,
And stopping up their ears with earth.
Now I make my own with silk and twine
From pictures in my books.  Sometimes I catch in oil
My delicate creations, then hang the still life on the wall
Above the flower vase original.
The effect greatly pleases me.

Martin Robbins

## Chicago Scene (1952, 1969)

Dawn in my mind.
It betrays no one.
But a man had died.
Ten were needed
So those behind
Could say Kaddish.

Again in dim, chill streets men rush,
In gray coats, again dispossessed.
Carrying velvet bags with stars

Of David woven gold, they rush
Through yellow, shrivelled leaves toward
A rented house, their House of Prayer.

Heavy steps on wood.  Then quick words
of morning worship.  Jewish arms bare—
Arms thick as a wagon driver's,
Fragile as a chemist's beaker,
Left arms (some with small blue numbers),
Thonged seven times with black leather.

Thonged near my heart, the black-boxed words
Of the Old Testament rubbed doubt
Of "Thy goodness to Thy creatures."
The Singer studying *Lieder*,
Mumbling lines, I questioned that rewards
And punishments come from our deeds.

And who had died?
At what black hour?
Prayers over,
In slow Yiddish
They told me: A birthday
Was commemorated—

The last fact of a Jew, Polish.
On this dawn I now remember
What a generation's buried.

Maurya Simon

# Munich, 1955

Mama, pick me up.
I dreamed I died again last night.
I dreamed the big men with guns,
the long walk, seven violins.
You said, *We'll take a bath.*

You held my hand,
I tried to cover myself.
How white your face was,
white like the soap she uses.
Mama, hold me tight.

Squeeze that dream out of me
before it eats me up.
There were big dogs behind us
sniffing a tower of shoes,
and a tinny taste in my mouth.

Such a long walk to the end.
My feet were chunks of ice.
Why won't the duchess talk to us?
She leaves a dark spot above me
on the ceiling when she takes a bath.

Van K. Brock

## The Nightmare

She and her parents escaped, but she still whispers
to herself: *Don't think.*
                              Karlsruhe was different
from the north, she said, the people lovelier, gentler.
She always smiles, her eyes vibrant and fervent.

Her two boyfriends were picked up by the state.

Now, with no shelter while incoming's explode always,
she knows what they who stayed behind learned
about survival and daily freezing and burning.

From a ravenous cavity, heat rises out of piteous cold,
pushing her back, always, saying, Live! Tell!

She wakes with a worried smile, flushed and pale.

"There's a monster in my sleep doesn't want its name known."
"It's bad," she says, simply, smiling, "evil."

Everything, all, as weightless as compressed air.

Steven Sher

## Sitting This One Out

for Sally Gleitman

Hours from the ceremony, laying out her dress,
she discovers happiness, a cousin's nuptial.
At the mirror she doubts her ability
to choose the least obtrusive
jewelry, her eyes unreliable

in such matters.  Her past dictates
pause, silence fixed.
She drifts, sees her young Joe
leading them from Poland, seeking
the future when the world had nothing.

Her nightmare resummoned, she enters
terror she balances more carefully than life,
eager to surface, for another glimpse.
Slapped to what survives, time
spreads its semblance of hope,

sends newlyweds into the darkest
memories.  Music filling the hall,
the numbers on her arm remind them
confinement doesn't end,
flashing caution at the celebration.

Patricia Garfinkel

## The Tailor

Ulezalka, Ulezalka,
your head, laced with cancerous
tentacles like a spider's endless
web, remembers in nightmares
the Gestapo snapping commands
like castanets.

Your small head
fit so snugly in the guard's
palm, baseball in a mitt,
heaved against the camp wall;
the cancer shaken loose, resounding
against the bricks.

In Buchenwald
your blood line was roasted
in ovens like the Christmas
goose, served in open graves,
the hot ashes melting
the snow to black water.

Only you,
last ink spot of the line,
were left, echoing the poison
of the walls.  They carried you
from camp, a mass of papier-mâché
unglued—shipped you to America.

They let you
keep your number and the threads
weaving in and out
of your brain.  The numbers
counted disappearing
faces in the night.

The threads
grew until you became the thread,
they the body.  After you put
the final stitches in my wedding
dress the thread rose and floated
through the open window.

V

**The Late Train: Memory**

Am I stricken by memory or forgetfulness?
Li-Young Lee

C. K. Williams

# Spit

. . . THEN THE SON OF THE "superior race" began to spit into
the Rabbi's mouth so that the Rabbi could continue to spit on the
Torah . . .

The Black Book

After this much time, it's still impossible.  The SS man with his stiff hair
    and his uniform;
the Rabbi, probably in a torn overcoat, probably with a stained beard the
    other would be clutching;
the Torah, God's word, on the altar, the letters blurring under the
    blended phlegm;
the Rabbi's parched mouth, the SS man perfectly absorbed, obsessed with
    perfect humiliation.
So many years and what is there to say still about the soldiers waiting
    impatiently in the snow,
about the one stamping his feet, thinking, "Kill him!  Get it over with!"
while back there the lips of the Rabbi and the other would have brushed
and if time had stopped you would have thought they were lovers,
so lightly kissing, the sharp, luger hand under the dear chin,
the eyes furled slightly and then when it started again the eyelashes of
    both of them
shyly fluttering as wonderfully as the pulse of a baby.
Maybe we don't have to speak of it at all, it's still the same.
War, that happens and stops happening but is always somehow right
    there, twisting and hardening us;
then what we make of God—words, spit, degradation, murder, shame;
    every conceivable torment.
All these ways to live that have something to do with how we live
and that we're almost ashamed to use as metaphors for what goes on in us
but that we do anyway, so that love is battle and we watch ourselves in
    love
become maddened with pride and incompletion, and God is what it is
    when we're alone

wrestling with solitude and everything speaking in our souls turns against
us like His fury
and just facing another person, there is so much terror and hatred that yes,
spitting in someone's mouth, trying to make him defile his own meaning,
would signify the struggle to survive each other and what we'll enact to
accomplish it.

There's another legend.
It's about Moses, that when they first brought him as a child before
Pharaoh,
the king tested him by putting a diamond and a live coal in front of him
and Moses picked up the red ember and popped it into his mouth
so for the rest of his life he was tongue-tied and Aaron had to speak for
him.
What must his scarred tongue have felt like in his mouth?
It must have been like always carrying something there that weighed too
much,
something leathery and dead whose greatest gravity was to loll out like an
ox's,
and when it moved, it must have been like a thick embryo slowly coming
alive,
butting itself against the inner sides of his teeth and cheeks.
And when God burned in the bush, how could he not cleave to him?
How could he not know that all of us were on fire and that every word we
said would burn forever,
in pain, unquenchably, and that God knew it, too, and would say nothing
Himself ever again beyond this,
ever, but would only live in the flesh that we use like firewood,
in all the caves of the body, the gut cave, the speech cave:
He would slobber and howl like something just barely a man that beats
itself again and again onto the dark,
moist walls away from the light, away from whatever would be light for
this last eternity.
"Now therefore go," He said, "and I will be with thy mouth."

Lisa Ress

## At Your Table. Vienna V, 1957

You serve me on plates marked with my grandmother's monogram
left with you for safekeeping the day she ran.
You have untied the letters, let our name out, it is gone.
The language we share cracks in my mouth.
Your home, you say, your dishes now, your tongue
curled like the long arms of the boxwood that would not hold us.
Your parks, your stone musicians.
You with your passion for music, crying as the bow
shudders over tight dried gut.

Christine Lahey

## Dan's Shoe Repair: 1959

We know who her father is,
that bully, pushing, shoving,
shouting on the playground
at recess like a Valkyrie.
The nuns are extra nice
to her in compensation:
*her father has no tongue.*

He cannot command her
to keep quiet, to behave,
to pull up her socks,
do her multiplication tables,
dry the dishes before
she can watch *Popeye.*

I live one block from his shop,
am terrified of him,
dream of him: *he is trying
to tell me something.*
Yet always beg the errand,

enter his shop, stinky
with worn-out leather,
lathes whirring, shoelaces
jumbled up in
glass display cases,
the Norman Rockwell print
of the smiling shoemaker,
shoes, shoes, shoes
piled up everywhere,
in barrows, on shelves,
the shoes of the dead,
bundles of belongings,
hats, jackets, boots, gloves.
He learned his trade
from those cast-off shoes
heaped up at Bergen-Belsen;
the dead schooled the living.

Sweaty sleeves rolled up,
forearms covered
with blond hairs
I look at secretly,
his blue eyes see me,
much more than see,
they *talk* to me,
ask me my errand,
but I cannot repeat
my mother's instructions,
my mouth falls open,
cat's got my tongue.
He grabs my sister's pumps
and my summer sandals,
nods at me, nods at me,
marking white X's on the soles
with a piece of chalk,

the card with the day circled.
They'll be ready Thursday:
*will I be there to pick them up?*

He jerks his head past me
to the next customer,
who's decided to wait
while his heels are replaced.
He's taking no chances,
won't let that shoemaker
out of his sight.

I dawdle by the door,
wonder what it's like
to have Dan for a father,
thin as barbed wire,
fingers always dirty,
the big glass ashtrays
filling up as customers
look at photos in *LIFE*:
eyes behind barbed wire,
pictures stuck in his mind
*that he cannot talk about.*




Philip Levine

**The Survivor**

in memory of my cousin,
David Ber Prishkulnick

Nîmes, August, 1966, and I
am going home.  Home is here,
you say; your hand reaches
out and touches nothing.
Russia, New York, back,
that was your father; you
took up the road, moving

at dawn or after dusk
in the corrugated Citroën
loaded with shirts and ties.
Light broke in the fields
of poplars and up ahead
was one more village fair
and the peddling.

Once upon a day in 1940
a little man had to leave
his dinner and save his life
and go with his house
on his back, sleeping nowhere,
eating nothing, a shadow
running, a dark stop. That's
how grandpa told the story.
Waking, I found you waiting,
your feet crossed and swinging,
like a child on the bench
outside the window, holding
a sack of warm rolls
for breakfast.

Gray suit, woolen vest,
collar, tie. Now you are
dispersed into the atoms
of gasoline and air
that explode an instant
and are always, dispersed
to the earth that never
warmed you and the rain
drumming down on the hoods
of trucks stalled on the bridge
to Arles. You stop a moment
in my hand that cannot
stop and rise and stumble
onward toward the heart
where there is no rest.

Marvin Bell

# The Extermination of the Jews

to Donald Justice

A thousand years from now
they will be remembered as heroes.
A thousand years from now
they will still be promised their past.

Objects of beauty notwithstanding,
once more they will appear
for their ruin, seeking a purse,
hard bread or a heavy weapon

for those who must survive,
but no one shall survive.
We who have not forgotten,
our children shall outremember:

Their victims' pious chanting—
Last wishes, last Yiddish, last dreaming—
were defeats with which the Gestapo
continues ceasing and ceasing.

Denise Levertov

# *from* During the Eichmann Trial

*i When We Look Up*
When we look up
each from his being
        Robert Duncan

He had not looked,
pitiful man whom none

pity, whom all
must pity if they look

into their own face (given
only by glass, steel, water

barely known) all
who look up

to see—how many
faces?  How many

seen in a lifetime?  (Not those
that flash by, but those

into which the gaze wanders
and is lost

and returns to tell
*Here is a mystery,*

*a person, an*
*other, an I?*

Count them.
Who are five million?)

'I was used from the nursery
to obedience

all my life . . .
Corpselike

obedience.'  Yellow
calmed him later—

'a charming picture'
yellow of autumn leaves in

## THE LATE TRAIN

Wienerwald, a little
railroad station
nineteen-o-eight, Lemburg,

yellow sun
on the stepmother's teatable

Franz Joseph's beard
blessing his little ones.

It was the yellow
of the stars too,

stars that marked
those in whose faces

you had not
looked. 'They were cast out

as if they were
some animals, some beasts.'

'And what would disobedience
have brought me? And

whom would it have served?'
'I did not let my thoughts

dwell on this—I had
seen it and that was

enough.' (The words
'slur into a harsh babble')

'A spring of blood
gushed from the earth.'
   Miracle

unsung. I see
a spring of blood gush from the earth—

Earth cannot swallow
so much at once

a fountain
rushes towards the sky

unrecognized
a sign—.

Pity this man who saw it
whose obedience continued—

he, you, I, which shall I say?
He stands

isolate in a bulletproof
witness-stand of glass,

a cage, where we may view
ourselves, an apparition

telling us something he
does not know: we are members

one of another.

Michael Waters

## Dachau Moon

1
There is a place like Germany in the body
that wants to remain a secret,
where all the tremendous weight of a life
is a kiss buried in the eyes,
pale moons that drift like heaven
across this bastard landscape

## THE LATE TRAIN

& I am flying to this place
on an overcast morning
when nothing is ready to rise,
so it's easy to imagine a moon
blue & romantic
as a dead woman.

This country is full of surprises.
My parents have told me to keep an eye
for the family star,
the remains of dark bone charcoal
thumbed like a mole
on the left side of the forehead.

2
Three days in Munich
and my head begins to split,
the beer tastes like a railroad
& I have been too fucking polite
like a child come home from death.

I am astonished by the number of gold teeth
taken from the mouths of the dead
and placed in the heads of fine German women.
There is a beauty in gold
when found in a dark forgotten place

and a fear
when the moon resembles a gold tooth
lodged in the skull like a light.

So the smile of the engineer is a killer,
precise as a military operation,
all the way to Dachau.

3

The stillness is so complete
not even the dead are here anymore.

All the fathers are gone,
having kissed their daughters like fever,
to a room where the moon is seen as a face
blue & almost romantic through mist.

So unlike the photograph in the museum:
someone, maybe an uncle,
strapped in a chair
with his forehead neatly sliced
& opened like a jewelry box,
the brain & its still water
exposed to the hands . . .

His mouth shapes a small *o*
that could be a moon
disappearing for the last time.

4

The sad Jews
who may be our fathers
haul themselves across New York City
as if weighted with stones,

and in my pocket is a stone
selected that day in Dachau
that contains all the darkness of a family

and I remember the moon is a skullcap
not placed properly on the head
like this, Lord, like this.

Carolyne Wright

# KZ

*Arbeit Macht Frei*
> motto over the entrance
of every Nazi concentration camp

We walk in under the empty tower, snow
falling on barbed-wire nets where the bodies
of suicides hung for days.  We follow signs
to the treeless square, where the scythe blade, hunger,
had its orders, and some lasted hours in the cold
when all-night roll calls were as long as winter.

We've come here deliberately in winter,
field stubble black against the glare of snow.
Our faces go colorless in wind, cold
the final sentence of their bodies
whose only identity by then was hunger.
The old gate with its hated grillwork sign

walled off, we take snapshots to sign
and send home, to show we've done right by winter.
We've eaten nothing, to stand inside their hunger.
We count, recount crimes committed in snow—
those who sheltered their dying fellows' bodies
from the work details, the transport trains, the cold.

Before the afternoon is gone, the cold
goes deep, troops into surrendered land.  Signs
direct us to one final site, where bodies
slid into brick-kiln furnaces all winter
or piled on iron stretchers in the snow
like a plague year's random harvest.  What hunger

can we claim? Those who had no rest from hunger
stepped into the ovens, knowing the cold
at the heart of the flame. They made no peace with snow.
For them no quiet midnight sign
from on high—what pilgrims seek at the bottom of winter—
only the ebbing measure of their lives. Their bodies

are shadows now, ashing the footprints of everybody
who walks here, ciphers carrying the place of hunger
for us, who journey so easily in winter.
Who is made free by the merciless work of cold?
What we repeat when we can't read the signs—
the story of our tracks breaking off in snow.

Snow has covered the final account of their bodies
but we must learn the signs: they hungered,
they were cold, and in Dachau it was always winter.

———————

(For Terrence Des Pres 1939-1987)


Mary Kathryn Stillwell

## Dachau

I was born within these confines,
between the stone watchtowers
and the barbed perimeters.
For all these years I have watched
like one might watch through the slats of a boxcar,
like the heart watches through the ribs.

Rain was never enough.
Ashes fall everywhere
turning the administration building
gray, the new chapel gray, even my hands.
The SS did not approve;

they wanted everything clean,
bedcovers smooth, benches and dead men
in straight rows.

Instead they built this monument of bone,
brittle and at sharp angles,
yes, clean, where the birds, were there birds,
might build nests,
flying up scraps of skin,
patches of hair for soft lining.

Mirrors were never allowed.
There was no need of them.
Death was a quick smile, a sure surprise.
Skulls bloomed like flowers
along the stream there,
suddenly and everywhere. You and I carry
them with us, on each knuckle, each knee.

Cold has held my hand for years,
has led me up and led me down
this gravel path between the barracks.
Listen to the voices we set free with each footfall,
sent to whisper across the lawn of stone.
Yes, there were birds then.
There were trees,
and the footbridge,
the hiding place until nightfall.
We must stop.
I am not allowed to go farther.
I will not go.

Aaron Miller

## Not Dachau

It is with curiosity, finally,
that man views his accomplishments:

as if this park
of spruce and new grass
were not of his own design;

as if these concrete markers
proclaiming acres of ashes,
mountains of bones,
concealed neither ashes nor bones,
but bits of moon
preserved in formaldehyde;

as if this statue
chiseled from death
were not of a man,
nor even man's work,
but some minor god's
ironic self-portrait;

as if these ovens
festooned with paper wreaths
never burned people;
old letters, perhaps,
bad books, rotten beams,
the refuse of a huge summer picnic—
but not people;

as if this were Atlantis,
not Dachau; a window,
not a mirror.

Robert A. Frauenglas

## Seriatim

Nazis
and friends
in drab olive green
in verdant green countryside
stoke red hot furnaces
while ashes of my
family cloud the sky.

Names
and histories
long, intricate and involved
are destroyed, tossed away
as deadwood, forgotten.

Nazis
and friends
in drab olive green
in verdant green countryside
stoke red hot furnaces
fire smoking machine guns
drive trainloads of cattle cars
while ashes of my
family fly across the world.

But
Wiesenthal says wait!—
they are not all destroyed.
He knows my name,
a German-Jewish name
and my family,
from Zbaraż?
Yes!

He
worked with my Cousin
on reparations

from the country and
the people
who can't buy
innocence with money—but try.

Nazis
and friends
in drab olive green
in verdant green countryside
stoke red hot furnaces
trying to destroy
all signs of my family.

Yet,
we still live,
we still breathe,
we become engaged,
we marry,
we have children . . .
still peopling
all the nations of the world,
and now . . . our own.

My family continues . . .

But
Nazis
and friends
in drab olive green
in verdant green countryside
survive.

William Heyen

## Riddle

From Belsen a crate of gold teeth,
from Dachau a mountain of shoes,
from Auschwitz a skin lampshade.
Who killed the Jews?

Not I, cries the typist,
not I, cries the engineer,
not I, cries Adolf Eichmann,
not I, cries Albert Speer.

My friend Fritz Nova lost his father—
a petty official had to choose.
My friend Lou Abrahms lost his brother.
Who killed the Jews?

David Nova swallowed gas,
Hyman Abrahms was beaten and starved.
Some men signed their papers,
and some stood guard,

and some herded them in,
and some dropped the pellets,
and some spread the ashes,
and some hosed the walls,

and some planted the wheat,
and some poured the steel,
and some cleared the rails,
and some raised the cattle.

Some smelled the smoke,
some just heard the news.
Were they Germans? Were they Nazis?
Were they human? Who killed the Jews?

The stars will remember the gold,
the sun will remember the shoes,
the moon will remember the skin.
But who killed the Jews?


## Simple Truths

When a man has grown a body,
a body to carry with him
through nature for as long as he can,
when this body is taken from him
by other men and women who happen to be,
this time, in uniform,
then it is clear he has experienced
an act of barbarism,

and when a man has a wife,
a wife to love for as long as he lives,
when this wife is marked with a yellow star
and driven into a chamber she will never leave alive,
then this is murder,
so much is clear,

and when a woman has hair,
when her hair is shorn and her scalp bleeds,
when a woman has children,
children to love for as long as she lives,
when the children are taken from her,
when a man and his wife and their children
are put to death in a chamber of gas,
or with pistols at close range, or are starved,
or beaten, or injected by the thousands,
or ripped apart, by the thousands, by the millions,

it is clear that where we are
is Europe, in our century, during the years
from nineteen-hundred and thirty-five

to nineteen-hundred and forty-five
after the death of Jesus, who spoke of a different order,
but whose father, who is our father,
if he is our father,
if we must speak of him as father,
watched, and witnessed, and knew,

and when we remember,
when we touch the skin of our own bodies,
when we open our eyes into dream
or within the morning shine of sunlight
and remember what was taken
from these men, from these women,
from these children gassed and starved
and beaten and thrown against walls
and made to walk the valley
of knives and icepicks and otherwise
exterminated in ways appearing to us almost
beyond even the maniacal human imagination,
then it is clear that this is the German Reich,
during approximately ten years of our lord's time,

and when we read a book of these things,
when we hear the names of the camps,
when we see the films of the bulldozed dead
or the film of one boy struck on the head
with a club in the hands
of a German doctor who will wait
some days for the boy's skull to knit, and will enter
the time in his ledger, and then
take up the club to strike the boy again,
and wait some weeks for the boy's skull to knit,
and enter the time in his ledger again,
and strike the boy again,
and so on, until the boy, who,
at the end of the film of his life

can hardly stagger forward toward the doctor,
does die, and the doctor
enters exactly the time of the boy's death in his ledger,

when we read these things or see them,
then it is clear to us that this
happened, and within the lord's allowance, this
work of his minions, his poor
vicious dumb German victims twisted
into the swastika shapes of trees struck by lightning,
on this his earth, if he is our father,
if we must speak of him in this way,
this presence above us, within us, this
mover, this first cause, this spirit, this
curse, this bloodstream and brain-current, this
unfathomable oceanic ignorance of ourselves, this
automatic electric Aryan swerve, this

fortune that you and I were not the victims, this
luck that you and I were not the murderers, this
sense that you and I are clean and understand, this
stupidity that gives him breath, gives him life
as we kill them all, as we killed them all.

## The Children

*I do not think we can save them.*
I remember, within my dream, repeating
*I do not think we can save them.*
But our cars follow one another
over the cobblestones. Our dim
headlamps, yellow in fog, brush past,
at the center of a market square,
its cathedral's great arched doors.
I know, now, this is a city
in Germany, two years

after the Crystal Night.  I think ahead
to the hospital, the children.
*I do not think we can save them.*

Inside this dream,
in a crystal dashboard vase,
one long-stemmed rose unfolds
strata of soft red light.
Its petals fall, tears, small
flames.  I cup my palm to hold them,
and my palm fills to its brim,
will overflow.
Is this the secret, then?  . . .
Now I must spill the petal light, and drive.

We are here, in front of the hospital,
our engines murmuring.  Inside,
I carry a child under each arm,
down stairs, out to my car.
One's right eyeball hangs on its cheek
on threads of nerve and tendon,
but he still smiles, and I love him.
The other has lost her chin—
I can see straight down her throat
to where her heart beats
black-red, black-red.
*I do not think we can save them.*

I am the last driver in this procession.
Many children huddle in my car.
We have left the city.  Our lights
tunnel the fog beneath arches of linden,
toward Bremerhaven, toward
the western shore.
*I do not think we can save them.*
This time, at the thought, lights
whirl in my mirror, intense

fear, and the screams of sirens.
I begin to cry, for myself, for the children.
A voice in my dream says
*this was the midnight you were born. . . .*

Later, something brutal happened, of course,
but as to this life I had to, I woke,
and cannot, or will not, remember.
But the children, of course, were murdered,
their graves lost, their names lost,
even those two faces lost to me. Still,
this morning, inside the engine of my body,
for once, as I wept and breathed deep,
relief, waves of relief, as though the dreamed

rose would spill its petals forever.
I prayed thanks. For one night, at least,
I tried to save the children,
to keep them safe in my own body,
and knew I would again. Amen.

## My Holocaust Songs

I
Some split SS backbones with axes,
but who can praise them?
Some filed like sheep into the corridors of the swastika,
but who can blame them?
Some found smoke's way to the cosmos,
but who can see them?
Some rose earth's way to grass and pond-pads,
but who can know them?

II
*Dead Jew goldpiece in German eye,*
*dead Jew shovel in German shed,*
*dead Jew book in German hand,*

*dead Jew hat on German head,*
*dead Jew violin in German ear,*
*dead Jew linen on German skin,*
*dead Jew blood in German vein,*
*dead Jew breath in German lung,*
*dead Jew love in German brain.*

III
Break down again, songs, break down
into pure melody, wind's way,
history sung in leaves almost lost,
atoms of singing darkness, the meanings,
the wailing songs of the holocaust,
themselves dying, returning with spring, the bleeding
notes, break down, break down again, my songs.

Carolyn Kreiter-Kurylo

## Leaving a Country Behind

i.
Rain over Munich, your plane's
clothed in a monk's black.
You look about the cabin
and wonder how the people
go on sleeping, rumors
over the radio of death
and hunger.  Staring
into darkness, you see
your aunt cupping a fresh
bouquet, saying goodbye
to a stranger, someone
who knew about Dachau,
how long it takes to burn
the eyes shut.  Again
there is lightning

and the murmur of her voice.
*Father, how many times*
*must you leave a country*
*where the eyes praise nothing?*

ii.
I will always remember
the way your aunt said *Hitler*,
her lips drawn into a hiss
and then freed.  Loving words,
I repeated *Hit* with a lilt
and then *ler*, too young
to understand the history
one man left behind
buried in this woman's heart.
I remember drawings hung
about the house, the time
she locked herself in the attic
to sketch a mad giant.
At the funeral, you placed
a rose in her lap.
The choirboy sang as if
the past were but a moment
he could bury with the dead.

iii.
*Drive twelve miles northwest*,
the villager said, pointing
the way to the death camp.
I was six years old,
and today my mind returns
to Dachau, to the barbed
wire, ovens, and wooden bunks,
to iron bodies writhing
in a sculpture displayed
for the world's children.
*Father, even now as the rains*
*fall, I hear sounds rising*
*from the dead and somewhere*
*beyond the rain, the voice*
*of a German offering her rose.*

Marina Roscher

## Going Back

The cathedral still rises
spires like music and columns
chants of a thousand voices
conversations of saints

in stained glass.  After
forty years in a foreign
country, I walk under chestnut
trees that endure.

Tonight I'll see
the sky through the spires red
again, the sunset
of my hometown burning

behind the cathedral at midnight
cracking its windows
when the synagogue towered
in flames.

Anneliese Wagner

## The Little Place

It is always there
always there for me,
on the night walk
across the hill
above the train, as it passes.

It is always there
and the train of my early years
on the other side of the Neckar,

the lit cars long thin roots
tunneling into the dark garden.

In the morning, boxcars.
The dead and dying.
They are always there:
my grandmother, my aunt.

The only light goes out
and I grope my way
on something slippery, cold
and hammer, I hammer
my fist on metal.

It is always night
on the street of the city
the houses high.
I see our window, the lamp,
the house rising
solid from the sidewalk.
There is no door.

It is dark
in the narrow street.
I must arrive at the corner
of Longview at six
just down this street
one more,
and then only one more.
I know exactly.
It is always there
the little place
where we meet.

I take off my jacket
order my meal.
In the light of the lamp
it is always here.
I did not expect the wine
to taste so soft, so flinty.

Miriam Offenberg

## Reforger

(REturn of FORces to GERmany—a U.S. military exercise)

I don't want to go
To streets that echo with 40-year-old cries
That went unheeded then
And go unheeded now,
Because who hears ghosts
But me?

I don't want to walk
On ground spongy with soaked up blood
Of my aunts and uncles and cousins.
There's no forgetting.

I can't eat the food
Heavy with pompous pride
Of a "new rebuilt Germany."
Nothing is new or rebuilt for me.
I still see the starved bodies
When I look at my full plate.

And how sleep at night
In a room too oven hot
Or too Black Forest cold.
I hear too many screams
And what others call a backfire
Sounds to me like gunshots.

Where can I hide
From memories of the tribe?
Why *should* I hide?
Let *them* hide
In shame.

Must I play hypocrite
And smile politely
As my hand is gripped

By a 60-year-old solid citizen
Who once wore a black shirt
He's now conveniently forgot?

Must I greet him
On behalf of the United States government,
When I want to bury him
On behalf of the Holocaust?

I don't want to go
And dig up memories I can't escape—
Aunt Helen's arm with the blue numbers
And the stories she never told
About her sister
Whose shower was cyanide.

I don't want to go.
It's bad enough to be here
And say *yiskor*
And cry tears that don't bring back the dead.

I don't want to be there
Walking the streets with them
Feeling their murder
Sharing their agony
Unable to lay their ghosts
Or give them peace.

I don' t want to go
Feeling their helplessness
Feeling the guiltiness
Of my being alive.

Alan Lupack

## Auschwitz Reportaż

a prose poem

    Today we went to Auschwitz. As we approached it, I could feel a heaviness, an oppressiveness in the air. We passed some railroad tracks. I could almost hear the screams and the moans and the dying gasps from trains where people had been crammed like souls satanically stolen from heaven because of a sleeping God.

    As I entered the lying gate and looked at the barbed wire—once electrified—and the zone of death, I could feel the bewilderment and the fear of those who had entered before, and then the anguish and terror when they were told by the sadistic SS officer that work would not make them free, that the only way out was through the poison gas and the ovens.

    I saw in the buildings of Auschwitz the torn, filthy clothing of the men who weren't allowed to end their days with the dignity of men. I saw the hair cut from the heads of women so that it could be turned into cloth or be used to stuff mattresses. (What dreams those who slept on such mattresses must have had.) I saw the clothing of children and a broken doll—head torn off and mangled, arm cracked—which, if it could feel, would have suffered less than its owner. And I saw the pictures of hundreds of the millions who died there. There were names with each of those faces. And there were families and friends and loves and hates, there were moods and habits, there were lives with each of those names. Until they came to Auschwitz, where there were no names. I saw the wall where men were murdered, and the posts where men were hung like hunks of meat in the shambles of civilization, and the cells where men were starved and suffocated for crimes like stealing food from the pigs of the SS—but where one man gave his life for another. I saw the chambers where the prisoners thought they could escape for a few moments the filth and the stench but where, chaos having come again, water became gas and fire, and people became ashes.

    I saw Barbara weep at Auschwitz. She wept for the faces of a family never seen, faces she could not find among the pictures on the wall and so would never see. She wept for the old who had worked and who had suffered the things that each man must, but who were not allowed to die with the dignity their endurance deserved. And she wept for the young who did not have a chance to suffer what men must because they were made to suffer what no man ever should, what it was once inconceivable that any man could at the hands of another. And she wept for a world where Auschwitz could exist.

Just across the road from Birkenau (Auschwitz II), whose wooden barracks and wooden bunk beds have none of the lying façade of Auschwitz I, whose gate, if it had a motto, would have said truthfully, "Abandon all hope . . ." —right across the road, I saw a farm with people working in the field.

As we drove away from Auschwitz, the farmers of the region were burning weeds. Billows of smoke filled the bus and burned our eyes. It was as if we were escaping across the fiery river surrounding hell.

May Sarton

## *from* The Invocation to Kali

3
The Concentration Camps

Have we managed to fade them out like God?
Simply eclipse the unpurged images?
Eclipse the children with a mountain of shoes?
Let the bones fester like animal bones,
False teeth, bits of hair, spilled liquid eyes,
Disgusting, not to be looked at, like a blight?

Ages ago we closed our hearts to blight.
Who believes now? Who cries, "merciful God"?
We gassed God in the ovens, great piteous eyes,
Burned God in a trash-heap of images,
Refused to make a compact with dead bones,
And threw away the children with their shoes—

Millions of sandals, sneakers, small worn shoes—
Thrust them aside as a disgusting blight.
Not ours, this death, to take into our bones,
Not ours a dying mutilated God.
We freed our minds from gruesome images,
Pretended we had closed their open eyes

That never could be closed, dark puzzled eyes,
The ghosts of children who went without shoes
Naked toward the ovens' bestial images,
Strangling for breath, clawing the blight,
Piled up like pigs beyond the help of God. . . .
With food in our stomachs, flesh on our bones,

We turned away from the stench of bones,
Slept with the living, drank in sexy eyes,
Hurried for shelter from a murdered God.
New factories turned out millions of shoes.
We hardly noticed the faint smell of blight,
Stuffed with new cars, ice cream, rich images.

But no grass grew on the raw images.
Corruption mushroomed from decaying bones.
Joy disappeared. The creature of the blight
Rose in the cities, dark smothered eyes.
Our children danced with rage in their shoes,
Grew up to question who had murdered God,

While we evaded their too attentive eyes,
Walked the pavane of death in our new shoes,
Sweated with anguish and remembered God.

Ephim Fogel

## Icon

Surely those eyes are of marble.
The exquisite hands
remember a score of mistresses in a dozen lands.
Who can believe that the lips—

merciless
thin—
have spoken except in the rasp of commands.

Impeccable uniform; face of ice;
staff work precise as angle of monocle;
statistics
at his fingertips.
He can tell you how many firing squads will execute a thousand Poles a
    day.
He can sacrifice a half a million troops without a tremor.
The murder of a million Jews is a problem in logistics
he has long ago considered, and solved.
Behind the marble eyes a hundred gallows glimmer.

Behold the man to conceive, and to gather and
consummate, new transfigurations in the mystery of killing.
And around the cérebrum ambitions revolve:
canonization in a Greater German Fatherland;
an Iron Cross for a more abundant chamber,
a quicker crematorium;
a bright medallion for weeding out a Region
*ad maiorem Germaniae gloriam.*

He would gleam in the amber of
a thousand-year chronicle.
His legends will be legion.
And millions of Aryan children
will contemplate his eyes, his dispassionate hands, his monocle.

—January 1945

Reva Sharon

## In the Absence of Yellow

The last, the very last
so richly, brightly, dazzlingly yellow,
     Perhaps if the sun's tears would sing
     against a white stone . . .
. . . Only I never saw another butterfly.
     Pavel Friedmann, 4 June 1942

It is summer and it is quiet
where I am standing in the yard
several feet from the wall
scarred by executions
It is quiet now . . .
more than forty years
have passed since you arrived
that Spring—late in April
Pavel—how long did you live
here . . . In only seven weeks
you grasped the universe
within these ramparts
and etched a page of sorrow
with your poem

Pavel—I have just come
from your city . . .
the glorious buildings of Prague
are unscathed by the War
In the narrow winding
streets of the Jewish Quarter
where you were born
centuries-old synagogues
are museums . . .
One thousand only
of your people live there now

On a wall in Pinkas Synagogue
your name is inscribed
with nearly 80,000 others

In remembrance
Pavel—the light
is tarnished with ashes
and every stone is stained
Here in Terezin
wings the color of rust
are fluttering . . .

Robert Mezey

## Theresienstadt Poem

In your watercolor, Nely Sílvinová
your heart on fire
on the grey cover of a sketchbook
is a dying sun or
a flower
youngest of the summer

the sun itself
the grizzled head of a flower
throbbing
in the cold dusk of your last day
on earth

There are no thorns to be seen
but the color says
thorns

and much else that is not
visible it says also
a burning wound at the horizon
it says Poland and winter

## THE LATE TRAIN

it says painful Terezin
SILVIN VI 25 VI 1944
and somehow
above the light body on its bed of coals
it says spring
from the crest of the street it says
you can see the fields
brown and green
and beyond them the dark blue line of woods
and beyond that smoke
is that the smoke of Prague
and it says blood
every kind of blood
blood of Jews
German blood
blood of Bohemia and Moravia
running in the gutters
blood of children
it says free at last
the mouth of the womb it says
SILVIN VI 25 VI 1944
the penis of the commandant
the enraged color
the whip stock the gun butt
it says it says it says

Petrified god
god that gave up the ghost at Terezin
what does it say but itself
thirteen years of life
and your heart on fire
                              Nely Sílvinová!

Frederick Feirstein

## "Grandfather" in Winter

The overcoats are gone from Central Park
—In the sudden Spring.
A clump of leaves, that lay in a white crypt
Of roots for months, loosens, looking for life.
Bare feet of hippies on the sunny walks,
Rock-heaps of pigeons bursting like corn, food
From brown bags, from white hands, from black hands,
Black and white kids kissing in the high rocks,
In the Rodin laps, in the hands of God
Above. Below, an old man, in a rough coat,
Wearing my grandfather's frown, lifts his face
Up to the sun and smiles smacking his lips.
His sky-blue Buchenwald tattoo has healed.
Below him, in the skating-rink, a small
Girl, Jewish, repeats the rings of the park:
The ring of her father skating around her,
The guard around him, the border of the rink
Around him, the rings of the pigeon-walks,
The rings of clouds, of jets, of the young
Sun around it. Me on the parapet,
The blood of the false Spring ringing my heart.
My wife beside me aims her camera at
The girl. The girl falls. The rope jerks. Nine
Iraqi Jews are falling through the air,
The Arab horde around them cheers. *Shema.*
The feet clump like leaves. The eyes turn up: white
Rocks. Israel in winter prepares again
For war. Around the gas-house are the guards,
Around the guards, pogroms: Deserts of dead,
Miles wide and miles thick. The rings around
Her border are of time. Grandfather knows.
His dead eyes scrutinize my eyes. He knows
Tomorrow snow will fall like lead, the news
Will be obituaries, Kaddish will
Be sung. It is the eve of war again:
*Shema.*

Susan Tichy

# Gaby at the U. N. Observation Post

> . . . you find yourself always standing
> Between the much-praised landscape
> And the one that praises and explains it
> > Yehuda Amichai

1.
On the border
you're posed and poised as a model
who has no idea where she is.

You cross your legs.  One elbow
rests on the telescope mount
where a newspaper is tucked
and folded: the news
is startling and old, news of a year
in which love joined hands with her sister
and both went down to death.

On the Day of Atonement
thirsty hands drank from the eyes,
and those who had nothing to grieve for
received a gift.

The gift you wanted? To win the world
by leaving it alone.

2.
You're not alone.

To one side, shadows of things that happened.
To the other, dreams that didn't come true.
The land is dry because of them.  They live
on the surface of things, like gypsies,
drinking all the moisture from the air.

Here, give them a loaf of bread
and wine from an earthen jar. Say,
"This is no longer the border.
   This is no longer the war." Tell them
in each of your four languages,

"I want to go home alone."
   What if a man is waiting for you?
   What if your body
   could be his whole country—
two countries, for night and for day?

On the Day of Atonement
you painted your face with make-up
and walked to the top of the city wall.
Everyone saw you mourn
for having your hands and feet.

3.
Two hands, two feet—
you are never alone.

Out of your father's country
you marched
at the head of a million dead.

But when you tried to lead them
to the future
they ran back, disappearing
through a small crack in the earth.

Don't rub your toe in the dust
like that. Show respect.
Turn your face away from the wind
when it blows
their loose hair in your eyes.

Edmund Pennant

## Yom Hazikaron

Day of Remembrance
for Israel's Fallen Soldiers

1.
Because every monstrosity
is diminished by the next
which is the pathos of monuments

you lay a pebble
on top the gravestone
before turning your back,

to tell the next visitor
you were there, to touch
the granite, to hear

the unspeakable, to leave
a forgotten nickname
inside a pebble.

2
The priests had to be fastidious
because the work of corrosion
goes on, all the washing of bodies
and donning of holy linens
was a war against corrosion.

And the blood and memory of blood
wash away best when done the same day.

Then the dirges and the elegies
are heard, and then they are drowned
by the sounds of children at play,
and the bleating of Azazel
by the silence of the desert.

3

Soldiers in the streets of Jerusalem
do not strut like Prussian officers;
you would have to look long
to find one whose body announces
he loves being a soldier.

They have the manner of quiet,
cool irregulars who would walk
away from camp at the drop of a hat,
like the farmer-fighters
of Washington's army;
and who could acquit themselves
well, under fire, for liberty.
They do not strut, neither do they slouch
like peddlars in the old ghettos
leaning against the pack.  And yet,
if you look carefully, you will find
a posture inherent in the weight-bearing
bones, the knees and the hips,
bespeaking a pack, a burden
not easy to carry with grace.

It is the burden of the Law
and the burden of memories
become immemorial, that lie heavy
even on the very young,
those too young to remember.

In the pomp and necessary ceremonials
of Yom Hazikaron, they march, they turn,
they blow the trumpets, they stare
straight ahead, trying not to see
the faces of parents who are mourners.

4.
In one lifetime we have cringed
and we have crowed.  Now, once again,
the surrounding, the moving in.
On the day of orations, between
the orations, is a silence
heavier than we have known before.

What was it the orators said?  "Tried by fire."
"Stronger by loss."  "Made brave by desperation."
The words disappear with the winds on Mount Herzl.

Not all the iron boxes buried in the ghetto
have been recovered.  One of them has the history
that will never be known.  The history eludes us.

5.
In the struggle not to forget,
we are forgetting what it is
we are struggling to remember,

the thing which is like a stone
covered with wet slime
which must be held with a limber
grip or be lost forever.

The stone wants to sink
to the seabottom and burrow
deep in primordial silt

because it is not a stone
but an eye that remembers
everything that happened
which we want to forget.

Diana Der Hovanessian

## The Anniversary Poem

The anniversary poem is a glass roofed
railroad station flooded
with false sunlight.  The trains are empty,
the conductors, dead, but
real passengers are waiting.

No,
the anniversary poem is the mark
of the teeth of the shark
on the arm of the swimmer
and the mark on the floating dismembered arm.
and the teeth of the smiling Turk
denying at the U.N.
the existence of sharks.

The anniversary poem
is the flow of the river Euphrates
60 years emptied of blood
but still running over red stones
in the mind of geographer.

The anniversary poem
is a caption under the paintings of Arshile Gorky
explaining why his broken world
could not be pressed into convention.

The anniversary poem finally acknowledges
for the 20th century its source
of fractured art,
the same source as Antonin Artaud's
theater of cruelty and the absurd,

the world that could not be shown
or painted or fictionalized except in excerpt
and in disguise.

No, the anniversary poem is made of steel
and rolls on wheels
through the streets of Erevan.

It is the thread of the novel
being written in Paris
and the short story in California.
It is the dance ensemble in Beirut
and the skyscraper in Buenos Aires
the symphonies in Vienna and Japan
and the football strategy at Notre Dame.
It is the political cartoon showing
a sick Turk being nursed by
an Armenian doctor nagging him
to get well and pay his bill.

The anniversary poem
is carved on exiles' gravestones and granite
library walls across North America.

The anniversary poem is a test tube
muscle flexing itself,
the lens of the observatory,
and the eye of the sculptor carving
new horses for David of Sassoun.

The rhythm of the poem is the same beat
as the pagan round dance.
It divides itself into two parts

like the scattered people,
half on a piece of home soil,
half sinking into warm friendly swamps.

The soul of the poem
is the breath of the Armenian language
being exhaled
waiting to be inhaled.

The heart of the poem is
Christian love that remembers obligation.

It recalls Christ rendered unto Caesar
Caesar's goods.  It remembers forgiveness
does not mean condoning
thievery and death.

The mind of the poem cries: Enough!
to anguish.
It searches solutions.

The anniversary poem is the shadow
of walls holding all the courts
in all the cities of the world.
The poem wants to come out of the shadows,
and asks a Nuremburg trial for 1915
so that with justice
the word forgiveness can be pronounced.

The anniversary poem points
at the world since 1915 and says it is time
that the legacy of 1915—
dehumanization—
be reversed.

It contains no laments.
It does not complain to all the TV-callous
ears of the world,

does not prod their conscience,
does not point-out bought historians,
warping facts.

It says merely: "Finish with the art of dying
Armenians."

The anniversary poem pledges itself
with the free will of Yeznick,
with the waters of Azad,
with the flowers of Avarair,
with the chains of Artavast,
with the sharagans of Gregory,
with the testament of Mashtots,
with the testimony of the revolutionary heart
to dedicate itself to Life.

And being neither threat nor promise,
ode nor eulogy,
narrative nor song of a small man
crying Akh,
the anniversary poem names itself
Question and Case,
that question that every human
must ask himself
before he can call himself human.


Richard Michelson

## The Jews That We Are

. . . you have inherited its burden
without its mystery.
                    Elie Wiesel

I.
March 1979 and I am watching Nazis
march through Chicago.  The bold type
of the *Sun-Times* describes a small band

of hoodlums, undereducated boyscouts, the better
to be ignored. My grandfather, back
hunched over his Bible, agrees. Jews like myself
should stay home, should lay down
our stones and pray like the Jews that we are.

II.
Grandfather, you are easy to love
with your long beard and the way you sway
like a palm branch in the storm. It is easy
to romanticize your spiritual search,
worldly naïveté and wise rabbinical words.
You belong in the books I read
by Singer, Peretz, Sholom Aleichem.
But their characters are ignorant
of the chapters to come. You know
where their prayers will lead.

III.
A circle. Six Nazis. Full military garb.
Your daughter naked in the middle. A gang-
rape and you're more ashamed than angry.
One soldier says all Jewesses are whores
and the others agree. You say nothing.
Years later you'll decide to speak:
"Do we not serve Hitler's purpose, we
who would sooner renounce our beliefs
than assume our burdens?" My mother
turns aside. Afraid
to answer. Silent even in her dreams.

IV.
A generation after the Holocaust
and I know no Hebrew, no Torah. I fast
only on the day of atonement
and even then I've been known to cheat.
A generation after the Holocaust
and I apologize for my grandfather's
bent back and wild gestures.
I used to tremble to the discordant

rhythm of his prayers.  I feared the mysterious
words that kept us from the devil.
Next to me my mother slept.  She never cried
out in her dreams for his protection.
From her window she watches Nazis
march.  Their feet strike the pavement
like the constant ticking of a clock.
I am a Jew a generation after the Holocaust.
Poorer, my grandfather says, without a past,
than he, who has no future.


Mark Nepo

## I Wake from a Dream of Killing Hitler

I
I have no numbers on my forearm.
I have only watched my Grandmother
with her thick tongue
sob in her Brooklyn apartment
while staring off.

I have watched her whisper
to her older brother, Louis,
butted off into a boxcar
no time for a wave or even a glance
just butt, butt, hop
the heavy door sliding
the padlocks fastened.

I only know of my Grandmother's sister,
Rifkah,
who sent back the steamship tickets
in 1933 because
Rumania was where she was born.
I only know of my Grandmother
ending the story there

sitting quietly
Rocking inside
a sad flutter in her lip
mezzuzah in her fallen hand.

I've thought too much.

II
There can be no revenge
only relief
from a tension wound
across an era;
a tension strung
like an imperceptible copper leash
through the corner of every Jewish soul.

Who can say Kaddish for six million
without ever mentioning the dead?
Yahrzeit marks every calendar I know
anniversaries of death outnumber the constellations,
the very planet marred
by a continent of scars
and only if the tissue
of every conscience
is seared;
only if for a century
we rub our lids with light;
only then might we not bleed in thought.

The sacred veils
behind which we walk this earth
are irretrievable.
Some gashes breach like canyons.

All my fathers' hands are broken
old prayers like knuckles broken
old prayers like bone resin.

Larry Rubin

## The Nazi in the Dock, at Sixty

Incensed, he clutches at his innocence,
Created out of years of careful lies.
The court is less important than his age:
Living with the skulls and cordoned flesh
Is possible; dying with them, something
Else. A poet of the past, he tames
The truth, shapes it to his need, makes
Lambs of dinosaurs. A Jewess on
The jury knows; she burns behind her eyes,
Like him. What more awaits?
The year grows thin; they lead him downward
To a camp where old men should not go—
To bits of hair and wire, acrid smells
Of something in his skin he can't recall.

William Trowbridge

## The Song of Iron Paul

from the specifications:
1) that, while serving as a guard at Buchenwald KZ,
he did cause the death or grievous bodily injury of
numerous inmates by beating, shooting, strangulation,
drowning, suffocation, trampling, whipping, and other means.
2) that, according to sworn testimony of surviving
inmate-witnesses, he was one of the "most dreaded and
bestial characters" among the guards, "often dispensing
his 'punishments' to the blare of martial or gypsy music."

You will notice that I do not deny,
have never denied any of these acts
of which I am accused. All the things
written on those papers, I could have done.
At my trial some spoke dully, some
stood up, uncovering puckered scars,
and bayed for my hide. I believed them all.

In the schoolyard, I was called Iron Paul,
a fool's name, no doubt, but what was I
to do? When my mother and my father left me
in Silesia with my Polack aunt, I had
only the name and my father's good coat.
She sang hymns in the Polack tongue
and skinned rabbits on her kitchen wall.

On winter nights, the wolves padded
boldly from deep in the forest and snuffled
the snow that drifted beneath my window.
Their scent seemed to rise from between the floorboards.
One morning I found a lamb by the footpath,
its private parts gnawed away,
its bowels naked and frozen to the ground.

So there was Breslau and my mad uncle, a street thug,
but a master huntsman, who clothed me like himself
and showed how a wolf, stripped of his coat,
looks as pitiful as any rabbit.
But I still had dreams of the skinned wolf,
its nails clacking on the pane,
my drained face reflecting from its eyes.

Why speak of Hitler? Where were the judges,
15,000 of them, when he tore away
the lawful state? Where were they
when Papa Eicke showed us how a hose
jammed down the gullet of an upstart
can burst his guts in thirty seconds
or thirty minutes, depending on the pressure?

And there were secrets, state secrets.
We were shown new maps of the Sudetenland
and Poland, marked like sides of mutton
ready for the butcher's saw. So how,
could we resign, knowing so much?
And how could we betray the uniform? Who
would take you in after such betrayal?

They were mannequins, of course, and clowns,
Himmler and the rest, poisoning themselves
like women.  But how could we have guessed
after the runes and the heroic toasts
and the silver Death's Head shining on our caps?
I wore mine till the Russians took it.
Bormann, I heard, fled as a Hebrew granny.

At Buchenwald I saw soft guards gassed,
looking, when stripped, like all the rest,
sheepish, eyes wild in the sockets.
Then I knew there was only the uniform,
that and my name to keep me from feeding
the stink that clung even to my blankets.
Duty was life there, sympathy a disease.

I will tell you, I was not well-suited.
I should have gone to Koch and told him
I was a simple man, not cut out
for such work. Yes, sick with sympathy,
and fear.  You have seen the lampshades perhaps,
but not the unscraped flesh and not the Bitch
watching it peeled away from fat and muscle.

And the thing that's left—God, what would you
call it?  My mother taught me the Commandments
but I could not face the others glaring
at my nakedness.  And, after all, Iron Paul
had volunteered, so Iron Paul stayed
to the end, vicious as a feral hound.
How they moaned when they heard my music.

Did I say Jews?  There's a joke for you!
We had no special feelings toward the Jews
till orders came down to hang everything
on the Jews.  Such foolishness, when one looks back.
They say Eichmann himself had Jew blood.
Oh yes, I read all about his trial, the poser,
slinking out to leave us to the Russians.

*They* were *soldiers*, from tunic to bone.
They were not like us; there was good order
in their camps, and they were fair: no random
selections, no flayings, no night rousts.
They gave me good wool clothes for winter.
I was a model prisoner, they said,
and still am, as you will notice in my official dossier.

Louis Simpson

## The Bird

*"Ich wünscht', ich wäre ein Vöglein,"*
Sang Heinrich, "I would fly
Across the sea . . ." so sadly
It made his mother cry.

At night he played his zither,
By day worked in the mine.
His friend was Hans; together
The boys walked by the Rhine.

"Each day we're growing older,"
Hans said, "This is no life.
I wish I were a soldier!"
And snapped his pocket-knife.

War came, and Hans was taken,
But Heinrich did not fight.
*"Ich wünscht', ich wäre ein Vöglein,"*
Sang Heinrich every night.

"Dear Heinrich," said the letter,
"I hope this finds you fine.
The war could not be better,
It's women, song and wine."

A letter came for Heinrich,
The same that he'd sent East
To Hans, his own handwriting
Returned, and marked *Deceased.*

\*

"You'll never be a beauty,"
The doctor said, "You scamp!
We'll give you special duty—
A concentration camp."

And now the truck was nearing
The place. They passed a house;
A radio was blaring
The *Wiener Blut* of Strauss.

The banks were bright with flowers,
The birds sang in the wood;
There was a fence with towers
On which armed sentries stood.

They stopped. The men dismounted;
Heinrich got down—at last!
"That chimney," said the sergeant,
"That's where the Jews are gassed."

\*

Each day he sorted clothing,
Skirt, trousers, boot and shoe,
Till he was filled with loathing
For every size of Jew.

"Come in! What is it, Private?"
"Please Sir, that vacancy . . .
I wonder, could I have it?"
"Your papers! Let me see . . ."

"You're steady and you're sober . . .
But have you learned to kill?"
Said Heinrich, "No *Herr Ober-
Leutnant,* but I will!"

"The Reich can use your spirit.
Report to Unit Four.
Here is an arm-band—wear it!
Dismissed! Don't slam the door."

\*

"*Ich wünscht', ich wäre ein Vöglein,* "
Sang Heinrich, "I would fly . . ."
They knew that when they heard him
The next day they would die.

They stood in silence praying
At midnight when they heard
The zither softly playing,
The singing of the Bird.

He stared into the fire,
He sipped a glass of wine.
"*Ich wünscht',* " his voice rose higher,,
"*Ich wäre ein Vöglein . . .*"

A dog howled in its kennel,
He thought of Hans and cried.
The stars looked down from heaven.
That day the children died.

\*

"The Russian tanks are coming!"
The wind bore from the East
A cannonade, a drumming
Of small arms that increased.

Heinrich went to Headquarters
He found the Colonel dead
With pictures of his daughters,
A pistol by his head.

He thought, his courage sinking,
"There's always the SS . . ."
He found the Major drinking
In a woman's party dress.

The prisoners were shaking
Their barracks.  Heinrich heard
A sound of timber breaking,
A shout, "Where is the Bird?"

\*

The Russian was completing
A seven-page report.
He wrote: "We still are beating
The woods . . ." then he stopped short.

A little bird was flitting
Outside from tree to tree.
He turned where he was sitting
And watched it thoughtfully.

He pulled himself together,
And wrote: "We've left no stone
Unturned—but not a feather!
It seems the Bird has flown.

"Description?  Half a dozen
Group snapshots, badly blurred;
And which is Emma's cousin
God knows, and which the Bird!

"He could be in the Western
  Or in the Eastern Zone.
  I'd welcome a suggestion
  If anything is known."

                    *

"*Ich wünscht', ich wäre ein Vöglein*,"
  Sings Heinrich, "I would fly
  Across the sea," so sadly
  It makes his children cry.

David Koenig

## Onkel Fritz Is Sitting

Onkel Fritz is sitting
Next to his cigarettes
On the table, here in Germany.
Onkel Fritz is sitting
On the terrace of his home
At dusk, smelling the
Tomato plants and roses,
Seventy-nine years old,
Staring out into the garden,
Thin shoulders propped up
On sharp bones, like barbed
Wire strung on posts.
Onkel Fritz, what are you seeing
As you wait for the dark
With your white handkerchief
Beside you on the table?
Do you see the white flag
Of surrender you couldn't
Wave when they came
And took you, the *SS*,
In Autumn, from your home?
Did you sit at a table, so

Long ago, next to your cigarettes,
And look up to see brown
Pants over black boots and
The red, hooked cross?
Did you smell food cooking
As they led you away
Without warm clothes,
Your stomach rumbling
With hunger you were yet
To feel, as they drove you
By the burning synagogue to jail?
Did you sit in jail, Onkel Fritz,
And wonder what you had done wrong,
Did you ask the jailer, an old Gentile
Friend, where you were being sent, and
Did he answer, "Buchenwald"?
Did you sit in Buchenwald
When you were not forced to stand
For hours in the dark, looking up
At a scaffold where the *SS* shouted down
At you all night about the man
They would hang before your eyes at dawn?
Did you sit at a table when
By some miracle your Dutch cousin
Brought you out, and the *SS* made
You swear in writing you had seen nothing?
Did you sit in the truck from Buchenwald
When the driver stopped for a moment
In memory of those left behind?
And then in the train where Jews
Were not allowed to sit, with
Shaved heads, while the conductor
Brought water for your dry lips
Because he too had a son in the camp?
Onkel Fritz, did you sit long
On the freighter to South America,
And years later, a sick old man,
On the ship back to Germany?
Did you sit with your fellow
Townsmen and neighbors and wonder

How you would ever feel at home again?
Did you sit in the dining room
Of city hall many times as the
Token remaining Jew?  Did you
Sit when the Queen of England
On a visit to the occupation forces
In the town asked you, "How have you survived?"?
Onkel Fritz, are you sitting
In the dark tonight,
Under the sun gone under the earth,
Are you thinking that every time
One goes under another
There is tyranny?  Are you feeling
The chill of the night air?
Onkel Fritz, are you thinking
Of the miracle
Of standing up again?

Luada Sandler

## The Gift

*after listening to Sonia address a gathering*
*of children of Holocaust survivors*

My life, she said at last, quietly,
when all her listeners were seated,
my life began in Poland, a few years
before the war.  When I was twelve
my mother and father and I, being Jews,
were taken to Auschwitz.  My father
was sent to the men's camp there, and
we never saw him again.

When I was fifteen, we were liberated
by the Russian Army.  To be free was incredible!
But today I am not going to talk about the camp.
Being of the Second Generation, you of all people

have no doubt read all that has ever been written
about Auschwitz. You have appropriately been called
A Generation Apart.

Some of you already know from your parents—at least,
those few who could bring themselves to talk about it—
what it was like in the camps. Like your parents,
I've thought about those years of my youth
every day since liberation, and I've dreamed about them
many long nights. My memories of that awful time
kept surging through my body like a—rushing stream.

For years I could not talk about my experience
with anyone except my husband, who was also a survivor.
But gradually, as our children grew older,
I told them a little, but only generalities,
no details. My experience remained lodged inside me
like a heavy stone that could not be dissolved.

So it is not about what happened at Auschwitz
that I speak today, for you have asked me here
to tell you how long it took me to find a meaning
to my experience and, when found, what I decided
to do about it.

It was only in 1983 at the American Gathering
of Survivors in Washington, D.C. that I noticed
the first stirrings around that stone, a feeling
that perhaps my experience was of some importance,
that what I was carrying within me was actually unique.
I remember half murmuring to myself,
*If I don't tell it now, it will soon be lost forever*
*because no one can tell about my experience but me.*
*After we are gone, there will be no one left*
*who witnessed those atrocities. People will then think*
*whatever they choose, or believe whatever*
*anyone tells them.* I remember a child who,
when asked what the Holocaust was, answered,
"Isn't that a Jewish holiday?" So, at best,

our history will be revised, either by accident
or design; at worst, it will be lost forever
if we don't speak out.

When I returned home, I began to speak
to young people at schools, sometimes going
to two or three schools a day. First, a Jewish man
shows a short film about the Holocaust; then I speak
about what I lived through and what happened to others I knew.
And as I speak, I begin to feel the healing power of release.
The children are quiet and listen; they are respectful
and interested. Curious, they want to see my numbers.
And they say, "We're very sorry it happened to you."

So, tell your parents, tell them to talk
about their trauma. Tell them there will be
no true meaning to their lives until their pain
is transformed into some medium that transcends them.
Tell them to use whatever talents they have, or can acquire,
to write a new chapter of Jewish history, a chapter
only they have experienced.

Tell them to think of their memories as a beacon—
a warning to others of the treacherous waters of hatred.
Please tell them—impress upon them—the importance
of commemorating their past in their own words
in order to inform the future,
of giving their past a voice so that others may learn
what happened to people in that dark place and time.

As for me, before my memories become mere echoes,
I shall write down for your children and mine
what it was like for an adolescent girl
to live with the burden of life at Auschwitz—

and I shall write how it took almost a lifetime
to realize that I alone had the power
to turn that experience into a living document.

*Let those of us who survived be worthy of our memories.*
*Let us rise to what life expects of us.*
*And tell your parents, tell them with love,*
*to make of their memories a gift to the world.*


David Ray

## A Couple of Survivors

He was a G.I. and she was huddled with the others
in their zebra suits, in a tin warehouse waiting
to be shot, all women and girls, when the noises
outside closed in and the shouts were not German
and the tin door slid open—a man framed in light.
She was the first to step out, into the sun
and he was there with his rifle, an American,
struck dumb, cagey, still looking about for the guards
who had run into the forest, and she said in German
I am a Jew and he said I am too, from Brooklyn, New
York, and he smiled, politely. And then, as she
now tells it, he asked if she would show him the others.
And with one gesture, the way she puts it,
he restored her to humanity. After those years,
the terrible years, he restored her
by taking one step back, waving her in,
letting her precede him, into the warehouse
where the women and girls stood, staring.
Now they are Americans and there are the two sides
to the memory, the soldier sliding open that door
of the warehouse, the sixteen year old girl
the first out, the meeting, the joy
of the first smile on the stunned face, and the other.

Ruth Whitman

## Maria Olt

On a hillside in Jerusalem
under the hammer sun, she lifts

a little carob tree, the tree of John
the Baptist, and sets it

into its hole.  Solid as a house,
she is called Righteous, a Christian

who hid Jews in Hungary.  Her hair clings
around her broad face as she bends

with the hoe, carefully heaping the soil
around the roots.  She builds a rim of dirt

on the downhill side and pours water from
the heavy bucket.  She waits until the earth

sucks the water up, then pours again
with a slow wrist.  The workmen

sent to help her, stand aside, helpless.
She straightens up.  Her eyes are wet.

Tears come to her easily.
The small Jewish woman she saved
stands beside her, dryeyed, beyond tears.
Thirtyfive years ago, as they watched

the death train pass, faces and hands
silent between the slats, the girl

had cried, I want to go with them!
No, said Maria, you must understand,

if you go, I will go with you.

Jorie Graham

## History

Into whose ear the deeds are spoken. The only
listener. So I believed
he would remember everything, the murmuring trees,
the sunshine's zealotry, its deep
unevenness. For history
is the opposite
of the eye
for whom, for instance, six million bodies in portions
of hundreds and
the flowerpots broken by a sudden wind stand as
equivalent. What more
is there
than fact? *I'll give ten thousand dollars to the man*
*who proves the holocaust really*
*occurred* said the exhausted solitude
in San Francisco
in 1980. Far in the woods
in a faded photograph
in 1942 the man with his own
genitalia in his mouth and hundreds of
slow holes
a pitchfork has opened
over his face
grows beautiful. The ferns and deepwood
lilies catch
the eye. Three men in ragged uniforms
with guns keep laughing
nervously. They share the day
with him. A bluebird
sings. The feathers of the shade touch every inch
of skin—the hand holding down the delicate gun,
the hands holding down the delicate
hips. And the sky
is visible between the men, between
the trees, a blue spirit
enveloping

anything.  Late in the story, in Northern Italy,
a man cuts down some trees for winter
fuel.  We read this in the evening
news.  Watching the fire burn late
one night, watching it change and change, a hand grenade,
lodged in the pulp the young tree
grew around, explodes, blinding the man, killing
his wife.  Now who
will tell the children
fairytales?  The ones where simple
crumbs over the forest
floor endure
to help us home?


Edmund Pennant

## Thoughts under the Giant Sequoia

(Yosemite National Park)

A shrub of tourists
gathers under "General Grant"
for the ranger's lecture.  This patriarch
is at least two dozen centuries old,
a loner in a corner of the grove.
The general has heard the talk before.

It will not be about death's durance
inherent in the living, a subject
he could respect.  It will not be
about strategies of attrition or political
whims of lightning lopping giants as if
they were dwarf skirmishers on the treeline.

The ranger—a romantic—commends us
to the lordly scene, citing
"silence of cathedrals"

which phrase we noted that morning
in the free brochure, pages made
from pulp of little brothers.

Thence to the usual chronicles building out
from natal core to delicate cambium:
William the Conqueror here, Charlemagne
and Columbus there, each to his ring concentric.
No mention, though, of the Massacre at York
of the Jews, while the tree was sleeping.

Francis Parkman and Emanuel Ringelblum:
there's a pair who took their scholarship al fresco.
One, pain-wracked on horseback, dared Indians
and forests, recapturing Pontiac's despair.  The other,
historian of the Warsaw ghetto, buried his diaries
in iron boxes before they took him in a bunker.

In what monstrosity of treetrunk, I wonder,
are all those martyrs marked, who died for
the Sanctification of the Name, unnamed?
Some day I'll come back alone and listen,
and look for a tree slightly older than Moses,
flaunting incredible veridians at the crown.

Tonight at Yosemite, though, I'll have to bushwhack
through dreams of the lovely greenbaums I have known
who rest securely under stone; and greenblatts
who huddled bleak by the grave they dug, waiting
for the guns; and greenwalds resting their tanks
in a grove of tamarisks near Sharm el Sheik.

John C. Pine

# The Survivor

(After Seeing "Kitty Hart: Return to Auschwitz" on Public TV)

She learned early that in order to survive
She would have to make herself
As small as possible and hide
Among the others, even if this meant
Concealing herself behind a corpse.
She learned also to appropriate
From the dead their bread
Ration and articles of clothing.
The sheer bureaucratic
Size and impersonality of the death camp
Worked to her advantage.
She survived also on animal instinct
And cunning. She knew that her elders
Thought too much about their situation.
Their fate could be read in the dazed
And vacant look on their faces.
After the inevitable selection they became
Spectral voices, disembodied hands
Between the iron bars of high windows.
Sometimes on warm spring days
When the foliage was beginning to turn green
And wildflowers were blooming in the woods,
She would sun herself within sight of the crematories
And observe the smoke rising from the chimneys,
And smell the stench of burning flesh
Which permeated the entire camp.
Almost thirty-five years later she returned
To Auschwitz-Birkenau with her son
From her home in Birmingham, England.
There was grass where before there had been only mud.
Some of the buildings had been torn down,
And the emptiness all round them
Was strange and unsettling. Nevertheless,
It soon came back to her. Unhesitatingly
She walked through the thick underbrush

To the pits which had been hastily dug
When the crematories could no longer
Dispose of people fast enough.
Many of those selected for extermination
Had been burned in these open pits—
Some of them while still alive.
Now poking in the ashes with a stick
She came upon a small fragment of bone
Bleached by the heat and cold of thirty-five years,
And gave it to her son as a memento
Of all that she had been witness to
And in memory of all those who nourished
The earth without even a whitish sliver
Of bone to be remembered by.

David Ray

## Kitty Returns to Auschwitz

A woman returns to Auschwitz
telling her son
who strolls beside her—
"This is where I shat—"
row upon row upon row
of holes in iron planks.
"This is where the S.S.
herded all my friends
into a truck—
This is where I said farewell
to my sister—
This is where I buried
gold off the bodies—"
And she stoops and digs
till a necklace
turns up. "And this is where
the shot bodies fell
into the ditch—" She claws

and hands him a bone
which he, being a doctor,
identifies—a man's elbow.
"Perhaps it is your grandfather,"
she tells him and briefly
weeps, adding her tears
to the puddle which already
holds molecules of bodies,
her sister's, her mother's.
We look over her shoulder
at the captured photograph
album, visit the warehouses,
pyramids of hair,
mountains of coats passed on
to the cold men of Stalingrad.
Here, stripped in the snow,
threatened with guns,
are the naked robbed
of their coats.  Once I knew
an old Jew who could whistle
the fourth *Brandenburg* through.
He was the kind
here herded like oxen.
And Kitty, who had
to return, listens by birches,
no Brandenburg there,
just wind of the great Nothing.

Myra Sklarew

## Blessed Art Thou, No-One

No one kneads us again of earth and clay,
No one incants our dust.
No one.
Blessed art thou, No-One.

                    Paul Celan

If I reach after you
into the darkness

will you stay put against my hand
or will I scrape against

the steady pulsing
of my own fingers

This day   held up
like a flag of warning

no-one made of words
soaked into the earth

stray words from the shrunken mouths
of those who sat down

in the forest
unlacing their shoes

Used up words
that we leaning

across a table wanted
to say to you

before the table
turned into a gun

before the chair fled
its house

If we attach the words
to our feet like a boot

will you walk on them
will they cry out

under you
like a woman

Will the faces of gravestones
call to you

when they are hammered into stairs
or set into roads

when the tanks run over
their names

Are you made of words no-one
shall I give you a name

or must your provisions
be metal and rope

or something to carry
these papers

so that you may cross
a border into your own life


Stephen Berg

*from* **Memory**

*Photograph:* families looking of all things shy
cupping their genitals with both hands
so we will never see—doesn't that mean they
still knew their own names?
grouped on the edge of the bottom half of the shot

that could be of the deep gray ocean
a pit that does not end with the shot
but flows out past its edges in the mind
as they try not to be there by looking as if nothing special
is going on
huddling in front of the amateur Sunday photographer's candid
visor-shaded blank eye

*Photograph:* whole bodies of bubbling wounds flung
across torsos down thighs like frozen cloth over backs faces
a patch of boiling skin so abstract
its patterns are your mother's face
or animals or an arm of twilit Cape Cod beach
embracing smooth water

*Photograph:* silent cloud mushrooming on your fat stem
caught swallowing whatever lived beneath you
the newsreel slows
how amazing harmless and beautiful you are in silence
as you blossom and rise and take everything with you
in the murky theatre on the screen.

*

To feel another's pain—
as a passenger in an airplane for the first time hesitates
to look out the porthole
then looks, because being afraid is childish, and sees the earth as
a wrinkled map interrupted by clouds, merely beautiful—
is, I suppose, human. Girlish, harmless, and beautiful.

If we stay up this far long enough we will stop on the moon.
The prisoners' faces glow like the moon
on any night in almost any weather—
in the photographs, though a few plead
or grimace or leer or seem to be finishing an urgent sentence—
heads jutting, eyes wide, half-smiling, half-open mouths—
the rest look drained of feeling, their faces ashen,
their souls fully resigned,
convinced,

surrendered to the endlessness of death,
abandoned by all of us.
They lean out at us,
their gray, ascetic faces
a shade darker than new snow,
than that star I saw watching us.


Richard Michelson

## Undressing Aunt Frieda

Undressing Aunt Frieda, I think of how,
undressing me, she would tilt back her head
as if listening for footsteps, the faint marching
of the S.S. men whose one great dream
was her death.  They must have feared
how her young Jewish fingers unbuttoned
and buttoned, as if they had continents
to cross, as if here, in East New York,
I was already tiring, and no one at home
to put me to bed.

Undressing Aunt Frieda, I try to imagine her
healthy, undressing herself, slowly at first,
as if for the love of a man, untying
her green checkered apron with the secret pockets,
unwrapping the frail "just shy of five foot" body
whose scarred beauty Rubens would surely have missed,
but Rembrandt, in the loneliness of his dying days,
might have immortalized.

My daughter at my side grows restless.
She unties her shoes, tugs at each sock.
She has learned, recently, to undress herself,
and pausing occasionally for applause,
does so now.  Naked, she shimmies up onto the bed,

curls her thin fingers around Frieda who,
as if she wished herself already dead,
doesn't coo or even smile.

"A dream of love," Frieda preached, "is not love,
but a dream." "And bad luck," I'd say, "follows
the bitter heart." But undressing her now,
I remember the lightness of her hands
and their strength which somehow lifted me
above the nightmares she had known.
*I'll care for you,* she whispered once,
*as if you were my own.* My daughter yawns.
I lift her gently, hoping she'll sleep
the hour drive home.

Annette Bialik Harchik

## Earrings

A Bialik tradition back home          was
for a woman to wear                              earrings
from birth to death.

Ears pierced in infancy          were
adorned in string;

small gold hoops for girlhood;
diamond studs with marriage.

When the trains pulled up
at Auschwitz
my mother was stripped, shorn,
and tattooed, leaving her                              earrings
in a huge glitter pile of jewelry.

Under her wavy white hair,
her lobes hang heavy,
the empty holes
grown shut.

Teresa Moszkowicz-Syrop

## The Tomatoes

Is it possible,
Do they still exist?
The real, red tomatoes
Which were shining in the sun
On some broken stands
In the corners
Of the ruined streets
In Warsaw.
I still remember,
When we were marching by
After the uproar,
Taken from the hiding places
By the Gestapo,
To be sent away
To the unknown.
We were so hungry—
Many days without food.
The houses were ruined,
The streets smashed in disorder.
But,
Mostly what I noticed—
What I longed for—
Were the juicy, red tomatoes
Shining in the sun.

Betty Wisoff

## Sanity

Jack, I never knew you
Until yesterday:
It was your face I saw on TV—
Holocaust survivor.

Your grocery store my weekly trysting place.
Your cheer the reason I return—
But now I know you.
You tell me of your sick dog, the fortune spent
To cure.
Why do you tell me *this*?

*

They traveled for ten days in a sealed boxcar.
On the tenth day, Auschwitz: not a dread word yet
—Here was daylight.

The cattle doors slid open.
Most were unable to move quickly from cramped
Positions, but moved toward fresh open air,
Unknowing, glad for anything.

A woman cradling her babe took cautious footholds,
Stumbled, prodded by an elegantly dressed SS man.
Before a thousand eyes, before she could scream,
Before realization, the terror, the shock,
Bayonet poised, he pierced her baby's breast,
Lifted it from her arms, tossed the child
As one tosses hay in a field.

I seek a word for the man's act.
I seek a word for the mother.
I seek a word for the then thirteen-year-old Jack,
Now grown, who says "I see that act daily
All of my days.  I must do mundane things
For the sanity of my days."


J. R. Solonche

## Another Book on the Holocaust

Is it the duty
Of every survivor

To write a book?
The stories are

The same.  Read one,
You've read them all.

Why should we be
Different from

The earth itself
That has already

Forgotten, in a shorter
Time than the life

Of a witness, how
Its new grass was grown,

Where its wounds
Had been, and what

Had filled them in?
I can't believe

They think we don't believe.
Surely we believed

## THE LATE TRAIN

From the very beginning,
At the sight of the first

Pictures: those shreds
Of people, fingers

Of bodies staring through
The wire as if it

Weren't there, those bodies
Of fingers curled around

The air in lost fists.
We sickened at the sight.

The bodies, the parts
Of the bodies, the whole

Bodies, the naked bodies,
The bodies recognizable

And the bodies unrecognizable,
The piles of bodies, bodies

Heaped on bodies heaped on
Bodies, bodies in mounds

As though swept there by
A broom made for sweeping bodies.

They sickened us. The facts
Of bodies. Statistics of

Bodies. Arithmetic of bodies.
They sickened us until

They numbed us. The dead proof.
How can they, the living proof,

Believe we don't believe?

Olga Cabral

## At the Jewish Museum

("Kaddish for the Little Children,"
An environment, consisting of a room 28 x 17 x 8 ft.,
by the sculptor, Harold Paris.)

Only what I bring to this room will exist here.
For the room is empty.
Empty as the inside
of a cold oven.
Narrow passageway in.
Narrow passageway out.
At the entrance, bronze scrolls.
Words:
the alphabet of mysterious
tablets.
May words guide me through this place.

Enter.
Did I expect to find
darkness?
Did I hope for blindness?
Worse than absence of light this
gloom and evil glint of some
metal object.  Is it
a box?
a receptacle for—
what?
An artifact
of a door in the mind?
(Metal door that
clangs, clangs—.)
Walls bare.

Naked brick.
Nothing to see.
Nothing.

In this room there were never clocks or calendars
or daily lists of little things to be done.
No one ever had any birthdays.
No one ever put on a hat.
Neither star nor spider came here.
Nor mouse nor cricket.
There is no trace of the memory
of a swirl of dust
of a fly
crawling on the wall.
A room without history of furniture
of broken plates or cups
of diaries
lost buttons
of shreds of cloth
of colors.
A room filled with absence
a room filled with loss
a room with no address
in a city in a country
unknown to mapmakers.

Once and only once
God
a trembling old man leaning on a cane
passed by but did not dare
look in.

Perhaps the black metal object
is a box with names.
Perhaps nobody had a name.
It was all done with numbers.
It meant less that way.
Perhaps the box is filled with numbers.
Perhaps the walls and ceiling—
shadow walls and shadow ceiling

bulging with emptiness
*are receding rapidly to the edge*
*of the visible universe where objects*
*tend to disappear—*

where all the names have gone
the diminutives
the sweet
nicknames
beyond reach of our most cunning
telescopes
and nets to catch the whispers
of the stars.

Marion Cohen

## Not a Dream, Just Thoughts ·

(March 11, 1983)

The child is the only one awake.  She decides not to kill.
The baby screams.  She decides to keep on screaming,
    to scream and scream until her mouth is big
    enough to contain everything she wants.
The war-baby cannot keep her daddy out of the war.
She is not even in the room when the letter arrives.
War planes are flying overhead.  Four of them in a
    horrible square.  Four so slow she can't tell
    which direction.
Warplanes *above* the sky, far too far above, war-
    planes over the sky of my mother's flesh.
And war lights shining red
And now it's *dark* red
And the ink in this pen turns red
And the ink in this pen turns white.
And I, in the dark, continue to scratch
to murder the pen
to murder the page

to murder the night
to murder the day.
To do.
To un-do.
To un-un-do.
I tell you, I did not create the war.
When I arrived, the war was already there.


Mari Alschuler

## In My Own Nightmares

I stand out in each nightmare
a dark Jew in an Aryan bed,
your too-white skin,
your henna-red hair.

I cup my breasts with dry hands
and let you fall
into your fast sleep.

Your bright hair is the only light,
the only thread
in our flat tapestry.

Your body is taut,
all angles,
a swastika turning
as you dream.

Lisa Ress

## The Family Album

Some pages have eyes, some mouths.  They desire.
*Put a platter on.  I want to dance at the Stadtpark Café.*
They have papers to complete.  Tax records haunt them.
Their secretaries, still on leave, were never notified
    when to return.
Each page has an aura of surprise.
*I was just putting dinner on the table.  Here is the book
I promised Max.  Sidi has not spoken to her father.*

They stare at me, move their lips.
Alive or dead, they ask,
their worried, torn-up faces stuck to the page.
I try to help.  I call up music,
wide brass notes that tear them free.
We put our arms back, and our faces, lace our flesh.
We are one body, whole.
The city walls keep time, they spin with us,
One clamorous gold mote, dancing away.

Enid Shomer

## Remembering

For my husband.  Israel.

Your mother hoards flour and sugar
whenever the news is grim.
No matter weevils get most of it.
It is stored in her heart and head,
fuel for a memory she stokes and fans.

I, too, keep expecting war
but each morning smells of

diesel, bread and donkeys.
All day at the zoo peacocks scream
but they are only laying eggs.

We take the train for Jerusalem.
The woman across the aisle
has those numbers on her arm,
but breathes deeply,
reads a paper.
Later at a roundhouse, you
watch an engine turn and
pass out cold, remembering men
gaffed and drowned near a platform
in Minsk.  The doctor says
it is memories that make you sick,
suggests next time you look away.

At Yad Vashem, memorial
to the six million, you close your eyes
as we grope our way along the damp walls,
past the silent brass roll call.
Later you tell me the engraved
names of the dead bloomed
like flowers in your hands.

Louis Phillips

## God Teaches Us How to Forgive, but We Forget

The Night & Fog Decree:
Under cover of darkness,
Persons I love are spirited away.
On this highway, no immunity.
Thru the February fog,
One can see
Valentines of barbed wire,
One is enchanted by

Waterfalls of blue gas,
Geysers of quicklime.
Soil takes on the smell of fat
& even the rain does not help.
What is the qood of men
Who dispatch their own kind?
Think of an answer.
I cannot.
God invented forgiveness
To shame His enemies,
But I am grieving planet
Blown off-course.
Look, you murdering bastards,
I shall not forget what you did,
What your fathers did,
& their fathers before them.
*Nacht-und-nebel erlass.*
What was once human
Is hurt forever.


Marc Kaminsky

## Medium

How do you do, delicate Roumanians!
You, with your large ovens,
where your girls sang, baking bread!

My grandmother sings your melodies,
but without your words:
they were in Hebrew, male and sacred,

which she never knew, and I,
sitting alone with her, on the other side
of two world wars, and two years

after the death of my grandfather,
am introduced to her grandfather:
Zalman of Kostuchohn, a lumber merchant,

and her father, Baruch, who sold wine
and farm tools, an old man
who couldn't keep up with the others,

forced to run towards the barbed wire—
fell,
and was shot.

Remembering her father's beautiful voice,
the silk *kapoteh* he wore, on Friday evenings,
and the Besarabian *tish mit mentshn,*

she sings as if her husky voice,
which can barely carry the *nign,*
is joyously nine years old and joining

in with her father's, and I, too,
will have sat at the Sabbath table
where my grandmother felt herself

happily loved, still happily loving,
in an old song,
though I will carry away

neither the words
nor the melody.
On the day that I met you,

Baruch of Kostuchohn,
how close you were
to never having existed.

Estelle Gershgoren Novak

## Yom HaShoah

A Visit to the Wiesenthal Center for Holocaust Studies
(in memory of the Loewe family)

I only read about you.
I want to piece you back together,
to make a new dress, new trousers,
a new hat for a head that smiles,
but I only read about you.

Your silence hurts.
Your death is here
in the photo
where the dirty water drips
out of a rusted faucet,
where the fields grow new grass
and pigs now grunt in the mud.

Over there
the watchman repairs in earnest
the old gates of your death.
Here
the museum displays on velvet
the last artifacts of your life.

But I cannot put together
what I never knew.
The fabric of your death is here.
Your life, the fever that made you,
the eyes that shone, wet with tears,
will never be mine.
I remain, my own tears
ignorant and astonished.

Reva Sharon

## Unanswerable Questions

Terezin—1984
Along the path where your light feet passed
your footsteps have been lost forever. . . .
                              Hayim Guri

It was here Jhirka
in that black yesterday
after your fists were torn

from your mother's shirt
and you were ripped
from her breast

. . . when your eyes were dark
and your mouth was full
of questions . . .

you shared the hard wood bunk
of a starving man
who had no answers

for a boy of five
with no memory
of life under a wide sky

beyond this
barbed electric fortress
But he captured you

in a sketch
that survives
framed and protected under glass

Oh Jhirka . . .
do your ashes
nourish wild vermilion poppies

or eddy endlessly in the River Ohre
Your image stays
and haunts

the silence
of an unlit place
where we walk now

and cry out "why"
. . . but Jhirka
*who will ask your questions*


Theodore Weiss

## The Late Train

What's it like?

A horn suddenly jammed
in a car junked years
ago.
        An alarm
gone off in a town
that a volcano leveled.

A siren snarling
out in me that must
belong to a time, a far-
off place
        I've
never known, shrieking
like a jet-black van
lurching
        to the wrecks
it's most successful in,

my countless relatives
minus
       faces, names,
crying out of flowers,
birds, this windy smoke
clotting up our sky.

Throttled before
they got the word out,
it must break through
some way.
       How satisfy
except to let it go,
listen
       till it runs
its course, father,
mother,
       else a curse
choking itself, choking
him it's locked up in.

Fran Adler

## Benny

for Benjamin Ben Yakov, and his father,
who survived Bergen-Belsen

It's not the length but the height of your days
and how much you could fill them with,
grabbing life between wars like a hungry child
who steals from a plate and runs.

You had envisioned death to be large like you
to be loud to be lion to be late

but it came disguised as a friend since birth.
It was *mayim*, it was water, it was life.

Benny, we've walked the desert
since you drowned at Eilat,
our mouths thick beneath our feet.

We've brought back your memory bleached
like Masada, stone alone in the sands.
We've brought back your memory like the sun
gaining weight as it climbs.

It's not the length but the depth of time since
your death and how loud your echo sounds.
Like a flash flood rushing in
you fill cisterns underground.

Philip Levine

## On a Drawing by Flavio

Above my desk
the Rabbi of Auschwitz
bows his head and prays
for us all, and the earth
which long ago inhaled
his last flames turns
its face toward the light.
Outside the low trees
take the first gray shapes.
At the cost of such
death must I enter
this body again,
this body which is
itself closing on
death? Now the sun
rises above a stunning

valley, and the orchards
thrust their burning
branches into the day.
Do as you please, says
the sun without uttering
a word. But I can't.
I am this hand that
would raise itself
against the earth
and I am the earth too.
I look again and closer
at the Rabbi and at last
see he has my face
that opened its eyes
so many years ago
to death. He has these
long tapering fingers
that long ago reached
for our father's hand
long gone to dirt, these
fingers that hold
hand to forearm,
forearm to hand because
that is all that God
gave us to hold.

J. L. Kubiček

## A Song

I sing a song of sorrow
    of cries for help,
        the silence that answered,

A song of remembrance . . .
    the innocent
        who wore all colors.

Victims, I sing for you—
    do you listen?
    Hear my song!

Evil lies not only
    in far lands:
    it flies between
    me and my friend
    as we sit, talk
    over a cup of coffee.

Deborah Hanan

## On Watching *Heritage: Civilization and the Jews*

for M. and A. S.

I.
It started outside, my seeing: the air—glass, fallen
leaves, paper easily rubbed to dust.
With each stroke of my rake, a cascade:
skin of Jewish hands, ready for needle and thread.
Fickle Europe needs many gloves.

One Jew, my dead stepfather.
A necktie of his, peacock feathers.
In splendid raiment, he enters The Garden.

II.
If Eden were this ground behind my house,
we'd stand near one another,
no trap door rigged in your skull
ajar beneath the skin, your stomach as if
it never ballooned from injections.  Sy, I tell you

Mother was like a furious King, a Pope.
Now they want their Jews, now they don't.

Being hers, the kid of a rich kid's kid—
I am saved by the job
of sharpening crayons, box by box,
talking to invisible you
as my youngest vanishes into the leaves.

On our walks through my recurring dream,
we give each other the good-bye we can:
mute agreement of love: together we feel safe.

III.
On T.V., men stand praying outside.  It's
midnight, when accuser angels go to bed and
hours of mercy wheel into place.
A bonfire sprays sparks back to God—Infinite
Universe—scattered not in one catastrophe, but
histories of catastrophe fixing
our spot on the ladder of worlds.
The mystics sing and the fire rushes skyward.
Light to light.  Ours, the unlasting moment
when God will be whole again and everyone, good.

Reg Saner

## Aspen Oktoberfest

Through an amber dazzle of aspen
the sun delves and paddles.  The eye opens,
walks with the sun in its circles,
and closes.

Along the streambed I listen: crag chunks, pebbles, boulders
breasting torrent, whacking back at it, memorizing
the full past of a creek trailing from them like robes
as their fracture lines blunt and decide
on the strange, voluptuous forms of believers in water.

Trunk shadows zebra the dirt.  Within planes of blue umber, then light,
then umber, the blurred twirl of a leaf
winks 20, 30 yards, descending.  A scintilla.  An eye,
like the others.  Autumn opens as radiance, closes
as stone.  Under a pressure nobody can imagine
there's a central cubic inch of this planet, a black incandescence
towards which everything falls
yet I've never been, can never be, happier
and no reason—or none weightier than mountain air
leaking gold.  Which no sooner seems an "Oktoberfest"
than out of the word's transparent German
a girl's smile comes to me, surviving only as name, Lily Tofler,
luckless, radiant—just as thinking of stone
I step into sunlight
traversing exactly these branches to reach me.

Ultramarine rings off the summits, their scree-slopes.

The eye opens to brilliance like that, animal and happy
it walks in the sun's perfect circles
helping photons pour from their center out of some vast, casual joy
while our share infinitesimal strikes this earth
and keeps going.  That I touched them for others
in me, the words on those gates, or passed through them,
wife and sons with me unharmed, reading "Arbeit Macht Frei"

written in iron on eyes closed as stone
back of the black hinges at Dachau
teaches nothing but luck.  Moment to moment
light's witnesses dismantle, annihilate, while every particle
illumined survives, eternal
as matter.

Along faults in this creek making gravity its entire career
fire breaks from pebbles that quench and rekindle
darkness in granite, this sparking
inside the stream.

With high tides and leaf spills flecking gorse clumps
like pollen, I see warehouses of shoeleather
emptied, bales of shorn hair, gold teeth shoveled up
like shelled corn.  But this isn't that light—
in which the shadow of a bullet nine millimeters small
entered the shadow of a girl.

It's just that within the outline of each, the sun
burns to a focus on me
for a moment, never happier.

And the ashen lids of Jewish women squint shut,
wombs injected with fine sand in quicklime, hardening
to history.  It happened.  My kinsmen, the Germans.

Further upslope toward the quarry
I tour the afternoon's plumed and luminous festival,
each aspen a sunburst, a shock, a fire curd I pass through
while October's least breath
offers windfalls of spattered translucence.

In a camp only my kinsmen the Germans could have imagined
I never saw Lily Tofler.  It's just her smile,
there, became by-word.  Talismanic and mine
now, as it was then for others.  A style, a daily, impossible courage

making even the officer's name a matter of record. Whose name
was Boger. Who raped her,
then killed her.

Lapping right up to timberline, the highest trees
seem a gray haze of twig, standing wind-stripped, naked,
accomplished.

In light so dustfree, so moteless these spruce cones
150 yards off cluster their bough tip, glittering
an absolute clarity
what would I know about suffering?
It's just that out of that firebrick and soot centered camp,
through this blind rightness of trees,
yellow-breasted as meadowlarks, the name of a girl
comes to me.

Within an amber dazzle of aspen, the sun's circle
half eclipses, trembles—then flares. The eye opens
and closes. And creekwater flashes, leaping down off the peaks,
making up new lives as it runs.

Hans Juergensen

## Yad Vashem

we had to enter

our veins ice-burned
with trepidation
our brains sparking
terror bursts

from sun to gehenna
a hesitance of step
past the burgeoning Trees
of the Just

walls meeting roof
in a tabernacle
portals a somberness
of sculpted splinters

our heart beats
slowly tolled us
inside

\*

six million minute squares
like random bits of coal

a world's soul
consumed
by inlaid letters:
        Majdanek
        Auschwitz
        Bergen-Belsen

this mosaic of anguish
encased
in that stark cube
of naked stone-heads

toward which
we turn

Liliane Richman

## After Claude Lanzmann's *Shoah*

It was always peaceful
in those deep fir woods
where the sun playfully shot arrows
into slowly shifting shadows,

quiet day and night in the woods not far from my village,
still peaceful after they burned two thousand daily,
after the screams, the barking of dogs,
the hissing of hundreds of bullets
rising to vaulting branches above,
caught there, hanging, trapped in the trees' green canopy.

I thought, then, and now,
don't they deserve axing, these trees,
not stretching their powerful limbs in protest,
not squelching the light twitter of birds?

When all was over
no one watched the mindless river
ferrying downstream kilos of powdered bones.

Luada Sandler

## A Scene from *Shoah*

for Claude Lanzmann

It is spring, and a boatman is rowing down the river
singing a song of his childhood, of the land
and his people, his sweet voice filling the air
with a haunting melody.

He moves serenely along the peaceful river
and a light wind that once had carried the ashes
of his family now wafts his song ahead of him
like a greeting to his village.

But, beneath his boat, the river is poisoned
with the refuse of war and the camp,
with the ashes of millions of victims.

There are wild flowers in the meadow that lies
between the camp and the village, a setting

of natural beauty bordered by the quiet river,
a landscape of innocence in pastoral Poland.

But the soil is tainted as deep down as silence.
The land is hallowed with its millions dead,
yet it is forever stained with their murder.

The boatman is gliding down the river, sweetly singing
in the midst of horror.  He is a survivor of those times,
but his memory—his memory perished in the camp,
except for the song he is singing.


Norbert Krapf

## The Name of a Place

Dachau, 1985: during Ronald Reagan's
visit to Germany.

Here the taste of ashes
that can never be swallowed,
or washed away by wine or beer.
Here a wound that still festers,
and silence that transcends language.

Here is no Oktoberfest
where people link arms
and sway to the melody
of a folksong handed down
by father to son,
mother to daughter.

One listens in vain
for the concertos of Bach
and the symphonies of Beethoven.
One cannot see the woodcarvings

of Riemenschneider or the watercolors
of Dürer.  And silence freezes
a camera against the chest.

The harsh name of this
sad place conjures up
the lamentation of children
torn from their parents.

And the taste of ashes
stays in the mouth.

Carolyne Wright

## After Forty Years

Don't tell me about the bones of Mengele,
the bones are alive and well.
                              Michael Dennis Browne

They've found the body
of the Angel of Death,
a bundle of brown bones
and scraps of skin
tossed like market produce
in the gravedigger's tray.

He can be himself now
for his loved ones—those
who took no chances
with the forged passports, bribes,
code words filing past the censors,
never breaking the family silence.

Himself now, for those
whose mouths gaped on silence,
survivors staring through barbed wire

in the abandoned camps, stumbling chance
their messenger, those for whom the bones
will always be alive and well.

Finally, the tribunal of Embú,
plain light of theTV anchor's day.
Cameras cross-haired on the throats of witnesses
who shrugged and said nothing, while for years
ash drift, fosses of lime,
the dead kept listening.

He was never sorry.
Death had grown old by the end,
familiar with his dreams:
water burning blue
off the coast of Brazil
like gas jets turned on full.

Strange how the bones are blameless,
the body dissolved as anyone's—
those who walked into the flames
with the prayer for the dead in their mouths,
the angel in his name
passing over the gates of the camps.

Harriet Susskind

**After That Time**

And it would never be over.  After that,
time would stay fixed at three-seventeen
when the hands of the surgery clock pierced

her, and the huge man in a white lab coat
dropped his pants and climbed up on her.
She was eleven, nipples small as daisy hearts.

The bells sound, MENGELE, Mengele, mengele,
and the sour hunger and the sweat,
grunt and clinical odor, alcohol, formaldehyde
and semen made her afraid of the froth
of any sea.  She was saved and would return,
over and over to the table in the surgery.

In the soft washed light of the evening news,
the grave digger stands in the pit, lifting
bones: a hip, two shanks and a rotting skull,
brown with soil.  And is this the end of pity?

Almost as the light deepens, she wants
all the children to rise up and return
stand in a ring about the bones.
Then each one will touch that dark wrist
and each one will take his own hand,
close those missing eyes and ask this of that sky:

*Is this the final justice?*
*The moment the clock can move on?*


Judith Irwin

## 1985—In a Small American Town

Sleeping beside you, I know a distance
without dimension.  I reach out—you say
you do not dream.  Your way is by no sound
I can follow.

I listen as you rise—your footfalls, throat clearing
and nose blowing, electric razor's whirr, change
jingling in your pocket where

I sometimes search
for answers in a wallet
stuffed with two forty-year-old photos—
faded, torn—of human skeletons tossed
in a common grave, piled too deep
for the eye to measure and, above,
someone in uniform holding between his fingers,
as you do now, a cigarette.

White as a bandage
rolled thin, it seems the smoke
is an inhalation, a kind of life
you draw into yourself
to cure the pain.

Irena Klepfisz

## Solitary Acts

for my aunt
Gina Klepfisz (1908?-1942)
> To garden is a solitary act.
>                     Michelle Cliff

1.
And to die
as you did   with the father
confessor   standing   waiting
patiently   for your death
for your final words
and you   watching the dissolution
around you   watching his eyes

his face   listening to his Latin words
said: "What have I to confess?
I am a Jew."

It was 1942   and you wanted someone
to know   though you'd be buried
in a Christian grave   with an Aryan name.

Such will to be known   can alter history.

2.
Today   I stand alone   planning my first garden
and think of you   buried on that other continent
rescued from the Christian plot
the only flesh of your family   to lie
in a marked grave   in the Jewish cemetery
in a Warsaw   almost empty of any Jews.
That ground   I know   is but a fragment
of the past   a place apart   the surroundings
long rebuilt   into a modern city
and I know   that even now
while I stand   and try to map this season's growth
that country   cleansed of our people's blood
intones the litany of old complaints.

Gina   they hate us still.

3.
You are to me   everything
that remains   outside my grasp
everything   in this world
that is destroyed   with no one
there to rescue the fragments
to hear the words.
So much of history   seems
a gaping absence   at best a shadow
longing   for some greater

definition   which will never come
for what is burned   becomes air
and ashes   nothing more.

So I cling   to the knowledge of your
distant grave   for it alone
reminds me   prods me   to shape that shadow.

4.
I have spent a life   disentangling from influences
trying to claim   what was original   mine:
from my mother's mastery   of daily survival
so subtly interwoven   with common gestures
few recognize it   for what it is
from my father's more visibly   heroic deed
of dying   recorded in memoirs   tributes
from the deaths of grandparents   aunts   uncles
anonymous   in a heap   indistinguishable
from all the others   who died unmourned.

And now   I remember you   and face another:
Gina   in those few months   when you watched
over me   before my consciousness learned
the danger   into which I had just been born
and the label   of who I was   and while my mother
sick and weak   teetered on the edge of life
in those few months   as the meaning of the ghetto
walls   grew more defined   as you inched people
out of the *umschlagplatz*   your chest contracting
gasping   with fear   yet certain that this needed to be done
I believe   that in that short time   something
passed between us   Gina   and you imparted to me
the vision   the firm sense of self   that gave
you strength   to state your name.

5.
And who would say   that I have mourned
enough   that I have looked at the old
photographs enough   yellowed and faded
and the green ink   now a grey dullness

where Marek   placed the flowers
on the rubble   where my father's body
was buried and disappeared   and Marek's head
looking down   his profile   etched against
an empty horizon   for there was nothing left

who would say   that I have mourned
enough?

And when I asked my mother if I
could have this album   that holds it all
holds more than most have   who are
without a witness   to mark their spot in green
or whose graves have been overgrown by weeds
or forests   or bulldozed for the sake
of modern cities   or whose bodies were never
buried   but were left for speechless animals
to devour   there is no piece of earth
that does not have its nameless   who lived
and died   unnoticed   beyond the grasp of history
who die today

And when I asked my mother   if I
could have this album   and she replied
this stays here   in this apartment
until I die   I glimpsed again the urgency
to be known.

6.
There have been many plots of ground
that formed me. This town's church
its cemetery   the bare   expectant earth
of my garden   all remind me   of that
other soil   on which I grew.

The first   was the green bush and grass
behind Marek's house in Lodz. It was
after the war   and Elza   orphaned   and just recently
claimed   from the Polish stranger   stood proud
before me   and brushed her long blond hair

her haughtiness  her only power.  I watched
ashamed  and awkward  my small hand trying
to hide  my bald head  shaved for reasons
I was never told.  It was our first meeting.

More than two years later  in the neutral
countryside that never saw the war  in Neglinge
Moti and I  crawled flat on our stomachs
to see the miniature wild flowers  hidden
beneath the blooming lilac bush.  They grew
for elves  I said  and bound him to me
with the secret  not wanting anyone else
to know.  He was alert then  but only months
before  had refused to eat  was force fed
in a Stockholm hospital.  When his appetite
returned  he clung to me  four years older
in a way  no one could ever understand
and I responded  as I never would again
unconsciously  selflessly  with complete
certainty.  I knew that he must live
and inched him along.

And again  a few years later  in a park  the Bronx
there was an unmowed field  near a metal fence.
My mother would bring me here  on warm summer Sundays
and spread a blanket  that would billow
over the high  resistant grass  then finally settle
and flatten with the weight of our bodies.
We brought things to read  books that warmed
with the sun  newspapers  that yellowed
as the day wore on.

These were the gardens of my childhood.

7.
Gina  I must tell you:  today I
felt hopeful  as I knelt close
to the earth  and turned it
inch by inch  sifting the soil
clearing the way  for roots

of vegetables. I felt so hopeful
Gina   that with repeated years
and efforts   the monotony of daily
motion   of bending   and someday
the earth   would be uncluttered
the debris cleared.

There is   I know   no reason
for such hope   for nothing destroyed
is ever made up   or restored to us.
In the earth   are buried histories
irretrievable. Yet what philosophy
can justify   any of our emotions?
Like the watercolors from Buchenwald—
if you can imagine! The stench
from the chimneys   just the sounds
of the place. And yet someone felt
a need to paint. And did.

So do not ask me to explain
why I draw meaning and strength
from these common gestures   why today
my hope is unwavering   solid   as if
I'd never lost it   or never would again
as if those dying   angry or stunned
at the stupidity of it   could be revived
as if their mortal wounds   could heal
as if their hunger   could be outlived
as if they were not dying   strangers
to others   strangers to themselves.

I need to hope. And do.

8.
I have been a dreamer   dreaming
of a perfect garden   of a family tree
whose branches   spread   through centuries
of an orderly cemetery   with no gravestones
missing. Tonight   as the sun sets   and I

turn towards evening   I have no such dreams.
Like the woman   who refused to trace
the ancient constellations   upon a clear
and crowded sky   because finding the stars
recording each in its place   the faint
and the brilliant   was enough
I too   Gina   have discarded all patterns
and blueprints.  This night   I want only
to sleep   a dark   rich   dreamless sleep
to shelter   in me   what is left
to strengthen myself   for what is needed.


John Z. Guzlowski

## How Early Fall Came This Year

Between the rows
of tomato plants
shrunken in their cages
and cannis bulbs
buried in the snow
my daughter follows me
asks me at last
why I wear a coat
without buttons
shoes without laces

I tell her I'm a fool
in a dream of magic

drop to my knees
like a penitent seal

and while she laughs
I make up more
tell her the buttons

were stirred into soup
the laces when sold
bought the secret of bread

she doesn't need
to know my thoughts
are always with my father
dying of the blood
that survived the camps
the memories of his mother
left in the field
with the beets

the real magic

only six she'd understand
his gray voice as I did
shaping a world out of
lightning and ashes

Monique Pasternak

**The Witness**

On November the eighth
    1942
the lights died.
Ice from the north
the Nazis froze the village.

In the dark, Tzvi, the Jew,
was holding a candle

while Fajtcha was giving birth.
The shadows were dancing in the room
and death on the body of Europe.

I began to breathe as the stench of
        Auschwitz
        Buchenwald
        Treblinka
was spreading over the world.
I was born while six million
were being led to humanity's slaughterhouses.
      —we were all condemned—

They came for my father,
he went into hiding.
My mother clothed her soul
in fear and courage
and raised her two yiddishe children.
She used to sing before the war
—she is silent now.

Her voice is my legacy.
I sing to celebrate and cry.
My sounds are prayers to be heard
by the living and the dead.
I bear witness to the light, to the dark
and claim the miracle
while the ocean whispers
that for each wave that dies,
another one rises
and breathes itself to the shore.

––––––––––

for my parents,
Tzvi and Fajtcha Pasternak

Melanie Kaye/Kantrowitz

## *from* Kaddish

and when I told the woman—a survivor, a fighter in the Warsaw Ghetto
Uprising—about the Holocaust conference in Maine, and how many
of the people there had known *nothing,* she said, *They still know nothing.*

*

> *Yisgadal v'yiskadash sh'me rabbo,*
> *b'olmo deevro chiruseh v'yamlick*
> *malchuseh*

if I said kaddish for each one

if I were to mourn properly
I would not be done

If I were to mourn
each artist   seamstress   *schnorrer*   midwife   baker
each fiddler   talker   tailor   shopkeeper
each *yente*   each Communist   each Zionist
each doctor   pedlar   beggar   Bundist rabbi
each prostitute   each file clerk   each lesbian
each fighter   the old woman in the photograph from
Hungary   holding the hand of the child whose
socks droop   each Jew

> *b'chayechon uvyo-mechon, uv'chayey*
> *d'chol beys yisroel*

I would not be done   yet
it was more than death   was more   the people's
heart   a language I have
to study   to practice speaking with
old people   songs   to collect   transcribing
from records or from the few
who know   a culture   which might have died
in this country   which eats culture   a death

346

we call normal   a culture   *astonishing*
*in its variety*   a taste   a smell   a twist of song
that was *Vilna*
        *Odessa*
        *Cracow*
        *Covner-Gberna*
        *Warsaw*
these were once Jewish sounds


Vera Weislitz

## Roses and the Grave

(for my father)

Someone, perhaps a friend,
Told me he would say Kaddish
For his father:
Roses he would bring to his grave

      I want to do the same
      But
      Here are no roses
      And
      You have no grave


Marie Syrkin

## The Reckoning

In the hour of reckoning
You will have to count them one by one.
Not a single figure dare be lost,
Not one old man

Or frightened child that ran.
You will have to count them everyone
Till the sum be done.

The total has been quickly made too long:
The lethal chambers filled; the ovens stoked,
And the six million tripping from the tongue.

But you will have to count them one by one,
Without a census or machines that add
A golden girl unto a golden lad.
Upon the fingers of your outstetched hand
The reckoning will stand.

Catherine de Vinck

## Kaddish

During a long march in the snow, in spite of myself, a prayer rose in my
heart to that God in whom I no longer believed.

Elie Wiesel, *Night*

It is dark and
I have no right to the flame
sputtering in a foreign tongue
in a room far away, out of reach;
have no right to the lamp
set in a window
behind frozen panes
in a house far away, out of reach.

The night covers me
like an ample hairy coat
a pelt smelling of dry blood.
The clasp between flesh and spirit
holds fast but for how long?
God of the tundra, of ice and snow

God of the wolves and of the crows
God of the stone tablets
flung from tall towers of sorrow
my God, far away, out of reach
I have no right to you.

But I make words:
picking animal bones, I blow
through the holes of wing-shafts
make sounds the wind sets flying
through the ragged trees.

For a long time I thought
I could spell your name
see it written in the stars
in the gauze of the northern lights;
I thought I could find under my fingers
the ancient letters of your good name
each one a gem polished
by centuries of patient care.
But what I touch now is hot:
your alphabet burns, releases smoke
melts huge rings of ice
through which the beasts of the deep
rise up for breath and food.

I know well, it has been invented
      the concert of ten thousand things musical
      free-floating in the air;
      flutes and violins under high ceilings
      the notes racing through the blood
      touching nerve endings
      opening in the flesh
      great wild roses of pleasure.

I will not deny
      the blessing of lichen and moss
      of small roots alive under the snow.
I will not forget
      the holy days of the bear and of the elk

    the rites of existence spent
    in deep burrows of sleep.

But as I advance on this road
everything changes:
the vastness of the universe
shrinks to the size of my footprints;
all sounds and sights vanish
sucked in by the mouths of pain.
Yet one last word hooks itself
on the last branch of memory
on the last tree of the lost garden
the God-Word I used to eat and drink
wine of the stars
sunburst of golden bread.

At the end
       —no, you do not come as the breeze
       wafted soft and whispering through the reeds—
you come as a whistle of flame
infinitely turning
       in the gyre of your power
a Falcon-God, crested with fire
burning in the tempest of its bright wings
and I become your prey
a small mammal, trembling
under your spirit-claws.

And again
       everything changes:
all that was leaning
toward a barren bleached north
all that was dying alone
out of reach and far away
—no right I had to the lamp
    to steaming cups, to circles of loving faces—
all that was broken, dumped

on garbage heaps, thrown away, shoved out:
piles upon piles of dry bones
can it all return to flesh and skin?

I do not know but I see:
in the glacial glassy distance
on the steel plate of the horizon
a faint exquisite light begins to glow.

Luba Krugman Gurdus

## We Seek You, One and Only God

In doleful tunes of autumn winds
In meek mumbles of entangled branches
In lengthy thunders of storms unleashed
In cannon's charge
And in shell's hiss
In the blast of guns, rushed by whistling air
In all the sounds of the universe
In songs of the sea and of the earth
We seek You, One and Only God . . .

In blue skies, swaddled by clouds,
In mingled pleats and misty wraps
In thinnest vapors and profuse gas
In the smoke of fires
And the dust of blasts
In the dense covers woven by fogs
In rays' glitter
And night's dusk
We seek You, One and Only God . . .

In tender looks and in sharp glances
In weary toil and in heart's beat
In blissful feeling of ominous end
In human vileness

351

And lustful play,
In the kaleidoscope of betrayal, hate
In meekness of spirit
In remorseful deed
It's You we seek, One and Only God
—1943

Charles Reznikoff

*from* Inscriptions: 1944-1956

Out of the strong, sweetness;
and out of the dead body of the lion of Judah,
the prophecies and the psalms;
out of the slaves in Egypt,
out of the wandering tribesmen of the deserts
and the peasants of Palestine,
out of the slaves of Babylon and Rome,
out of the ghettos of Spain and Portugal,
          Germany and Poland
the Torah and the prophecies,
the Talmud and the sacred studies, the hymns and songs of
          the Jews;
and out of the Jewish dead
of Belgium and Holland, of Rumania, Hungary, and Bulgaria,
of France and Italy and Yugoslavia,
of Lithuania and Latvia, White Russia and Ukrainia,
of Czechoslovakia and Austria,
Poland and Germany,
out of the greatly wronged
a people teaching and doing justice;
out of the plundered
a generous people;
out of the wounded a people of physicians;
and out of those who met only with hate,
a people of love, a compassionate people.

Leslie Woolf Hedley

## Chant for All the People on Earth

Not to forget not to ever forget so long as you live
so long as you love so long as you breathe eat wash
walk think see feel read touch laugh not to forget
not to ever forget so long as you know the meaning
of freedom of what lonely nights are to torn lovers
so long as you retain the soul heart of a man so long
as you resemble man in any way in any shape not to
forget not to ever forget for many have already
forgotten many have always planned to forget fire
fear death murder injustice hunger gas graves for
they have already forgotten and want you to forget
but do not forget our beloved species not to forget
not to ever forget for as long as you live carry it
with you let us see it recognize it in each other's
face and eyes taste it with each bite of bread each
time we shake hands or use words for as long as we
live not to forget what happened to six million Jews
to living beings who looked just as we look men
people children girls women young old good bad evil
profound foolish vain happy unhappy sane insane
mean grand joyous all dead gone buried burned not
to forget not to ever forget for as long as you live
for the earth will never be the same again for each
shred of sand cries with their cries and our lungs
are full of their dying sounds for god was killed in
each of them for in order to live as men we must not
forget for if they are forgotten O if they are forgotten
forget me also destroy me also burn my books my
memory and may everything I have ever said or done
or written may it be destroyed to nothing may I
become less than nothing for then I do not want even
one memory of me left alive on cold killing earth for
life would have no honor for to be called a man
would be an insult—

Gerald Stern

## Adler

The Jewish King Lear is getting ready
for some kind of horror—he is whispering
in the ears of Regan and Goneril: I know
the past, I know the future, my little hovel

will be in Pennsylvania, I will be
an old man eating from a newspaper,
I will stop to read the news, my fish
will soak the petty world up, it will stretch

from Sears on the left to Gimbels on the right,
my table will be a crate and I will cover
the little spaces with tape, it is enough
for my thin elbows.  They will look at him

with hatred reminiscent of the Plains
of Auschwitz—Buchenwald—and drive him mad
an inch at a time.  Nothing either in England
or Germany could equal his ferocity,

could equal his rage, even if the Yiddish
could make you laugh.  There is a famous picture
of a German soldier plucking a beard; I think
of gentle Gloucester every time I see

that picture.  There is a point where even Yiddish
becomes a tragic tongue and even Adler
can make you weep.  They sit in their chairs for hours
to hear him curse his God; he looks at the dust

and asks, What have I done, what have I done,
for Him to turn on me; that audience murmurs,
Daughters, daughters, it cries for the sadness that came
to all of them in America.  King Lear,

may the Lord keep him, hums in agony,
he is a monster of suffering, so many holes
that he is more like a whistle than like a king,
and yet when sometimes he comes across the stage

crowned with burdocks and nettles and cuckoo flowers
we forget it is Adler, we are so terrified,
we are so touched by pity. It is said
that Isadora Duncan came to worship him,

that John Barrymore came to study his acting,
that when he died they carried his coffin around
from theatre to theatre, that people mourned in the streets,
that he lay in a windsor tie and a black silk coat.

One time he carried Cordelia around in his arms
he almost forgot his words, he was so moved
by his own grief, there were tears and groans
for him when they remembered his misfortune.

I thank God they were able to weep
and wring their hands for Lear, and sweet Cordelia,
that it happened almost fifty years
before our hell, that there was still time then

to walk out of the theatre in the sunlight
and discuss tragedy on the bright sidewalk
and live awhile by mercy and innocence
with a king like Adler keeping the tremors alive

in their voices and the tears brimming in their eyes.
Thank God they died so early, that they were buried
one at a time, each with his own service,
that they were not lined up beside the trucks

or the cattle cars. I think when they saw him put
a feather over her lips they were relieved
to see her dead. I think they knew her life
was the last claim against him—the last delusion,

one or two would say.  Now he was free,
now he was fully changed, he was *created,*
which is something they could have to talk about
going back to their stairways and their crowded tables

with real streaks of remorse on their faces—
*more* than forty years, almost fifty,
before the dead were dragged from their places
and dumped on the ground or put in orderly piles—

I think they used a broom on the charred faces
to see if there was breath—and a match or two
was dropped on the naked bodies.  For the sake of art
there always was a German or Ukrainian

walking around like a dignified Albany,
or one made sad repentant noises like Kent
and one was philosophical like Edgar,
giving lectures to the burning corpses,

those with gold in their mouths, and those with skin
the color of yellow roses, and those with an arm
or a hand that dropped affectionately on another,
and those whose heads were buried, and those whose black tongues—

as if there were mountains, as if there were cold water
flowing through the ravines, as if there were wine cups
sitting on top of the barrels, as if there were flowers—
still sang in bitterness, still wept and warbled in sorrow.


Teresa Moszkowicz-Syrop

## Lullaby

On a sleepless night
When the past and present
Mix together

As in a moving play,
Pictures from the Nazi horrors
Follow me,
Suffering
Beyond the limit
Of human endurance
Comes alive again.
I often
Don't believe that
All we experienced
Existed.
I still cannot speak
About it
In any clear way.
On such a night
I wish to be a child again,
To feel safe, without fear,
To reach out for my mother's
Soothing hands,
Resurrected from the ashes,
And listen to the lullaby
She used to sing for me:
*Lulu lul, Lulu lul, Lulu lul* . . .

Marina Roscher

## The Lanternman

Every evening without fail he
appeared and brought sleeptime
not by the clock
but according to the amount of darkness.
It was good at that hour to watch
by the window until
he arrived in his smock and red cap
climbed his ladder against
the gas-lantern post and made

light by the touch
of a magic wand.  He was a gnome and lived
in a fairytale, in a kind town
this friend of the sandman
and he loved children.  Sometimes
you might knock at your window pane just
to see him doff that red cap.
He was better than a lullaby.  His name was
Yaacov.  Not a German name.

Once upon . . .
the nursery turned into schoolroom
the street grew wide
the comfort of lanterns
was chopped down.  They gave him a broom
for his ladder and wand
but he kept the red cap.  Now
doffing it often at all kinds of people
sweeping hard when tanks and boots
muddied the street.  His name
was Yaacov.  Gone one day
as if you'd only imagined him.  It would
have been good in the hour of darkness
if the lanternman had come back
again.  It would have been
good to think of ladders to heaven instead
of the gas-flame.

Tamara Fishman

## I Did Not Know, but I Remember

I can hear the clatter of the cattle cars.
It echoes forever in my mind.
My ears have never heard the sound,

and yet it is ingrained in my soul.
I did not know those who died.
I did not know those who were tossed into the flaming inferno
and taken out,
black ashes,
I did not know those whose burning flesh smelled
for miles around,
still in the air.
I did not know those who were made to walk the death march,
slowly dying,
and were then gunned down not because of what they had done,
but because of what they had been born.
I did not know those who were live guinea pigs for "doctors"
such as Joseph Mengele
and later died or were permanently scarred
from the effects of the silent torture.
I did not know those who bravely fought
against a monstrous tyrant
and did not live to see it dwarfed.
I did not know those marked for death,
and yet they are a part of me.
I am bound to them with a special bond,
as still I think, "It could have been my grandparents,
parents, friends.
It could have been me, too."
A part of me died with those people whose faces I have never seen.
A part of me is dead and buried
in the grave of millions.


Marilyn Mohr

## Tsena Tsena (Second Generation)

There you are dancing with your child,
The one you thought never could be born
Whirling her in tattooed arms,
Your faces flushed with the joy

Of her first year, rose-colored
Sunrise after the long night,
Twirling to the music of the *Tsena*,
Holding her high, as if in thanks
To the God you thought had forsaken you.

This child, fondled and touched with awe—
Each strand, each finger, a miracle—
The three of you dancing in the dim lights
Of a Brooklyn apartment, dancing away
the ashen smoke and hopeless years . . .
This child, this dance, this song
Sweeping back the darkness,
Tsena!

Katherine Janowitz

## The Third Generation

(for Jessie)

And no blight on her
anywhere from the
beginning, almost
too bright as if
out of my packet
of mixed seeds
the most extravagant
was sown and
my father told me
not to wear red
and I listened
but I gave birth to
this red bird
impossible to miss,
I gave birth to this crimson flower
from my secret blood.

David Shapiro

## For Victims

They have used the bodies
Of children as improvised bridges
Which, later, they cross
First the sun and the moon,
       then the earth comes in
But they have lost the atmosphere
Which belongs to them

Light passers-by

# Acknowledgments

**Carol Adler:** "We Are the Echoes" from *Arioso* (Pentagram Press), copyright 1975 by Carol Adler.

**Fran Adler:** "Benny," copyright 1983 by Fran Adler; first appeared in *Shirim.*

**Mari Alschuler:** "In My Own Nightmares," copyright 1985 by Mari Alschuler.

**Inge Auerbacher:** "I Am a Star" and "Something to Remember Me By" from *I am a Star: Child of the Holocaust* (Prentice-Hall Books for Young Readers), copyright 1985, 1986 by Inge Auerbacher.

**Julius Balbin:** "Tonight" and "Lament for the Gypsies" from *Strangled Cries* (Cross-Cultural Communications), copyright 1981, 1986 by Charlz Rizzuto. Reprinted with permission of Julius Balbin and Charlz Rizzuto.

**Willis Barnstone:** "Miklos Radnoti" and "The Rose of Blue Flesh," copyright 1985 by Willis Barnstone.

**Marvin Bell:** "The Extermination of the Jews" from *A Probable Volume of Dreams* (Atheneum), copyright 1969, 1985 by Marvin Bell.

**Lora Berg:** "Maschlacki," copyright 1985 by Lora J. Berg.

**Stephen Berg:** From "Memory," from *With Akhmatova at the Black Gates* (University of Illinois Press), copyright 1983 by Stephen Berg.

**Michael Blumenthal:** "Juliek's Violin" from *Days We Would Rather Know* (Viking-Penguin), copyright 1984 by Michael Blumenthal.

**George Bogin:** "Pitchipoi," copyright 1985 by George Bogin; copyright 1989 by the Estate of George Bogin; first appeared in *Jewish Currents.*

**Emily Borenstein:** "The Shoah," "The Excavator," and "I Must Tell the Story" from *Night of the Broken Glass* (Timberline Press), copyright 1981 by Emily Borenstein.

**Van K. Brock:** "The Hindenburg," copyright 1985 by Van K. Brock; first appeared in *New England Review/Bread Loaf Quarterly.* "The Nightmare," copyright 1985 by Van K. Brock; first appeared in *Crazy Horse.*

**Olga Cabral:** "At the Jewish Museum" from *In the Empire of Ice* (West End Press), copyright 1980 by Olga Cabral Kurtz.

**Esther Cameron:** "Exposure," copyright 1985 by Esther Cameron.

**Joan Campion:** "To Gisi Fleischmann," copyright 1985 by Joan Berengaria Campion.

**James William Chichetto:** "Etchings," copyright 1985 by James William Chichetto; first appeared in *Gargoyle.*

**John Ciardi:** "The Gift" from *Thirty-nine Poems* (Rutgers University Press), copyright 1959 by John Ciardi.

**Vince Clemente:** "From the Ardeatine Caves," copyright 1985 by Vince Clemente.

**Helen Degan Cohen:** "A View from the Ghetto (Or, On Either Side)," copyright 1985 by Helen Degan Cohen; first appeared in *Rhino;* "In Hiding" and "I Remember Coming into Warsaw, a Child," copyright 1985 by Helen Degan Cohen; first appeared in *Spoon River Quarterly.*

**Marion Cohen:** "Not a Dream, Just Thoughts," copyright 1985 by Marion Cohen.

**M. Truman Cooper:** "At a Mass Grave," copyright 1985 by Marsha Truman Cooper.

**R. M. Cooper:** "Rebecca 1942," "Eli 1943," and "Rebecca 1944," copyright 1985 by R. M. Cooper.

**Stanley Cooperman:** "The Children of Terezin," copyright 1985 by Jenifer Svendsen. Reprinted by permission of Jenifer Svendsen.

**Susan Dambroff:** "There Were Those" from *Memory in Bone* (Black Oyster Press), copyright 1984 by Susan Dambroff.

**Sister Mary Philip De Camara,** V.H.M.: "Yellow Starred," copyright 1985 by Sister Mary Philip De Camara, V.H.M.

**Theodore Deppe:** "School of Music," copyright 1985 by Theodore Deppe; first appeared in *Poem in a Pamphlet* (Andrew Mountain Press).

**Diana Der Hovanessian:** "The Anniversary Poem" from *How to Choose Your Past* (Ararat Press), copyright 1978 Diana Der Hovanessian.

**Catherine de Vinck:** "Kaddish," copyright 1985 by Catherine de Vinck.

**Owen Dodson:** "Jonathan's Song" from *Powerful Long Ladder* copyright 1946 by Farrar, Straus & Giroux, Inc.; renewed 1974 by Owen Dodson. Reprinted with permission from Farrar, Straus & Giroux, Inc.

**Olga Drucker:** "The Brooch," copyright 1985 by Olga M. Drucker.

**Shelley Ehrlich:** "Vilna 1938," copyright 1981 by Shelley Ehrlich; first appeared in *Jewish Currents.*

**Kenneth Fearing:** "AD" from *New and Collected Poems*, copyright 1956 by Indiana University Press. Reprinted with Permission of the Estate of Kenneth Fearing.

**Frederick Feirstein:** "'Grandfather' in Winter" from *Survivors* (David Lewis), copyright 1975 by Frederick Feirstein.

**Irving Feldman:** "Scene of a Summer Morning" and "The Pripet Marshes" from *New and Selected Poems*, copyright 1964 by Irving Feldman. Reprinted with permission of Viking-Penguin, Inc.

**Ruth Feldman:** "Survivor," copyright 1972 by Ruth Feldman; first appeared in *European Judaism.*

**Frank Finale:** "Digging," copyright 1983 by Frank Finale; first appeared in *Visions.*

**Charles Fishman:** "The Death Mazurka," "September 1944," and "Weltanschauung" from *The Death Mazurka* (Timberline Press), copyright 1987 by Charles Fishman. Variations on the prose of Arnost Lustig published with his permission.

**Tamara Fishman:** "I Did Not Know, but I Remember," copyright 1989 by Tamara Fishman.

**Ephim Fogel:** "Shipment to Maidanek" and "Icon" (originally "Portrait of a General") from *Cross Section 1945*, ed. by Edwin Seaver (L. B. Fischer Co.), copyright 1945, 1957, 1984 by Ephim Fogel.

**Carolyn Forché:** From "The Angel of History," copyright 1989 by Carolyn Forché.

**Robert A. Frauenglas:** "Seriatim" from *The Eclectic Musings of a Brooklyn Bum* (SOMRIE Press), copyright 1980 by Robert A. Frauenglas.

**Florence W. Freed:** "God's Death," copyright 1985 by Florence W. Freed.

**Mike Frenkel:** "Quiet Desperation," copyright 1985 by Michael W. Frenkel.

**Sari Friedman:** "Skin," copyright 1985 by Sari Friedman.

**Carol Ganzer:** "Taking Leave," copyright 1985 by Carol A. Ganzer.

**Patricia Garfinkel:** "The Tailor," copyright 1979 by Patricia Garfinkel; first appeared in *Seattle Review.*

**Kinereth Gensler:** "For Nelly Sachs" from *Threesome Poems* (Alice James Books), copyright 1976 by Kinereth Gensler.

**Jacob Glastein:** "Without Jews" translation by Nathan Halper. Reprinted with permission of Helen Marjorie Windust Halper. "Dead Men Don't Praise God," "I'll Find My Self-Belief," and "Nightsong" from *The Selected Poems of Jacob Glatstein* (October House), copyright 1972 by Ruth Whitman. "Little Boy," translation copyright 1985 by Doris Vidaver.

# ACKNOWLEDGMENTS

**Gloria Glickstein:** "Diary of a Tashkent Jew" and "The Ghetto," copyright 1985 by Gloria Glickstein.

**Barbara Goldberg:** "Survivor," copyright 1985 by Barbara Goldberg.

**Thomas A. Goldman:** "Rotterdam—1946," copyright 1985 by Thomas A. Goldman.

**Jorie Graham:** "History," copyright 1985 by Jorie Graham.

**Ber Green:** "The Martyrs Are Calling," translation copyright 1985 by Aaron Kramer.

**Luba Krugman Gurdus:** "We Seek You, One and Only God" from *Painful Echoes: Poems of the Holocaust* (Holocaust Publications), copyright 1985 by Luba Krugman Gurdus.

**John Z. Guzlowski:** "Cattle Train to Magdeburg," copyright 1984 by John Z. Guzlowski; first appeared in *Blue Unicorn.* "How Early Fall Came This Year," copyright 1988 by John Z. Guzlowski; first appeared in *Farmer's Market.*

**Leo Hamalian:** "Boghos Sarkissian, a Watchmaker of Karpet, Remembers the Turkish Atrocities of 1915," copyright 1985 by Leo Hamalian.

**Cecile Hamermesh:** "Trilogy," copyright 1983 by Cecile Hamermesh; first appeared in *The Third Wind.*

**Deborah Hanan:** "On Watching 'Heritage: Civilization and the Jews'" copyright 1985 by Deborah Hanan.

**Annette Bialik Harchik:** "Earrings" from *Ghosts of the Holocaust* (Wayne State University Press), copyright 1985 by Annette Bialik Harchik.

**Anthony Hecht:** "'More Light! More Light!'" from *The Hard Hours* (Atheneum), copyright 1967 by Anthony Hecht.

**Leslie Woolf Hedley:** "Chant for All the People on Earth" from *On My Way to the Cemetery* (Ampersand Press), copyright 1964, 1981 by Leslie Woolf Hedley.

**Julie N. Heifetz:** "The Blue Parakeet," "The Wheel," and "Harry Lenga" from *Oral History and the Holocaust* (Pergamon Press), copyright 1985 by Julie N. Heifetz.

**William Heyen:** "Riddle," "Simple Truths," "The Children," and "My Holocaust Songs" from *Erika: Poems of the Holocaust* (Vanguard Press), copyright 1977, 1984 by William Heyen.

**Edward Hirsch:** "Paul Celan: A Grave and Mysterious Sentence" from *Wild Gratitude* (Alfred A. Knopf), copyright 1983, 1986 by Edward Hirsch.

**Barbara Helfgott Hyett:** "You Know the Funny Thing Is," "In Some of the Bunks," and "And There Were Pits" from *In Evidence: Poems of the Liberation of Nazi Concentration Camps* (University of Pittsburgh), copyright 1986 by Barbara Helfgott Hyett.

**David Ignatow:** "1905" from *New and Collected Poems: 1970-1985,* copyright 1986 by David Ignatow. Reprinted by permission of Wesleyan University Press.

**Judith Irwin:** "1985—In a Small American Town," copyright 1985 by Judith Irwin.

**Katherine Janowitz:** "The Third Generation," copyright 1985 by Katherine Janowitz; first appeared in *Jewish Currents.*

**Randall Jarrell:** "A Camp in the Prussian Forest" from *The Complete Poems by Randall Jarrell,* copyright 1946 by Randall Jarrell; renewed 1973 by Mrs. Randall Jarrell. Reprinted by permission of Farrar, Straus & Giroux, Inc.

**Laurence Josephs:** "Passover at Auschwitz" from *Cold Water Morning* (Skidmore College), copyright 1964, by Laurence Josephs.

**Hans Juergensen:** "The Scar—August, 1934" from *Hebraic Modes* (Olivant Press), copyright 1972 by Hans Juergensen. "Yad Vashem," from *Journey Toward the Roots* (Valkyrie), copyright 1976 by Hans Juergensen.

**Marc Kaminsky:** "Medium," copyright 1977, 1982 by Marc Kaminsky; first appeared in *Response.*

**Peretz Kaminsky:** "Bramble" and "Identifications," copyright 1985 by Peretz Kaminsky.

**Rosa Felsenburg Kaplan:** "Kol Nidre," copyright 1982 by Rosa Felsenburg Kaplan; first appeared in *Shirim.*

**Laura Kasischke:** "For Malka Who Lived Three Days Dying," copyright 1985 by Laura K. Kasischke.

**Dori Katz:** "Line-Up" and "The Return," copyright 1985 by Dori Katz.

**Melanie Kaye/Kantrowitz:** From "Kaddish," copyright 1984 by Melanie Kaye/Kantrowitz; first appeared in *Sinister Wisdom.*

**Miriam Kessler:** "Yahrzeit," copyright 1985 by Miriam Kessler.

**Irena Klepfisz:** "Solitary Acts" from *Keeper of Accounts* (Sinister Wisdom), copyright 1982 by Irena Klepfisz. *"Di Rayze Abeym/*The Journey Home," copyright 1985 by Irena Klepfisz; first appeared in *Lilith.*

**David Koenig:** "After the Holocaust, No Poetry" and "Onkel Fritz Is Sitting," copyright 1985 by David Koenig.

**Yala Korwin:** "The Little Boy with His Hands Up," copyright 1982 by Yala Korwin; first appeared in *Martyrdom and Resistance.* "Passover Night 1942," copyright 1985 by Yala Korwin; first appeared in *Bitterroot.*

**Aaron Kramer:** "Westminster Synagogue" and "Zudioska" from *Carousel Parkway and Other Poems* (A. S. Barnes & Co.), copyright 1980 by Aaron Kramer.

**Norbert Krapf:** "The Name of a Place," copyright 1985 by Norbert Krapf.

**Carolyn Kreiter-Kurylo:** "Leaving a Country Behind," copyright 1985 by Carolyn Kreiter-Kurylo.

**J. L. Kubíček:** "A Song," copyright 1985 by J. L. Kubíček.

**Maxine Kumin:** "The Amsterdam Poem" from *The Nightmare Factory* (Harper & Row), copyright 1970 by Maxine Kumin.

**Aaron Kurtz:** "A Million Pairs of Shoes," copyright 1965 by Olga Cabral Kurtz; first appeared in *Jewish Currents.*

**Christine Lahey:** "Dan's Shoe Repair: 1959 from *Sticks and Stones* (Urban Despair Press), copyright 1980 by Christine Lahey-Dolega.

**Carole Glasser Langille:** "Babi Yar," copyright 1985 by Carole Glasser.

**Cornel Adam Lengyel:** "Independence Day: Eureka" from *Fifty Poems,* copyright 1965 by Cornel Adam Lengyel.

**Denise Levertov:** From "During the Eichmann Trial" from *Denise Levertov: Poems 1960-1967,* copyright 1961 by Denise Levertov Goodman. Reprinted with permission of New Directions Publishing Corporation.

**Philip Levine:** "On a Drawing by Flavio" from *Ashes,* copyright 1979 by Philip Levine. "The Survivor" from *The Names of the Lost,* copyright 1976 by Philip Levine. Both reprinted with permission of Atheneum. "In Saxony" from *Not This Pig,* copyright 1968 by Philip Levine. Reprinted with permission of Wesleyan University Press.

**Leatrice H. Lifshitz:** "A Few More Things about the Holocaust," copyright 1985 by Leatrice H. Lifshitz.

**Abraham Linik:** "The Thief," copyright 1985 by Abraham Linik.

**Geraldine Clinton Little:** "Meditation after Hearing the Richard Yardumian Mass, 'Come, Creator Spirit,'" copyright 1983 by Geraldine C. Little; first appeared in *Ararat.*

**Alan Lupack:** "Auschwitz Reportaż," copyright 1985 by Alan C. Lupack.

# ACKNOWLEDGMENTS

**Yaacov Luria:** "There Is One Synagogue Extant in Kiev" from *Not a Piano Key* (Shira Press), copyright 1979 by Yaacov Luria.

**Arlene Maass:** "Opa the Watchmaker," copyright 1985 by Arlene G. Maass. "In Remembrance of the Children of Izieu" from *A Book of the Year 1986, Book 64* (The Poetry Society of Texas, NFSPS, Inc.), copyright 1985 by Arlene G. Maass.

**Lois Mathieu:** "Counting Sheep by Night," copyright 1979 by Lois Mathieu; first appeared in *Connecticut River Review.*

**David Mckain:** "For the Children" from *The Common Life* (Alice James Books), copyright 1982 by David McKain.

**Bert Meyers:** "Pigeons" is reprinted from *Sunlight on the Wall* (Kayak), copyright 1976 by Bert Meyers.

**Robert Mezey:** "Theresienstadt Poem" from *The Door Standing Open* (Houghton Mifflin), copyright 1970 by Robert Mezey.

**Richard Michelson:** "The Jews That We Are" is reprinted from Richard Michelson, *Tap-Dancing for the Relatives* (Orlando: University of Central Florida Press, 1985), by permission of the author. Copyright 1985 by Richard Michelson. "Undressing Aunt Frieda," copyright 1985 by Richard Michelson.

**Bernard S. Mikofsky:** "1945," copyright 1975 by Bernard S. Mikofsky; first appeared in *Friday Forum.* "Mame-Loshen, Yiddish," copyright 1977 by Bernard S. Mikofsky; first appeared in the *Detroit Jewish News.*

**Aaron Miller:** "Not Dachau," copyright 1964 by Aaron Miller; first appeared in *World Union* published in India.

**Marilyn Mohr:** "Tsena Tsena (Second Generation)," copyright 1985 by Marilyn Mohr; first appeared in *Response.*

**Teresa Moszkowicz-Syrop:** "The Tomatoes" and "Lullaby," copyright 1985 by Teresa Syrop.

**Elaine Mott:** "The Last Visa for Palestine," copyright 1985 by Elaine Mott. "On the Wings of the Wind" from *Day Tonight/Night Today,* copyright 1985 by Elaine Mott.

**Gerald Musinsky:** "Drawing the Blinds," copyright 1982 by Gerald Musinsky; first appeared in the *Bay Area Jewish Newsletter.*

**Mark Nepo:** "I Wake from a Dream of Killing Hitler," copyright 1985 by Mark Nepo.

**Amos Neufeld:** "A Shade of Night" and "In the Heaven of Night," copyright 1985 by Amos Neufeld. "A Shade of Night" first appeared in *Forum* published in Israel.

**Estelle Gershgoren Novak:** "Yom HaShoah" copyright 1985 by E. G. Novak.

**Miriam Offenberg:** "Reforger," copyright 1985 by Miriam Offenberg.

**Gregory Orfalea:** "The Poacher" from *The Capital of Solitude* (Ithaca House/Greenfield Review Press), copyright 1988 by Gregory Orfalea.

**Gary Pacernick:** "Why I Write about the Holocaust," copyright 1985 by Gary Pacernick.

**Linda Pastan:** "Response" and "Rachel" from *PM/AM: New and Selected Poems* (W. W. Norton), copyright 1982 by Linda Pastan.

**Monique Pasternak:** "The Witness," copyright 1985 by Monique Pasternak. Reprinted with permission of Monique Pasternak.

**Mark Pawlak:** "Unforgettable," copyright 1985 by Mark Pawlak.

**Edmund Pennant:** "Thoughts under the Giant Sequoia" from *Dream's Navel,* copyright 1979 by Edmund Pennant. Reprinted with permission of Lintel Press. "Yom Hazikaron," copyright 1984 by Edmund Pennant; first appeared in *Moment.* Reprinted with permission of *Moment.*

**Louis Phillips:** "God Teaches Us How to Forgive, but We Forget," copyright 1985 by Louis James Phillips, Jr.

**Ronald William Pies:** "Voices," copyright 1978 by Ronald William Pies; first appeared in *The Literary Review*. Reprinted with permission of *The Literary Review*.

**William Pillin:** "The Ascensions," "Farewell to Europe," "Miserere," "The Requirement," and "The Terrified Meadows" from *To the End of Time* (Papa Bach Editions), copyright 1980 by William Pillin. Reprinted with permission of Polia Pillin.

**John C. Pine:** "The Survivor" from *Cliff Walk* (Moveable Feast Press), copyright 1985 by John C. Pine.

**Ginger Porter:** "I Am Babi Yar," copyright 1985 by Ginger Porter.

**David Ray:** "Kitty Returns to Auschwitz" from *The Touched Life* (Scarecrow Press), copyright 1982, 1985 by David Ray. "A Couple of Survivors," copyright 1985 by David Ray; first appeared in *Associated Writing Programs Newsletter*.

**Richard C. Raymond:** "And Nothing Moved" from *A Moment of Bells* (The Plowshare Press), copyright 1970 by Richard C. Raymond. Reprinted with permission of Laura Raymond.

**Norah Reap:** "Numbers," copyright 1985 by Norah Boyle Reap.

**Naomi Replansky:** "The Six Million" from *Ring Song* (Charles Scribner's Sons), copyright 1952 by Naomi Replansky.

**Lisa Ress:** "The Family Album," "U.S. Army Holds Dance for Camp Survivors. Germany, 1945" and "At Your Table. Vienna V, 1957" from *Flight Patterns,* copyright 1985 by the Rector and Visitors of the University of Virginia. Reprinted with permission of the University Press of Virginia.

**Charles Reznikoff:** From "Mass Graves" and from "Massacres" from *Holocaust* (Black Sparrow Press), copyright 1975 by Charles Reznikoff. From "Inscriptions: 1944-1956" from *Poems 1937-1975*, vol. 2 of *The Complete Poems of Charles Reznikoff* (Black Sparrow Press), copyright 1977 by Marie Syrkin Reznikoff. Reprinted with permission of Black Sparrow Press and Marie Syrkin Reznikoff.

**Liliane Richman:** "To My Mother Who Endured," copyright 1989 Liliane Richman; first appeared in *Response*. "After Claude Lanzmann's *Shoah*," copyright 1989 by Liliane Richman; first appeared in *Z Miscellaneous*.

**Michael D. Riley:** "Hands: Abraham Kunstler," copyright 1984 by Michael D. Riley; first appeared in *The Third Eye*.

**Nicholas Rinaldi:** "Auschwitz" from *The Luftwaffe in Chaos* (Negative Capability Press), copyright 1985 by Nicholas Rinaldi.

**Martin Robbins:** "Chicago Scene (1952, 1969)" from *A Reply to the Headlines* (Swallow Press), copyright 1970 by Martin Robbins. "A Cantor's Dream before 'The Days of Awe,'" copyright 1985 by Martin Robbins.

**William Pitt Root:** "Late Twentieth Century Pastoral," copyright 1983 by William Pitt Root; first appeared in *Southern Poetry Review*.

**Marina Roscher:** "Going Back" and "The Lanternman," copyright 1985 by Marina L. Roscher.

**Menachem Z. Rosensaft:** "The Second Generation," copyright 1980 by Menachem Z. Rosensaft; first appeared in *Midstream*.

**Larry Rubin:** "The Nazi in the Dock, at Sixty," copyright 1981 by Larry Rubin; first appeared in *Midstream*.

**Luada Sandler:** "The Gift," copyright 1985 by Luada Sandler. "A Scene from *Shoah*," copyright 1989 by Luada Sandler.

**Reg Saner:** "Aspen Oktoberfest" from *Essay on Air* (Ohio Review Books), copyright 1984 by Reg Saner.

**May Sarton:** From "The Invocation to Kali" from Collected Poems: 1930-1973 (W. W. Norton), copyright 1974 by May Sarton.

**Ruth Lisa Schechter:** "The Hungarian Mission," copyright 1985 by Ruth Lisa Schechter.

**David Shapiro:** "For Victims," copyright 1989 by David Shapiro.

**Gregg Shapiro:** "Tattoo," copyright 1983 by Gregg Shapiro; first appeared in *The Reconstructionist.*

**Harvey Shapiro:** "Ditty" from *This World,* copyright 1971 by Harvey Shapiro. Reprinted with permission of Wesleyan University Press.

**Reva Sharon:** "In the Absence of Yellow" from *Berekhat Tzefira: Pool of the Early Morning Wind* (Shemesh, Jerusalem), copyright 1989 by Reva Sharon. "Unanswerable Questions," copyright 1985 by Reva Sharon; first appeared in *Jewish Frontier.*

**Steven Sher:** "Sitting This One Out," copyright 1985 by Steven Sher; first appeared in *Midstream.*

**Pearl B. Sheridan:** "Little Lamb," copyright 1985 by Pearl B. Sheridan.

**Enid Shomer:** "Remembering," copyright 1983 by Enid Shomer; first appeared in *Shirim.* "Women Bathing at Bergen-Belsen: April 24, 1945," copyright 1985 by Enid Shomer; first appeared in *Negative Capability.*

**Maurya Simon:** "Munich, 1955" and "Letter to Vienna from Paris, 1942," copyright 1985 by Maurya Simon.

**Louis Simpson:** "The Bird" from *A Dream of Governors,* copyright 1957 by Louis Simpson. "A Story about Chicken Soup" from *At the End of the Open Road,* copyright 1963 by Louis Simpson. Both reprinted with permission of Wesleyan University Press.

**Frieda Singer:** "Saving the Children," copyright 1985 by Frieda Singer.

**Myra Sklarew:** "Blessed Art Thou, No-One" from *The Science of Goodbyes* by Myra Sklarew, copyright 1982 by the University of Georgia Press. Reprinted with permission of the University of Georgia Press.

**Joan Jobe Smith:** "Hollow Cost," copyright 1985 by Joan Jobe.

**Deborah S. Snyder:** "Carolyn's Neighbor," copyright 1985 by Deborah S. Snyder.

**Kirtland Snyder:** "City Children at a Summer Camp. Slonim, 1936" and "Selma . . . a Pot of Soup . . . a Bottle of Milk. Lodz, 1938," copyright 1985 by Kirtland Snyder.

**J. R. Solonche:** "Another Book on the Holocaust," copyright 1985 by J. R. Solonche.

**Gizela Spunberg:** "Memories of December," copyright 1979 by Gizela Spunberg; first appeared in *Martyrdom and Resistance.*

**Martin Steingesser:** "The Three," copyright 1978, 1980 by Martin Steingesser; first appeared in *The American Poetry Review.*

**Gerald Stern:** "Soap" and "Adler" from *Paradise Poems,* copyright 1984 by Gerald Stern. Reprinted by permission of Random House, Inc.

**Mary Kathryn Stillwell:** "Dachau" from *Moving to Malibu* (Sandhills Press), copyright 1988 by Mary Kathryn Stillwell.

**Bradley R. Strahan:** "Yom Kippur," copyright 1979 by Bradley R. Strahan; first appeared in *The Jewish Spectator.*

**Yuri Suhl:** ". . . And the Earth Rebelled" from *Jewish Life Anthology, 1946-1956,* copyright 1956 by Max Rosenfeld.

**Harriet Susskind:** "After That Time," copyright 1985 by Harriet Susskind.

**Marie Syrkin:** "Niemand" and "The Reckoning" from *Gleanings* (Black Sparrow Press), copyright 1979 by Marie Syrkin. Reprinted with permission of Black Sparrow Press.

**Marilynn Talal:** "Being Children" and "For Our Dead," copyright 1985 by Marilyn Talal.

**Elaine Terranova:** "1939," copyright 1985 by Elaine Terranova; first appeared in *Spoon River Quarterly.*

**Susan Tichy:** "Gaby at the U.N. Observation Post" from *The Hands in Exile,* copyright 1983 by Susan E. Tichy. Reprinted with permission of Random House, Inc.

**William Trowbridge:** "The Song of Iron Paul," copyright 1982 by William Trowbridge; first appeared in *The Beloit Poetry Journal.*

**Alfred Van Loen:** "Auschwitz #1," "Auschwitz #5," "Auschwitz #6," copyright 1985 by Alfred Van Loen.

**Anneliese Wagner:** "The Little Place," copyright 1983 by Anneliese Wagner; first appeared in *The Jewish Spectator.*

**Derek Walcott:** XXXVIII from *Midsummer '81,* copyright 1981, 1982 by Derek Walcott. Reprinted with permission of Derek Walcott. First appeared in James Atlas, *"Derek Walcott:* Poet of Two Worlds," 23 May 1982, New York *Times* Magazine (sect. *vi* ), 38.

**Morrie Warshawski:** "Sonia at 32," copyright 1985 by Morrie Warshawski. First appeared in *Ghosts of the Holocaust* (Wayne State University Press).

**Burton D. Wasserman:** "1945," "The Silence," copyright 1985 by Burton D. Wasserman; first appeared in *Pomegranate.*

**Michael Waters:** "Dachau Moon" from *Fish Light* (Ithaca House), copyright 1975 by Michael Waters.

**Florence Weinberger:** "The Dancing Dog," copyright 1982 by Florence Weinberger; first appeared in *Poetry/LA.* "Survivor," copyright 1985 by Florence Weinberger; first appeared in *Poetry/LA.* Reprinted with permission of Helen Friedland.

**Vera Weislitz:** "Roses and the Grave," copyright 1985 by Vera Weislitz-Lustig.

**Theodore Weiss:** "The Late Train" from *Fireweeds* (Macmillan), copyright 1976, 1987 by Theodore Weiss.

**Ruth Whitman:** "Maria Olt" from *Permanent Address: New Poems 1973-1980* (Alice James Books), copyright 1980 by Ruth Whitman. "The Death Ship" from *The Testing of Hanna Senesh* (Wayne State University Press), copyright 1986 by Ruth Whitman.

**C. K. Williams:** "Spit" from *With Ignorance* (Houghton Mifflin), copyright 1972, 1974, 1975, 1977 by C. K. Williams.

**Betty Wisoff:** "Sanity," copyright 1985 by Betty Wisoff.

**Carolyne Wright:** "After Forty Years," copyright 1985 by Carolyne Wright and "KZ," copyright 1989 by Carolyne Wright.

**Jeffrey A. Z. Zable:** "To the End," copyright 1984 by Jeffrey A. Z. Zable; first appeared in *Ally.*

**David Zucker:** "Entrance to the Old Cracow Ghetto," copyright 1983 by David Zucker; first appeared in *Shirim.*

# Notes to poems on pages 4-8

For the most part, I have limited these annotations to factual details that are not common knowledge or easily gleaned from a good college dictionary, and I have placed more personal reflections in the section immediately following this one, Additional Notes.

## I. After the Holocaust—No Poetry?

The title of this section—which echoes the title of David Koenig's poem—is a reference to the famous statement by German sociologist and music critic, T. W. Adorno, in "Engagement," in *Noten zur Literatur III* (Frankfurt: Suhrkamp Verlag, 1965): "I do not want to soften the proposition that continuing to write lyric poetry after Auschwitz would be barbaric; negatively expressed in it is that impulse which inspires a committed poetic work"(125, my translation). For a valuable discussion of Adorno's remarks, see Laurence Langer, *The Holocaust and the Literary Imagination* (New Haven: Yale University Press, 1975), 1-3.

**Why I Write about the Holocaust**. *SS insignia:* The indelible numbers tattooed on the arms of concentration camp prisoners. *SS:* The *Schutzstaffel*, Hitler's elite guard.

**I Must Tell the Story.** *Warsaw:* When Warsaw came under siege 1 September 1939, "some 20,000 Polish Jews lost their lives during the invasion and bombardments; Jewish homes, stores, buildings, workshops, factories, and other installations were destroyed . . . about one-third of Jewish-owned buildings were demolished and the main centers of Jewish trade were reduced to rubble" (Lucy S. Dawidowicz, *The War against the Jews 1933-1945* [New York: Holt, Rinehart and Winston, 1975], 198). In October 1940, the Warsaw ghetto for Jews was established. Despite the heroic resistance by surviving Jewish partisans, this ghetto was systematically destroyed under the direction of SS Brigadeführer Jürgen Stroop, between 19 April and 16 May 1943. Stroop was awarded the Iron Cross First Class for his role. According to Abram L. Sachar, "The Warsaw Ghetto uprising of 1943 was the first mass open rebellion on the continent against the Nazis, except for the resistance of the Yugoslav guerrillas under Tito" *(The Redemption of the Unwanted: From the Liberation of the Death Camps to the Founding of Israel* [New York: St. Martin's/Marek, 1983], 51). Sachar provides a fine overview of the uprising (50-56). *Chaim Kaplan:* Kaplan was a Polish Hebrew teacher who perished not long after the last entry in his diary, *The Scroll of Agony*, which recorded the day-to-day destruction of the Warsaw ghetto and its Jewish inhabitants. This historical record, which covers the period from 1 September 1939 to August 1942, was reprinted as *The Warsaw Diary of Chaim Kaplan* (New York: Macmillan, 1965). *Bruno Schulz:* Polish writer, author of *The Street of Crocodiles* and *Sanatorium under the Sign of the Hourglass*. Schulz, a teacher of drawing and handicrafts at the boys' high school in Drogobycz, was shot on the street by a gestapo officer in November 1942. He was fifty years old. *Emanuel Ringelblum:* Historian of the Warsaw Ghetto. "At Emanuel Ringelblum's initiative and under his direction, a secret Jewish archive was established under the code name *Oneg Shabbat* (Pleasures of the Sabbath). Its purpose, as Ringelblum described it in his letter of 20 May 1944, was to gather 'materials and documents relating to the martyrology of the Jews of Poland.' A large staff worked systematically to this end, stimulating the production of diaries, chronicles, all sorts of descriptive and analytic writings on every phase of Jewish life under German occupation. . . . Much of the assembled material was buried in crates in the ghetto and uncovered after the war" (Dawidowicz, 259). *See also* Emily Borenstein in Additional Notes.

## II. The Terrified Meadows

**Meditation after Hearing the Richard Yardumian Mass, "Come, Creator Spirit."** *Maydan:* An open square or marketplace. *Hitler's remark:* It appears in Michael Arlen's book, *Passage to Ararat* (New York: Farrar, Straus & Giroux, 1975). The Turks perpetrated genocide on the Armenians at the beginning of the twentieth century. When Hitler was about to invade Poland (22 August 1939), he used the Turkish genocide as partial justification of his lethal intentions.

**1905.** *Prince Igor:* An opera invented by the poet. *See also* David Ignatow in Additional Notes.

**The Terrified Meadows.** *Black Hundreds:* Monarchist societies, such as the Union of Russian People, the Double-headed Eagle Society, and others, which played a significant role in the organization of the pogroms of 1903-1906. These savage attacks against Russian Jews began with the Kishinev pogrom, which occurred during Passover 1903. The pogroms of 1903-1906 stimulated a great nationalist awakening among the Jews of Europe.

**Boghos Sarkissian, a Watchmaker of Karpet, Remembers the Turkish Atrocities of 1915.** *Hamadiyeh cavalry:* The sabre-swinging Kurdish horsemen that Ottoman officials used to maintain "order" among the deportees. *Aydin Bitlis Malatya Kharpet Moush:* Villages in Turkey with large Armenian populations before the massacres. *Museum of Deir-e-Zhor:* According to some reports, this "museum," the final destination of the death marches of 1915, contained a pyramid made of Armenian skulls. For a recent overview of the genocide, see Peter Stine, "German Complicity in the Armenian Genocide," *Witness* 1 (Spring 1987):98-106. *See also* Leo Hamalian in Additional Notes.

**Scene of a Summer Morning.** *Ten Tribes:* The Hebrew tribes that broke away from the kingdom of Judah to form their own kingdom in the post-Solomonic period. Later, they became known as the "Lost Tribes" of Israel.

**The Scar—August, 1934.** *Death's-Head men:* The SS had silver death's heads on their caps. This emblem goes back to the Wars of Liberation (1813-1815) when a number of Free Corps and the Brunswick Hussars (Totenkopf Husaren) initiated its use. In World War I, a famous cavalry regiment carried the death's head. Crown Prince Friedrich Wilhelm wore it on his fur cap. Dawidowcz adds: "The Totenkopfverbände originated from the guard unit at Dachau, the first concentration camp in National Socialist Germany" (75). *See also* Raoul Hilberg, *The Destruction of the European Jews,* rev. and definitive ed., 3 vols. (New York: Holmes & Meier, 1985), 864; and Hans Juergensen in Additional Notes.

**City Children at a Summer Camp. Slonim, 1936.** *Slonim:* The name of the city (in White Russia, near the Polish border) where the summer camp was located. The camp was operated by the Jewish Health Society and ministered to the needs of poor, handicapped, and retarded children. *Dresden dolls:* Dresden china (porcelain) has been world famous since 1710. *See also* Kirtland Snyder in Additional Notes.

**The Hindenburg.** LZ-129 was completed in 1936 and offered the first commercial air service across the North Atlantic. It was 803 feet long, had a cruising speed of 78 m.p.h., and could transport up to 1,002 passengers. On 6 May 1937, while landing at Lakehurst, New Jersey, on the first crossing of the 1937 season, it burst into flames and was completely destroyed. *Thousand Year Reich:* Hitler had predicted that the Third Reich would last for a thousand years. *See also* Van K. Brock in Additional Notes.

**Entrance to the Old Cracow Ghetto.** *Appia and Reinhardt:* Adolphe Appia, Swiss theoretician (1862-1928) who emphasized scenic designs in which shadow was as important as light. Max Reinhardt (1873-1943), German expressionist director in theater and film (including Hollywood). *See also* David Zucker in Additional Notes.

**Vilna 1938.** In 1938, Roman Vishniac traveled secretly to photograph the Jews of Poland. Edward Steichen (Roman Vishniac, *A Vanished World*. New York: Farrar, Straus & Giroux, 1983) wrote of this trip: "It gives a last-minute look at the human beings he photographed just before the fury of Nazi brutality exterminated them." According to the poet's husband, Dr. Frederick M. Ehrlich, the photograph that inspired this poem is entitled "Vilna, Poland" and appears on page 62 of *Roman Vishniac*, ICP Library of Photographers (New York: Viking, 1974). *Vilna:* In a short period in 1941, more than 20,000 of the 70,000 Jews from Vilna were massacred at Ponary, a small village outside the ghetto (Dawidowicz, 201). Vilna, now called Vilnius, had been a leading center of Jewish culture in Eastern Europe since the sixteenth century. Napoleon had called it "the Jerusalem of Lithuania." The shifting geopolitical borders of Eastern Europe during the twentieth century account for the fact that Vilna has been identified as Polish, Lithuanian, and Russian within the course of a single lifetime.

### III. Crystal Night

For many scholars, *Kristallnacht* ("Crystal Night" or "Night of Glass") signals a major intensification of the Nazi mission to disfranchise, humiliate, and—ultimately— destroy the Jews of Germany. This explosive pogrom was unleashed, as if on cue, by the report that Ernst vom Rath, a third secretary in the German embassy in Paris, had been assassinated by Hershl Grynszpan, a seventeen-year-old Polish student whose parents had just been expelled from Germany. On 8 and 9 November, in the wake of vom Rath's death, "night fires were ignited all over Germany, and the shattered plate glass that was to give the pogrom its name littered the streets of German towns and cities. . . . Synagogues and Jewish institutions were burned to the ground. Over seven thousand Jewish businesses were destroyed. Nearly one hundred Jews were killed, and thousands more subjected to wanton violence and sadistic torments" (Dawidowicz, 100-103). Dawidowicz stresses the power of *Kristallnacht* as a metaphor or template for future actions: "The Germans reenacted the Kristallnacht in every town and city they invaded and occupied. All over Poland synagogues went up in flames. (Those spared the fire were desecrated, turned into stables, garages, and public latrines.) Everywhere the Germans organized pogroms, rounding-up the non-Jewish population to witness and learn how to mock, abuse, injure, and murder Jews" (200).

**Weltanschauung.** *Twisted clockwise:* The Nazi version of the ancient mystical symbol, the swastika, used as the party emblem and as a symbol of anti-Semitism. *Shtetls:* (Yid.) Little cities, towns, and villages—the Jewish communities of Eastern Europe, where Ashkenazic culture flourished prior to World War II. *Shuls:* (Yid.) Synagogues. *Himmelstrasse:* (G.) Heaven Street. The same brand of malevolent humor evidenced in the placing of *"Arbeit Macht Frei"—Work Makes [You] Free*—over the gates of concentration camps.

**The Shoah.** *The Hineni:* (Heb.) A prayer, "Here I am [as I stand before God]." *TEKIAH! SHEBARIM! TERUAH! TEKIAH!:* The notes of the shofar—the ram's horn— sounded in the synagogue during Rosh Hashanah (the New Year) and at the end of services on Yom Kippur (the Day of Atonement). *Ovenu Malkenu!:* (Heb.) Our Father, our King. A prayer recited on the New Year and Day of Atonement in which worshippers acknowledge their sins and pray for God's forgiveness. *Yaahleh:* (Heb.) Let us go up: a High Holiday prayer—that our words might ascend to God. *Shema Kolenu:* (Heb.) Hear our voice: a plea for God to listen to our prayers.

**Babi Yar.** *Babi Yar:* On 29 and 30 September 1941, the Nazis systematically machine-gunned nearly 34,000 Jews from the Kiev ghetto at this ravine near the captured Russian city (Sachar, 60). *Anatoly Kuznetzov:* Author of *Babi Yar*, first published in *Yunost* in 1966. An uncensored and expanded version was translated by David Floyd and published by Farrar, Straus & Giroux in 1970.

**The Death Ship.** *Lord Moyne:* The British official who refused to allow the ship to land in Istanbul. He was later assassinated in Cairo by members of the Stern Gang

(Hilberg, 1140n). For a concise account of the fate of the *Struma*, see Sachar, 178-180.

**I Am a Star.** Auerbacher reports: "As of September 1, 1941, Jews in Germany were ordered to sew the yellow Star of David on their clothes as a distinguishing mark. On the star the word 'Jude' [Jew] was written in Hebrew-like letters." *See also* Inge Auerbacher in Additional Notes.

**Little Lamb.** *Umschlagplatz:* (G.) Reloading point. Jews who had been rounded up in one of the "actions" were gathered at the designated place, typically a train depot, where guards swinging truncheons and leading large dogs often clubbed protesting captives onto the trains and then bolted the boxcars after them.

**Opa the Watchmaker.** The ten Boom family of Holland ran a watchmaker's business and maintained living quarters in an old three-story building in the heart of Haarlem. During the Nazi occupation, they concealed a number of Jewish people in an obscure attic room. "Opa," the ten Boom patriarch, was a devout Bible-believing Christian; his convictions and love for the Jewish people led to his eventual arrest, incarceration, and death at the hands of Dutch traitors and Nazis. *No justice in the streets:* A reference to Lam. 4:18: "Men stalked us at every step so we could not walk in our streets; our end was near, our days numbered, for our end had come." *Hiding place:* "Thou [the Lord] art my hiding place" (Ps. 32:7). *Root of Jesse:* A messianic reference from Isa. 11:1: "A root [shoot] will spring up from the stump of Jesse; from his roots a branch will bear fruit." *Moriah:* A place of sacrifice, and the setting for the *Akeda*, the binding of Isaac. Abraham was commanded by God to bind his son Isaac and offer up his life. Abraham stood ready to obey the command; however, God circumvented the order and, at the last moment, spared Isaac. In place of the son, a ram was sacrificed.

**The Little Boy with His Hands Up.** In the ghettos of former Poland, Jews were ordered to wear a white cotton band with a blue Star of David (not a yellow star).

**"More Light! More Light!"** The title is composed of what are reputedly the last words of Johann Wolfgang von Goethe (1749-1832), German poet, scientist, critic, man of letters, and probably chief representative of what was once called "the German Enlightenment." The first three stanzas concern details conflated from several executions, including those of Latimer and Ridley (Anglican bishops executed for heresy in 1555), whose deaths at the stake are described by John Foxe in *Acts and Monuments* (S. R. Cattley and George Townsend, eds. [New York: AMS Press, Reproduction of 1849 edition (no date given), 8 vols.]), a Protestant martyrology. Neither of these men wrote poems just before their deaths, though others did. *Kindly Light.* A phrase from a hymn by Cardinal Newman, "Lead, Kindly Light." According to Hecht, the events described in the remaining stanzas of the poem are transcribed as exactly as possible from a book called *The Theory and Practice of Hell* by Eugen Kogon (translated by Heinz Norden [New York: Farrar, Straus & Co., 1950]). Buchenwald concentration camp was built only a few miles from Goethe's home at Weimar, and prisoners sent to that camp were unloaded from trains at the Weimar station and marched the rest of the way to the camp.

**Saving the Children.** *Gizelle Hersh:* "You are the oldest, Gizelle. Save the children!" were the last words sixteen-year-old Gizelle Hersh heard from her mother as she and her three younger sisters, Mitzi, Lenci, and Katya, were separated from their parents at Auschwitz. The story of the survival of these Hungarian children is told by Gizelle Hersh, in collaboration with Peggy Mann, in *Gizelle, Save the Children!* (New York: Everest House, 1980). *Zeile Appell:* (G.) Roll call. This refers to straight lines or rows for daily roll call in the camps, usually held between 5 A.M. and 10 A.M. *Selection to the left:* This meant "designation crematorium." According to Singer, to confuse Auschwitz prisoners during daily roll call, the selectees (those who appeared too weak or sickly, too old or too young to survive) were occasionally sent to the right, instead of to the left. Therefore, "to the left" is a metaphor for the end of the line. At Auschwitz, this meant starvation, torture, death by asphyxiation.

**The Children of Terezin** The fifteen thousand children were assembled by the Germans and wedged into Terezin, a camp in Czechoslovakia and way station to Auschwitz. Approximately one hundred survived. Poems and drawings were found in the Terezin barracks after the war. Inge Auerbacher, one of the surviving children (see her poems in this section), adds this note: "The Nazis masked the camp as a 'model ghetto' for propaganda purposes. In actuality, it was a gruesome place. Thousands of people died of malnutrition and disease. Many transports left Terezin for the East and fed the gas chambers at Auschwitz. The most frequent deportations were in the fall of 1944, when almost the entire camp was emptied."

**The Three.** "The Three," Miroslav Kosek, Hanus Löwy, and Bachner, have four poems in *I Never Saw Another Butterfly: Children's Drawings and Poems from Terezin Concentration Camp 1942-1944* (Hana Volavkova, ed., Jeanne Nemcova, trans. [New York: McGraw-Hill, 1964]). *Koleba:* A blend of the children's three names that also evokes the Czechoslovakian *koleda*, a children's fairy tale, and *chleba*, bread. According to Steingesser, they wrote the poems together, signing them Koleba, while imprisoned in Terezin.

**To My Mother Who Endured** *Munch's scream:* Edvard Munch (1863-1944), Norwegian painter. The reference is to Munch's famous print in which a distorted figure holds its hands to its head and screams in anguish. Richman remarks, "To me, it is a quintessential representation of despair, a symbol of the suffering of the victims of the Holocaust." *Petite fille:* (Fr.) Little girl—an expression of endearment. *See also* Liliane Richman in Additional Notes.

**From the Ardeatine Caves.** *Monet at Giverny:* Claude Monet (1840-1926), French painter and one of the founders of the Impressionist school. He settled at Giverny in 1883 and died there in 1926. The garden at Giverny inspired some of his best works.

**In Remembrance of the Children of Izieu.** *Obersturmführer:* A high-ranking commander of the SS, the elite military arm of the National Socialist Party. *Rachel weeping:* A biblical reference found in both testaments—Jer. 31:15; Matt. 2:18. *Afikomen:* (Gk.) Dessert. The middle matzah is broken during the Passover Seder; the *afikomen* is the half of matzah that is wrapped in a linen cloth and hidden. Later in the Seder, the children look for the "dessert," and the child who succeeds in finding it is rewarded by the father, who redeems (or buys back) the missing piece of matzah. Additional references in the poem recall the Exodus, when the children of Israel prepared unleavened bread and hastily ate the meal of roasted lamb before fleeing from the land of Egypt.

*from* **The Angel of History.** "This is Izieu." *Izieu:* See above note. Izieu and Bregnier-Cordon were villages in the Free Zone. The children were arrested on 6 April 1944 by the Lyon Gestapo and were sent to Drancy, for deportation to the extermination camps. *Comment me vint . . . hiver:* (Fr.) A line from the poet Rene Char: How does writing come to me? Like a feather to the window pane in winter. *Le silence de Dieu est Dieu:* from Elie Wiesel's poem "Ani Maamin." *Pithiviers, Beaune-la-Rolande, Les Tourelles:* Internment camps in Vichy France, or the Free Zone. Most of the Jews rounded up—including thousands of children under sixteen—were deported to Auschwitz by order of Adolf Eichmann, a major figure in the Reich's transport ministry. For a detailed discussion of the French camps and the deportation process, see Hilberg, 609-660 ("The Semicircular Arc"). *Vous n'aurez . . . Lorraine:* (Fr.) You shall not have Alsace-Lorraine. During the German occupation, the provinces of Alsace-Lorraine were ruled as quasi-incorporated areas, which facilitated the deportation of the Jewish population of the region. According to Hilberg, "twenty-two thousand Jews were involved in these movements from Alsace alone. The victims were piled on trucks, driven across [borders to unoccupied France], and dumped out at night on a deserted country road" (614).

**Miklos Radnoti.** *Miklos Radnoti:* Hungary's major poet of the century. He was a Jewish slave laborer during the war. In 1944, on a forced march, he was beaten to death by his German captors and left in a ditch. He was identified two years later by a letter and postcard poems to his wife, found in his overcoat pocket. These postcard poems are among the most beautiful in the Hungarian language. **September 1944.** *Die Fledermaus:* (G.) *The Bat.* The Strauss opera. **Voices.** *Birkenau:* A Polish death camp. *Buno:* Altered spelling of Buna, another concentration camp. *Hepzibah:* A proper name. Also note that Hepzibah is mentioned twice in the Bible—2 Kings 21:1; Isa. 62:4. *Kapo:* A Jewish prisoner appointed by the Nazis to police other Jews. *Shabbas:* (Heb.) The sabbath (an Ashkenazic variation). *Tefillin:* The phylacteries used in morning prayer. They contain Biblical scriptures, including the words said three times a day (and before death) by observant Jews: "Hear, O Israel, the Lord our God, the Lord is One." They are made up of two small, square black boxes that are put on the forehead and on the left bicep with flat, black leather thongs attached to the boxes. On the left arm, the thong, or thin strap, is wrapped seven times down the forearm and then around the left hand. *See also* Deut. 6:8.

**The Hungarian Mission.** *Children's Cadre:* An underground movement of children (age 10 to 18), anti-Nazi, highly disciplined, and organized to follow orders of dangerous espionage; active throughout Europe. *The Road of Martyrs:* Matirok Utja in Hungarian. *Tovarish:* (Rus.) Comrade. *See also* Ruth Lisa Schechter in Additional Notes.

**On the Wings of the Wind.** *Hannah Senesh:* Born 1921, Budapest. In 1939, she went to Palestine to live on a kibbutz and help build a land for the Jewish people. After news of the persecution and slaughter of European Jews reached her, Senesh joined a British parachute corps that had been trained to locate British pilots who had been shot down over Yugoslavia. Once this mission was completed, she used her vantage point in Yugoslavia to return to her native Hungary in order to help in the resistance; but, almost immediately, she was caught, imprisoned, tortured, and, just as liberation was at hand, shot. She was twenty-three when she died.

**To Gisi Fleischmann.** *Gisi Fleischmann:* Leader of the Slovakian Jewish resistance group known as the *Arbeitsgruppe* (Working Group) and one of the great unsung heroic figures of the Holocaust. She is especially known for her efforts to save children and to negotiate with the Nazis for Jewish lives. She was murdered at Auschwitz 18 October 1944.

**You Know the Funny Thing Is.** *Buchenwald:* Liberated by American troops on the morning of 11 April 1945, this was the first concentration camp to be breached by the Allies (Sachar, 3). Sachar provides a concise overview of conditions in the camps prior to and at the time of liberation in the opening chapters of *The Redemption of the Unwanted* (1-45). *See also* Barbara Helfgott Hyett in Additional Notes.

**A View from the Ghetto.** The ghetto, in Nazi-occupied Lida, White Russia, was a neighborhood of houses surrounded by barbed-wire fencing into which all Jews were packed upon the arrival of the Nazis—and where, often, several families had to share a single room. During "selections," hundreds or thousands were marched out of the ghetto, through the town, to the edge of a field, where they were shot. Thus the ghetto kept shrinking. Ultimately, what remaining Jews were left in the town—that is, in the ghetto within the town—were shipped off to the camps. In the poem, the ghetto borders the farmlands on one side. *See also* Helen Degan Cohen in Additional Notes.

**. . . And the Earth Rebelled.** *Tallis:* (Heb.) Ashkenazic variation of tallit, prayer shawl.

**A Million Pairs of Shoes.** The camps were death factories. With macabre efficiency, inmates were stripped of everything of the slightest use to the home front of the Third Reich. Everything was sorted and carefully warehoused. A roomful of long hair, cut from the heads of women prisoners, was saved for stuffing mattresses. The dead were rifled of the gold fillings in their teeth. Eyeglasses were saved. Most pathetic were the shoes of the victims, ready to be shipped for reuse by citizens of the Third Reich. This poem was published in 1945, in Yiddish, when the camps had been liberated and the atrocities revealed.

## IV. Without Jews

**The Gift** (Ciardi). *Josef Stein:* According to American poet Miller Williams, Ciardi based his poem on the experience of an actual poet-survivor.

**Women Bathing at Bergen-Belsen.** This sonnet is based on *A Memory of the Camps*, a documentary film made by British troops and edited by Alfred Hitchcock. The film was not made public until April 1985, on the fortieth anniversary of the Allied liberation of the camps. *See also* Enid Shomer in Additional Notes.

**U.S. Army Holds Dance for Camp Survivors. Germany, 1945.** *Czerny exercises:* Finger exercises, created by Karl Czerny (1791-1857), Austrian composer. Commonly assigned to piano students. *See also* Lisa Ress in Additional Notes.

**Mame-Loshen, Yiddish.** *Mame-Loshen:* Mother tongue. Mikofsky reports the following history: *Mame-Loshen* (pronounced *MAH-meh LAW-shun*) has nearly a millennium of history, Yiddish having started as the Middle High German that Jews invited into medieval Poland spoke. This period of time is about the same as that of the development of English out of Anglo-Saxon, following the Norman conquest of England in 1066. And just as English was enriched by Old French (itself from Latin) as well as savant Latin and Greek words, just so was Yiddish tremendously enriched by Hebrew and Aramaic words (the *Loshen-Koydesh*, the Holy Language) as well as words from Slavic and other European languages.

**Paul Celan: A Grave and Mysterious Sentence.** Paul Celan (born Autschel, in Czernovitz, Bukovina, Romania, 1920) is best known for his "Totenfugue" ("Fugue of Death"). His parents were murdered by the Nazis, and he was sent to forced labor. After the war, Celan went to Paris and became a French citizen, though he continued to write in German. He killed himself in 1970. During the last twenty years of his life, Celan published seven volumes of poetry in German, in addition to various translations. *See also* Edward Hirsch in Additional Notes.

**Survivor** (Feldman). *Giorgio Bassani:* Contemporary Italian writer, author of *Il Giardino dei Finzi Contini* (The Garden of the Finzi Contini), made into a film with the same title by Vittorio de Sica, and *Storie Ferraresi* (Stories of Ferrara). *See also* Ruth Feldman, in Additional Notes.

**Niemand.** *Zbonzyn:* Variant of Zbaszyn, a small town in western Poland, 45 miles west-southwest of Poznan (Posen). From 1919 to 1939, it was a frontier station on the German border on the main Berlin-Warsaw line. Dawidowicz comments: "On October 28 [1938] the Gestapo, on orders from the Foreign Office, began rounding up Polish Jews in Germany to transport them to the Polish border. Prevented from entering Poland, they were kept in appalling conditions in a no-man's-land on the Polish side at Zbaszyn, near Posen" (100).

**Without Jews.** *The Thirty-Six:* In Jewish mystical tradition, the *Lamed Vav Tsaddikim:* the 36 righteous individuals in each generation, whose very existence in the world protects it from destruction.

**God's Death.** *Kristallnacht:* See explanation at beginning of notes to Section III. *Emanuel Ringelblum: See note* to "I Must Tell the Story," p. 371. *Zyklon B gas:* At first carbon monoxide was used in the gas chambers, but cyanide gas, known by its German trade name, Zyklon B gas, proved to be more effective. Jews were made to undress and have their hair cut. Then they were forced, with whips and guns, to the gas chambers where they were locked in, one person per square foot. The gassing lasted from ten to thirty minutes, after which the bodies were thrown out and burned, either in the open air or in the crematoria. Zyklon B was manufactured by Degesch, a German pesticide company and a subsidiary of I. G. Farben *(Response*, Simon Wiesenthal Center, 10 [April 1989]: 10). For detailed information on the production and distribution of Zyklon B, see Hilberg, vol. 3, 886-889.

**Lament for the Gypsies.** Martin Gilbert, in *The Holocaust* (New York: Hill and Wang, 1978), states: "In 1939, there were more than 700,000 gypsies living in Europe. At least 200,000 of them were murdered by the Nazis, as part of a deliberate policy aimed at 'ridding' Europe of both its gypsies and its Jews. A gypsy was defined by the Nazis as a person with at least two gypsy great-great-grandparents" (22). Gilbert continues: "By 1939, many German and Austrian gypsies had been sent to Buchenwald and Dachau. In 1940, all surviving German gypsies were deported to Poland and forced to live in special sections set aside for them in the ghettos being established for Jews. Several thousand Serbian gypsies were murdered during German 'field operations' in 1941, and many Crimean and Ukrainian gypsies were killed in January 1942 at mass-murder sites intended primarily for Jews. On 16 December 1942, a Nazi decree ordered gypsies from all over Europe to be deported to Auschwitz, where 16,000 were murdered on arrival at the camp" (22).

**For the Children.** *Führerbunker:* (G.) Hitler's bunker. The fortress and hideout of Adolf Hitler during the final stages of the war.

**The Amsterdam Poem.** *Concertgebouw:* The name of the hall. *Eroica:* Beethoven's Symphony no. 3, op. 55 (1803); first performed 7 April 1805. *Mijnheer and mevrouw:* (D.) Mr. and Mrs. *Bittere Jaren:* Bitter years. *Walker Evans:* Like Ben Shahn and Edward Steichen, Evans (1903-1975) was an important portrayer of the social forces at work in the United States during the thirties. A photographer, editor, and teacher, he was best known for his photographic documentation of poverty in rural America during the Depression. His work is collected in *American Photographs* (1938) and *Let Us Now Praise Famous Men* (1941). *Vondelpark:* The name of the park. *Westerkirk:* The name of the church.

**Westminster Synagogue.** *Westminster Synagogue:* Perhaps the prime center of Jewish worship in Britain. As soon as it was possible, following the war, this synagogue became headquarters for archiving and restoring many central and eastern European Torahs that had belonged to annihilated congregations. Among the functions of this great center has been the transfer of restored Torahs to new congregations, generally in North and South America.

**Zudioska.** *The Placa:* A main square in Dubrovnik; we would call it "the plaza." According to Kramer, many side streets, step by step, lead down into that superb square from the hills on all sides that are topped by the city's ancient circling wall. Thus, he suggests, one might think of the Placa as the hub of a great concave wheel. *Rab:* An island off the Dalmatian coast of Yugoslavia.

**The Rose of Blue Flesh.** *Terrible 1492:* In March 1492, the Jews of Spain were given the choice between renouncing their faith—and submitting to baptism as Christians—and exile from their home country. As many as 165,000 Spanish Jews (Sephardim) preferred exile and emigrated to Portugal, Italy, Greece, Turkey, and North Africa. *Agonia:* (Gk.) Agony.

**There Is One Synagogue Extant in Kiev.** *Ninth of Ab:* In Hebrew, *Tisha b'Ab.* A Jewish fast day that commemorates the destruction of the Temple in ancient Jerusalem, as well as more recent tragedies. *Queen of Sabbath:* In Jewish tradition, the Sabbath is known as the "queen" (royalty) of the days of the week. *See also* Yaacov Luria, in Additional Notes.

**For Our Dead.** *Herraus!:* (G.) Turn out! An order to move out from a place.

**Yahrzeit.** *Yahrzeit:* (Yid.) Yiddish variant of *Jahrzeit:* year's time. The anniversary of someone's death, usually a parent or other close relative whom one is obligated to mourn. On this day, a memorial candle is lighted in the home and another in the synagogue, where it burns from sunset to sunset. Leo Rosten suggests a link with Prov. 20:27: "The spirit of man is the candle of the Lord" (*The Joys of Yiddish* [New York: McGraw-Hill, 1968], 448).

**Identifications.** *"Lord, from the depths I call":* A prayer asking God to hear us in our moments of despair.

**Yom Kippur.** *Yom Kippur:* The Day of Atonement when Jews gather in their places of worship to confess their sins before God and to ask forgiveness for sins against God and against their fellow man.

**A Cantor's Dream before "The Days of Awe":** *"Days of Awe":* Refers to the Jewish High Holidays, Rosh Hashanah (the New Year) and Yom Kippur. *"Return, my heart, as in days of old":* A prayer, asking for the power to return to God in love. The Sabbath between the New Year and the Day of Atonement is the "Sabbath of Return." *Bim-bom:* The refrain of a song, welcoming the Sabbath.

**Passover at Auschwitz.** *The Guest:* Elijah (in Hebrew, Eliyahu), a prophet of Israel in the ninth century B.C., who is believed to return, in spirit, to visit each Jewish home during the Passover Seder. *See also* Laurence Josephs in Additional Notes.

**The Ghetto.** *Rue de Belleville:* A street that runs through the Jewish section of Paris. *Rehov Yehuda:* A main thoroughfare in Jerusalem. *Warsaw pickle factory:* Glickstein remarks: "When the Nazis invaded Poland, a bomb tore open the Warsaw pickle factory in the Jewish Quarter—scores of people ran in to grab what they could."

**Dead Men Don't Praise God.** *The Rambam:* Maimonides, born Moses ben Maimon (1135-1204), a great rabbi, philosopher, writer, and physician. *Vilna Gaon:* Rabbi Elijah Ben Solomon Zalman. One of the leading figures of world Jewry in the late eighteenth century. Vilnius, formerly Vilna, was a capital of European Jewish culture. One of its streets was named Gaon Street. "Gaon" is Hebrew for "genius." *Mahram:* (Heb.) Our master. As with "Gaon," used when referring to a great rabbinical teacher. *Abraham Geiger:* A nineteenth-century German rabbi and teacher (1810-1874), who helped frame the philosophy of Reform Judaism. *Marshal the Seer:* A famous rabbi in eighteenth-century Poland, but possibly a further reference to an ancient Jewish sage who was reputed to have the ability to see into the future.

**Soap.** *Amelia Earhart:* A famous U.S. pioneer aviator (1898-1937) who disappeared mysteriously over the Pacific in the forties, but also, according to Stern, the name of a former restaurant in Iowa City.

**The Pripet Marshes.** *The Pripet Marshes:* The area near Lake Narocz in Poland, east-northeast of Vilnius (Vilna), and the site of a great, but disastrous, offensive by the Russian Second Army in the spring of 1916. Concerning World War II, Hilberg states: "We know that only a few thousand Jews escaped from the ghettos of Poland and Russia; that only a few hundred Jews hid out in the large cities of Berlin, Vienna, and Warsaw; that only a handful of Jews escaped from camps. Von dem Bach mentions that in Russia there was an unguarded escape route to the Pripet Marshes, but few Jews availed themselves of the opportunity. In the main, the Jews looked upon flight with a sense of futility. The great majority of those who did not escape early did not escape at all" (1036).

**The Death Mazurka.** *Judenrein:* (G.) Cleansed of Jews. A chief goal of the *Nationalsozialistische Deutsche Arbeiterpartei* (National Socialist German Workers Party) was to "purify" Germany of its Jews and other "undesirables."

**The Ascensions.** *Clair-de-lune:* (Fr.) Moonlight. Possibly also an oblique reference to a song by this name composed by Claude Debussy, from a poem by Paul Verlaine.

**Farewell to Europe.** *The Presence:* God (Jewish mystical tradition). *Basta! Genug! Assez! Dostatochno!:* (It.; G., Yid.; Fr.; Rus.) Enough! *The mark of our ancient covenant:* The *bris*, the circumcision of the Jewish male on the eighth day after birth. *See also* Gen. 17:10-14. *Blood mysteries:* The ancient "blood libel" against the Jewish people that accuses Jews of preparing the Passover matzoth (unleavened bread) with the blood of Christian children and similarly obscene libels used for centuries to incite violence against Jews.

**Rachel.** *The Pequod:* The principal ship in Melville's *Moby Dick*, under the command of Captain Ahab, but also a place mentioned in Jer. 50:21. The word means "to punish."

**Quiet Desperation.** *Allegro di bravura:* Used to mark a technically difficult piece or passage to be executed swiftly and boldly (in contrast to "bagatelle," a short piece of light music).

**Kol Nidre.** *S'lach lanu, m'chal lanu, kaper lanu:* (Heb.) Forgive us, be with us, help us atone (for our sins). A prayer from the High Holiday prayer book. *Onkel:* (G.) Uncle. *Tante:* (Yid.) Aunt. *Kati Neni:* (Hun.) Aunt Kathrin. *See also* Rosa Felsenburg Kaplan in Additional Notes.

**For Nelly Sachs.** Gensler reports this background: In 1966, at age 75, Nelly Sachs shared the Nobel Prize for Literature with Israeli novelist S. Y. Agnon. Sachs was a German Jewish poet who found asylum in Sweden during World War II. She received the award for her life's work as a poet, playwright, and translator—work that culminated in the moving lyrics of *O the Chimneys*, a deeply metaphoric book of elegies for the victims of the Holocaust. *See also* Kinereth Gensler in Additional Notes.

**Line-up.** *Andrzei Munk:* Polish filmmaker who was born in Cracow in 1921 and died near Warsaw in a car accident in 1961 while filming *Pasazerka (The Passenger)*. *See also* Dori Katz in Additional Notes.

**The Return.** *Malines:* A city in Belgium; a clearing center for deportation during the war. All Jews arrested were first sent to Malines, registered, and "cleared"; then they were assigned to a transport to a concentration camp. *See also* Dori Katz in Additional Notes.

**The Second Generation.** *Ponar:* Ponary. During the Holocaust, site of the mass execution of Lithuanian Jews by the Nazis. *See also* "Vilna 1938," p. 372.

**The Blue Parakeet.** *Lager:* (G.) Camp.

**Hands: Abraham Kunstler.** *Neue Strasse:* (G.) New Street. Riley states: "The character and specifics are imaginary, though closely resembling actual occurrences."

**Chicago Scene (1952, 1969).** *Ten were needed:* Refers to the *minyan*, a group of ten (or more) Jewish males over 13 years old that traditional Judaism requires to conduct a communal prayer service. *Left arms . . . thonged seven times . . . : See also* note to "Voices," p. 376.

### V. The Late Train: Memory

**Spit.** *The Black Book:* Subtitled *The Nazi Crime against the Jewish People, The Black Book* was one of the first publications to include captured wartime documents of the Holocaust period (New York: Jewish Black Book Committee, 1946).

**i When We Look Up,** *from* **During the Eichmann Trial.** *Eichmann:* Adolf Eichmann. One of the key architects of the "Final Solution"—the plan to exterminate the Jewish people—and, following the war, near the top of the list of escaped Nazi criminals sought by Israeli Intelligence. Sachar states: "It was the trial of Adolf Eichmann in 1961, conducted in [Jerusalem] Israel, that most effectively recreated for the short-memoried world all the bestiality of the Nazi period" (140). The basis of Eichmann's defense against the charge that he was responsible for mass murder was that he had merely been a loyal functionary in the party—that he had acted upon the orders of his superiors. He did not deny that he was implicated in the genocide, nor did the judges accept his defense. Their judgment that Eichmann had, in fact, been "amongst those who pulled the strings," found an appropriate correlative when he was hanged on May 21, 1962 (Sachar, 143). *Lemburg:* Variant of Lemberg, the German name for the city of Lvov (in Polish, Lwów). Formerly Polish, it is now in West Ukrainian Republic USSR. Its Jewish population of 100,000 was largely exterminated in World War II. *Franz Joseph:* Franz Josef.

**KZ.** *KZ:* (G.) Abbreviation for *Konzentrations Lager:* concentration camp. *"Arbeit Macht Frei":* (G.) Work Makes [You] Free. *See also* note to "Weltanschauung," p. 373.

**Seriatim.** *Wiesenthal:* Simon Wiesenthal. Well-known Nazi-hunter and founder of the Simon Wiesenthal Center for Holocaust Studies in Los Angeles. *Zbaraz:* Zbarash. Formerly Polish, now Ukrainian Republic USSR, 11 miles northeast of Tarnopol.

**Riddle.** *Albert Speer:* Hitler's minister of armaments. He was given a twenty-year sentence by the tribunal at Nuremberg for planning and supervising the war economy (i.e., using masses of foreign workers as slave labor) and for his complicity in hastening the "Final Solution" (Sachar, 121).

**The Little Place.** *Neckar:* The name of a river in southwest Germany.

**Reforger.** *Yiskor:* (Heb.) Remember. The word designates a service for the dead, conducted on the Day of Atonement and on a number of other important occasions, including the anniversary of a loved one's death. *See also* Miriam Offenberg in Additional Notes.

**Auschwitz Reportaż.** *The lying gate: See* note to "KZ," above. *"Abandon all hope . . . ":* Words from the inscription on the gate mentioned at the opening of Canto III, "The Vestibule of Hell," in Dante's *The Inferno* ( John Ciardi, trans. [New York: Mentor, 1954], 42). The opening stanzas read:

I AM THE WAY INTO THE CITY OF WOE.
I AM THE WAY TO A FORSAKEN PEOPLE.
I AM THE WAY INTO ETERNAL SORROW.

SACRED JUSTICE MOVED MY ARCHITECT.
I WAS RAISED HERE BY DIVINE OMNIPOTENCE,
PRIMORDIAL LOVE AND ULTIMATE INTELLECT.

ONLY THOSE ELEMENTS TIME CANNOT WEAR
WERE MADE BEFORE ME, AND BEYOND TIME I STAND.
ABANDON ALL HOPE YE WHO ENTER HERE.

**Icon.** *Ad maiorem Germaniae gloriam:* For the greater glory of Germany; a takeoff from the motto of the Jesuit Order, "For the greater glory of God" (sometimes abbreviated A.M.D.G.).

**In the Absence of Yellow.** *Pavel Friedmann:* Born 7 January 1921 in Prague. He was deported to Theresienstadt (Terezin) on 26 April 1942 and died at Auschwitz 29 September 1944. *See also* Reva Sharon in Additional Notes.

**Theresienstadt Poem.** The concentration camp Theresienstadt was located at the edge of Terezin, Czechoslovakia, the town itself having been converted into a camp in which many thousands of Jewish children were confined before being sent to various death camps. Only a handful of the Terezin children survived the war. Mezey comments: "My poem is a response to a watercolor by a girl named Nely Silvinova, of whom we know only her age and barracks number and that she died in 1944. To keep the children from despair, the adult prisoners in Terezin organized secret classes in music, painting, and so on. The watercolor of my poem, along with a good many other paintings, drawings, and poems, can be found in *I Never Saw Another Butterfly* [New York: McGraw-Hill, 1964]." *See also* notes to "The Children of Terezin" and "The Three," p. 375.

**"Grandfather" in Winter.** *Nine Iraqi Jews:* Nine Jews were hung publicly in Iraq in 1978, the year this poem was written.

**Gaby at the U. N. Observation Post.** This poem is part of a series of poems set on the Golan Heights.

**Yom Hazikaron.** *Mount Herzl:* A burial hill in Jerusalem. Yad Vashem, the Holocaust Martyrs' and Heroes' Remembrance Authority, is also located there. *Iron boxes: See* note to "I Must Tell the Story," p. 371.

**The Anniversary Poem.** *The Anniversary:* The sixtieth anniversary of the genocide of the Armenians by the Turks, which began 24 April 1915 when 200 poets and other leaders were executed—before the mass killings started. *Arshile Gorky:* Armenian-American painter (1904–1948), a native of Van and a survivor of the genocide. Der Hovanessian states: "My theory is that his fractured style—and that of French-Armenian playwright, Antonin Artaud—was their way of dealing with the horrors of what happened." *Theater of cruelty:* In 1946, Artaud, a film actor, director, and playwright, was released from nine years in asylums for the insane. He died two years later. "The Theater of Cruelty (First Manifesto)" is included in his important work of criticism, *The Theater and Its Double* (New York: Grove Press, 1958). *Erevan:* Yerevan, the Armenian capital. *David of Sassoun:* Hero of a folk epic (the second oldest after *Gilgamesh*) whose wild adventures provide a prototype of the brave and foolhardy hero. *Yeznick:* Armenian philosopher whose treatise on will is an important document. *Azad:* (Armenian) Free. One of the main rivers of Armenia. *Avarair:* The Battle of Avarair (or Avarayr) occurred on 2 June 451. Sixty-six thousand Armenians under Prince Vartan (or Vardan) Manikovian encountered an army of two hundred twenty thousand Persians, reinforced by squadrons of armored elephants. Although the Persians won the day, the carnage was so great that they gave up their dream of converting Armenia (a Christian nation) to the Zoroastrian religion. According to the poet, the blood of Vartan's army is said to have stained the flowers of Avarair red, and Armenians say that nightingales there weep, "Vartan, Vartan." *Sharagans:* Chains of hymns. The early church fathers, beginning with Gregory, were also poets who wrote these hymns. *Mesrob Mashtots:* Mesrop Mashtotz, a saint. He was born in A.D. 361 in the province of Taron and died in 440 (he is buried in the crypt of the church at Oshakan). He was commissioned by the Armenian king to form a new alphabet (Greek had been used until then) to keep the Armenian church distinct from the Greek. *Akh:* Alas! Oh, what a pity! *See also* Diana Der Hovanessian in Additional Notes.

**The Jews That We Are.** *Nazis march through Chicago:* In 1977, a group of neo-Nazis, a branch of the National Socialist Party of America (NSPA), created a furor by announcing its intention to stage a march through Skokie, the most substantially Jewish of Chicago's suburbs and the home of many Holocaust survivors. Although court battles and public pressure forced the demonstration to Chicago's Marquette Park, the confrontation became a *cause célèbre* when the American Civil Liberties Union defended the First Amendment rights of the NSPA to march. *Peretz:* I. L. Peretz (1852–1915) was an important Yiddish writer who, along with Mendele Mocher Seforim and Sholem Aleichem, helped set the standard of artistic expression for Russian Yiddish literature in the late nineteenth and early twentieth centuries.

**The Nazi in the Dock, at Sixty.** In the late 1970s and into the 1980s, several Nazi war criminals finally were brought to trial in the United States, after living under assumed names in America for thirty years or longer. *See also* Larry Rubin in Additional Notes.

**The Song of Iron Paul.** *Street thug:* Many of Hitler's early followers, especially those in the SA (*Sturmabteilung,* the Storm Troopers), were former street toughs, employed to beat up those who opposed the Nazis. *Papa Eicke:* Theodor (Tehodor) Eicke. Eicke was in charge of some of the earliest concentration camps, including Dachau, where—among other things—he trained SS personnel in torture methods. He was known as "Papa" Eicke by his trainees. *See also* Dawidowicz, 75–76. *The Sudetenland:* Part of Czechoslovakia inhabited largely by ethnic Germans and annexed into Germany as part of Hitler's expansionism. *Himmler:* Heinrich Himmler (1900–1945), German police official and, by 1929, leader of the *Schutzstaffel* (SS), Hitler's elite guard. By summer 1941, Himmler "had become the chief receiver and transmitter of Hitler's orders for the Final Solution and its operational principal" (Dawidowicz, 129). Following Hitler's death, Himmler went into hiding, but he was soon arrested by British soldiers and, on 23 May 1945, he committed suicide by biting into a vial of cyanide. *Runes:* The twin lightning bolts insignia on SS uniforms; also runic letters for SS. *Silver Death's Head:* The skull and crossbones insignia used by the SS. *See also* note to "The Scar—August, 1934," p. 372. *Bormann:* Martin Bormann. He headed the National Socialist Party Chancellery under Hitler. Believed killed in the Battle of Berlin in 1945. *Koch:* Karl Koch, commandant of Buchenwald and husband of Ilse, the "Bitch of Buchenwald," remembered for her cruelty. She ordered lampshades and gloves to be made from the skins of tattooed prisoners. *Eichmann: See* note to "When We Look Up" p. 380.

**The Bird.** *Ich wünscht', ich wäre ein Vöglein:* (G.) "I wish I were a little bird." *Wiener Blut:* (G.) "Vienna Blood"—a famous Strauss waltz. *Herr Oberleutnant:* (G.) Lieutenant, Sir. *See also* Louis Simpson in Additional Notes.

**The Gift** (Sandler). *The Second Generation:* Like "one generation after," a term used to denote the children of survivors of the Holocaust. Sandler states: "The adult children of survivors were meeting to learn what they could do, individually or as a group, to help their parents accept their experiences in the camps and to find a way to transform them into something positive."

**Thoughts under the Giant Sequoia.** *Francis Parkman:* Renowned American historian (1823–1893), whose two-volume *Conspiracy of Pontiac* is considered a classic. He suffered from severe headaches but insisted on traveling in the territories he wrote about. *Emanuel Ringelblum:* Emanuel Ringelblum, historian of the Warsaw ghetto, who perished at the hands of the Nazis. *See also* note to "I Must Tell the Story," p. 371. *Sharm el Sheik:* The southern tip of the Sinai peninsula.

**Kitty Returns to Auschwitz.** *Fourth Brandenburg:* (c. 1720). The fourth of six concertos by Johann Sebastian Bach composed between 1711 and 1720 in Weimar, Cöthen, and dedicated to Christian Ludwig, margrave of Brandenburg.

**At the Jewish Museum.** At an exhibition of art on the theme of the Holocaust, one of the exhibition pieces was a large, brick-lined, darkened room that was totally empty. This environment was the sculptor's monument for the children who had perished in the death camps that dotted Germany, Poland, and parts of Eastern Europe during the Hitler terror.

**The Family Album.** *Stadtpark:* The city park in Vienna. *See also* Lisa Ress in Additional Notes.

**Remembering.** *Yad Vashem:* (Heb.) [The] hand of God. The Holocaust memorial museum in Israel. *See also* Enid Shomer in Additional Notes.

**God Teaches Us How to Forgive, but We Forget.** *Nacht-und-Nebel erlass:* (G.) Night and fog decree. A reference to the powerful documentary film *Night and Fog* (1955) by the French filmmaker Alain Resnais and an allusion to the deportations. "Nacht und Nebel" was "an official Nazi term for organized roundups of Jews" (James E. Young, "Holocaust Memorials: Memory and Myth," *Moment* 14 [June 1989], 25).

**Medium.** *Kapoteh:* Caftan. A long gaberdine coat worn by observant Jews. *Tish mit mentshn:* (Yid.) Literally, "table with people." *Nign:* (Yid.) Melody.

**Yom HaShoah.** *Yom HaShoah:* (Heb.) Day of Destruction. The day (usually in April) set aside for remembering the Holocaust. *Wiesenthal Center: See* note to "Seriatim" p. 381. *Loewe family:* Novak's husband's mother's family. According to Novak, they "lived in Czechoslovakia, and all who did not immigrate to America were destroyed by the Holocaust." *See also* Estelle Gershgoren Novak in Additional Notes.

**Unanswerable Questions.** *River Ohre:* After the Nazis burned the bodies of Jews in the crematoria, they put the ashes in boxes and numbered them to identify them. When the Nazis knew that their atrocities at Theresienstadt would be discovered, they emptied as many of those boxes as they could into the surrounding fields and into the River Ohre, which flows not far from the camp. *Jhirka:* Jhirka was five years old and shared a bunk with Norbert Troller, an artist. Troller's sketch of Jhirka has been preserved. Troller survived and described Jhirka as a "clever companion" with a thousand questions nobody could answer. Jhirka died at Theresienstadt.

**Benny.** *Mayim:* (Heb.) Water. Also the name of a popular Hebrew song. *Eilat:* Elat. A resort area in southern Israel. The southernmost city of Israel, it is named for the ancient town and port of Elath, which was situated nearby; it was one of the places through which the Israelites passed in their wanderings through the desert.

**On a Drawing by Flavio.** *Flavio:* Flavio Constantini (born in Rome, 1926); a contemporary Italian political artist.

**On Watching *Heritage: Civilization and the Jews.*** "Heritage: Civilization and the Jews" was a series aired on Public Television during the fall of 1984. *See also* Deborah Hannan in Additional Notes.

**Aspen Oktoberfest.** *Lily Tofler:* According to war crimes witnesses' testimony, Lily Tofler was nineteen when she died. Her usual answer to the question, "How's it going?" was "With me, it always goes well." *Arbeit Macht Frei:* (G.) Work Makes [You] Free. A slogan hung on the gates of the concentration camp. Boger: The German lieutenant who raped Tofler, then shot her to death with his pistol. *See also* Reg Saner in Additional Notes.

**Yad Vashem.** *Trees of the Just:* At Yad Vashem, the commemorative trees planted to honor those Germans and other non-Jews who saved Jewish lives during the Holocaust, at risk to their own. *Majdanek:* Polish spelling of Maidanek, the notorious death camp near Lublin, Poland.

**After Claude Lanzmann's *Shoah.*** The episode described is based on Lanzmann's 1985 documentary film. Lanzmann interviewed survivors and witnesses of the Holocaust, as well as concentration camp guards and residents of towns near the camps. Richman states: "The poem is based on the recollection of a man who was a boy when the Nazis liquidated the people in his village."

**The Name of a Place.** The headnote refers to Ronald Reagan's controversial visit to the Bitberg cemetery where *Waffen SS* officers are buried. Krapf remarks: "I was in Germany at the time and wrote the poem in my journal, in response." According to Deborah E. Lipstadt: "The attempt to reformulate German history has its roots in Reagan's visit to Bitburg. . . . Chancellor Kohl's invitation to Reagan was issued as a means of linking [the murderers and the murdered as victims]. After having been snubbed by the Allies' Normandy commemoration, the German leader wanted Reagan at his side as a means of indicating to the world that postwar Germany no longer carried the moral burdens of the Holocaust. The object of the visit to the cemetery in which members of the Waffen SS [armed SS] are buried was to obliterate the distinction between victims and perpetrators" ("What Is the Meaning of This to You?" *Tikkun* 4 (May/June 1989):68. *Riemenschneider:* Tilman Riemenschneider (1460–1531), the great woodcarver, lived and worked in Krapf's ancestral region of Franconia—especially in Würzburg, where he served as *Burgermeister.*

**After Forty Years.** *Mengele:* In June 1985, the body of Nazi death camp doctor Josef Mengele was discovered in a grave in Embú, Brazil, where he had lived in hiding with his family and local people who knew his identity. *Angel of Death:* Embedded in Mengele's name is the German word *Engel,* angel. This irony was not lost on those who suffered and died at his hands.

**Solitary Acts.** *Umschlagplatz:* Place of deportation—in this instance, for Treblinka. *See also* note to "Little Lamb," p. 374. *Neglinge:* A place in Sweden.

*from* **Kaddish.** *Yisgadal V'yiskadash sh'me rabbo, b'olmo deevro chiruseh v'yamlick malchuseh:* (Heb.) The opening words of the mourner's prayer: "Let the name of God be glorified and sanctified in the world, which He hath created according to His will. May He establish His kingdom [His rule]." *Schnorrer:* (Yid.) Cheapskate; moocher. *Yente:* (Yid.) A shrew or busybody. *Bundist:* A member of the Jewish Labor Zionist movement, especially in Warsaw, prior to World War II. *B'chayechon uvyo-mechon, uv'chayey d'chol beys yisroel:* Continuation of the

Kaddish: "During your life and during your days, and during the life of all the House of Israel."*Covner-Gberna:* A province in Poland. In Polish, Kowno Gubernia.

*from* **Inscriptions: 1944–1956.** *Ukrainia:* The Ukraine.

**Adler.** *Adler:* Jacob Adler (1855–1926), the founder of the acclaimed U.S. theatrical family and one of the leading Jewish actor-managers and reformers of the early Yiddish theater. According to Stern, Adler "was the most famous of all Jewish [Yiddish] actors—Lower East Side—a hero among women—who wrote, and acted in, *The Jewish King Lear.*" *Regan, Goneril, Gloucester, Cordelia, Albany, Kent, Edgar:* Characters in Shakespeare's great tragedy *King Lear.*

**Tsena Tsena (Second Generation).** *Tsena Tsena:* (Heb.) Go forth. A popular Hebrew song.

# Additional Notes

Unless otherwise indicated, all entries in this section are excerpts from the poets' correspondence with the editor.

***Carol Adler*** **"We Are the Echoes"**: In 1961, I, a fourth-generation American Jew, stood on the Judenplatz in Vienna, at the site of the old synagogue, and heard the echoes that continue to repeat themselves throughout my life whenever I visit holy places in Europe that—for reasons of hatred and bigotry—have been decimated. I live and suffer these echoes. Their sound has hammered a message on my soul and compelled me to cry out against all war and human suffering. These echoes are universal and multilingual, and should by no means ever be mistakenly identified only with the history of the Jewish people. [Nonetheless,] my commitment to the strength of the Jews, to their strange capacity to rise to the occasion of survival, to "overcome"—my commitment to Judaism—is at the heart of everything I write.

I do not like to be morbid about the Holocaust, nor do I like to wallow in suffering. Rather, I choose to write poems that use this period of Jewish history as content or as metaphor, simply because it is part of the fabric of my Jewishness. I am not a political poet. I write what I feel, and through those feelings I hope to express what it has been like to have lived through these years in America when the Jews were being destroyed in Europe.

My message is always that we must go on from here, in order to prove that Hitler truly was defeated.

***Mari Alschuler*** **"In My Own Nightmares"**: This poem is dedicated to the memory of the several thousand gay men and lesbians who were persecuted in the Holocaust. Their symbol, the pink triangle, is now captured as a universal gay/lesbian rights symbol to memorialize those who were executed simply for their sexual orientation.

I use the swastika in the poem as a reminder of the anti-Semitism which occurs in subtle ways in some intimate relationships. It is also a term for a common sleeping position, in which the sleeper's body resembles the shape of a swastika.

***Inge Auerbacher*** **"I Am a Star"**: As of September 1, 1941, Jews in Germany were ordered to sew the yellow Star of David on their clothes as a distinguishing mark. On the star, the word "Jude" was written in Hebrew-like letters. I was only six years old. This branding had a profound effect on me.

I wore this badge of shame, humiliation, and degradation with silent pride and fear, and tried to turn an ugly symbol into something positive. In my heart, I felt that no one could take away my humanity and dignity.

**"Something to Remember Me By"**: The most frequent deportations [from Terezin to Auschwitz] were in the fall of 1944, when almost the entire camp was emptied. One particular stranger and chance meeting touched me greatly. A strange man's fear of the unknown and feeling of helplessness made a tremendous impression on me. He seemed satisfied to be remembered by someone, even an unknown young girl, and to achieve some kind of immortality through her.

***Julius Balbin*** **"Tonight"** (From correspondence with the translator, Charlz Rizzuto): For Dr. Balbin, as with many who suffered the horrors of the Holocaust, the present tense was an all-consuming phenomenon. Never certain of the next hour, let alone the next day, one either consciously or unconsciously was ironically prone to savor the moment with thoughts which would help to alleviate it. In the poem, "Tonight," Julius Balbin's memories of joy and heartache, pain and agony, as well as Divine abandonment, live with him as the actual experience.

***George Bogin*** **"Pitchipoi"** (From correspondence with the author's wife, Ruth Bogin): This poem was set to music by Lloyd Ultan in a 1983 work for chamber orchestra and soloists entitled *Pitchipoi* (*The Children of Drancy*).

***Emily Borenstein*** **"The Excavator," "I Must Tell the Story,"** and **"The Shoah"**:
Like all interested Jews, I had read about the Holocaust, but I did not actively seek
out the horrific facts of the slaughter of the Six Million Jews, or immerse myself
deeply as a writer in this critical wound of my people until one ordinary day. It was
a chance encounter in the Shoprite supermarket in Middletown, New York that
changed me as a poet. While in the supermarket shopping for groceries, I stopped
as usual at the magazine rack off to the side. As I riffled through the pages of
magazines, cookbooks, and how-to books, my attention was suddenly seized by a
World War II Special Publication: "The Warsaw Ghetto No Longer Exists"—Jürgen
Stroop, SS Brigadeführer and Majorgeneral of Police—from the Warsaw Ghetto
Archives of Alexander Ben Bernfes.* Here, in starkly dramatic photographs and in
the words of the victims and victimizers, was the terrible story of the Nazis'
extermination of the Polish Jews of the Warsaw Ghetto. That chance encounter with
the actual photographs of the U.S.A. Exhibit 275, filed December 13, 1945, with the
International Military Tribunal in Nuremburg, Germany, indelibly marked and
changed me. . . . It was as if I had been struck by a thunderbolt or lightning.

I began writing the Holocaust poems for *Night of the Broken Glass* [Timberline
Press, 1981] simultaneously with the writing of the poems that comprised my first
published book, *Cancer Queen*. I felt "driven" to write both books, that is, to bear
witness. It was like answering a "call," to go on a journey into the depths of
terrifying human conditions and destiny and still assert the indestructibility of the
human spirit. Even eleven and one-half years later [September 1985], it is painful for
me to discuss it. At that time, my beloved mother was dying of terminal cancer and
from a form of cancer for which there is no hope yet of an extension of life through
remission or cure.

My mother's dying and death and my helplessness to prevent her death . . .
reinforced the profound hurt I felt and the painful feelings I carry with me always in
regard to the victims of the Holocaust. I undertook, in 1974, to set out on two
journeys at one and the same time—the journey into the hell of terminal cancer and
the journey into the hell of Hitler's Final Solution for the Jews. From this dual
traumatic experience, with the revival of the memories of personal family loss in
Europe during the Holocaust years, I wrote the poems of *Cancer Queen* and *Night
of the Broken Glass*.

*[According to Borenstein, Dr. Bernfes presented his copy of the Warsaw Ghetto
archives to Yad Vashem, the Holocaust Martyrs' and Heroes' Remembrance
Authority in Jerusalem. (The book discovered by Borenstein was published in 1973
by Orbis Publishing in London and by Marshall Cavendish in the United States. It
was printed in Great Britain by Oxley Press.)]

***Van K. Brock*** **"The Hindenburg"**: In "The Hindenburg," the dirigible, begun
before Hitler came to power, symbolizes the valuation of technology over nature,
the sacrifice of life to technology, and man's inflated ego and sense of power. I see
only small steps from the mass slaughter of mammals for their hides and other uses,
other than survival, to the development of mass burials, machine-gunnings, Zyklon
B, etc., with regard to human beings. That is why "The Hindenburg" is the initial
poem of my unpublished *Unspeakable Strangers*—[the making of this dirigible] was
one of the beginnings of the attitude toward life which could accommodate the idea
of the Holocaust.

***Theodore Deppe*** **"School of Music"**: Zhanna Dawson—direct source of "School
of Music"—was 13 when the Germans arrested some 13,000 Jews in Kharkov
(southern Russia). She remembers being lined up, six in a row, and marched out of
town during a snowstorm. In her row were her father, her mother, her grand-
parents, her sister, and herself. Her father managed to bribe a Ukrainian guard with
a family heirloom, a gold watch, allowing her to escape. Later, her sister also
escaped—the others were killed in the death camps.

After making her way across Europe, playing concerts under assumed names, she
finally made it safely to the U.S. and taught music at Indiana University. I knew her
as the mother of one of my childhood friends, and later took a few lessons from her.

**Diana Der Hovanessian "The Anniversary Poem"**: This poem was written on the 60th anniversary of the Armenian massacres in 1915. Here it is the 70th [1985], and the Turks are trying to rewrite the whole thing. I think that is the reason that so many Armenians are incensed. If there had been an acknowledgment and apology, people several generations away from the genocide could start to heal. But the way it is, to deny the victims ever lived, is another crime, and outrage. And it is that outrage that creeps into some of my work.

**Olga Drucker "The Brooch"**: After [my father] was taken to Dachau during "Crystal Night," my mother arranged for me to be sent to England via the "Children's Transport." I was still home when my father returned from Dachau, after six weeks. There was a change in him, and he wouldn't or couldn't talk about his ordeal. I lived in England from 1939 to 1945, during which time my parents escaped together, via Portugal, to New York, in August 1941. One day after they left Germany, the American Consulate in Stuttgart closed. The next day would have been too late. We were reunited in 1945 in New York.

**Ruth Feldman "Survivor"**: "Survivor" was inspired by a short story by Giorgio Bassani about a man who returns unexpectedly to Ferrara on the day in which a marble plaque is being put up on the synagogue wall with the names—including his—of the Jews who have perished in concentration camps. The story, "Una Lapide in Via Mazzini" ["A Memorial Tablet in Via Mazzini"] haunted me for two years, and I finally "exorcized" it by writing the poem.

**Robert A. Frauenglas "Seriatim"**: The poem, "Seriatim," is mainly autobiographical. The Wiesenthal comment arises from my meeting him during my 1,200 mile solo backpacking trek through seven W. European nations on behalf of Soviet Jewry. We were both featured speakers at a gathering at the Jewish Community Center in Brussels, Belgium. After I was introduced to the gathering and said a few words, Wiesenthal came up to me on the stage and greeted me in German. I said I didn't speak German and he replied, "Pick a language." I chose English and he said he previously said in German, he knows my family. I replied, you mean you knew my family; because, I had always thought that all my European relatives had been killed in the Holocaust.

Wiesenthal said no, he didn't mean "knew"; he meant "knows." He told me that he was still friends with the Frauenglas family in Vienna. I was so happy to learn that I had family alive in Europe that I began jumping up and down on the stage, and when people nearby learned the reason they began clapping and cheering. It was through Wiesenthal that I eventually contacted and met with my surviving cousins in Vienna, Paris, and Romania.

**Kinereth Gensler "For Nelly Sachs"**: I [think of] the poem as a form of personal exorcism, as well as a belated response to *O the Chimneys*. I was an American teenager during World War II, brought up in the late 1930s, during my high school years, in Palestine (we lived in Jerusalem). When the news of the concentration camps trickled out, and then the full magnitude of the Holocaust became known, I was a college student at the University of Chicago. I felt then, as I still feel: "There but for the grace of God go I." Surely all Jews of my generation share that feeling. So that, although I am not a member of One Generation After [children of Holocaust survivors], I *am* a member of the generation of the Jews of the Holocaust, and have always felt part of them, one of the lucky ones. Nelly Sachs, too, managed to find a safe harbor during the war; her book spoke for me, and I was sorry not to have written to her before her death.

**Barbara Goldberg "Survivor"**: I didn't find out until I was twenty that I was named after my mother's mother who, at the time of my birth, had already perished at Auschwitz, although my mother didn't know that for sure until some years later. Which is to say, that during the earliest years of my life, my mother didn't know what had happened to her family, and of course, this must have been the cause of much anxiety and depression for her. And most likely interfered with her ability to feed me (literally and metaphorically). Since according to Jewish custom one cannot name a child after a living relative (so as to not confuse the angel of death) she named me Barbara, just taking the first initial. Thus, the speaker of "Survivor" is my mother; Blanka, the name of her mother; and the "you" in the poem is me.

My interest in the Holocaust: my (German) father dragged my mother out of the Sudetenland (Prague, Czechoslovakia) in 1938 because he was sufficiently paranoid to be able to guess what was going to happen to the Jews. Most of the Jews in that area of Czechoslovakia were living quite well at the time, and could not believe in "horror stories." My mother's parents refused to leave the country. As my grandfather (the one Jewish "notaire" in the area) said, "What would I do at my age in a foreign country? Sell sausages?" My parents made it out of Europe in time—my mother is Czech, my father, German—they emigrated first to Paris, then Portugal, came to the U.S. on Portuguese visiting visas, then went to Brazil, and entered the U.S. *I think* in 1941 on Brazilian visas. Forest Hills had a sizable refugee community and became the new home of many survivors. My uncle (my mother's brother) stayed behind to care for his parents, was spared by Joseph Mengele at Auschwitz because he knew how to weld, was sent to another camp (Friedlander? I think that's the name) to work on German rockets (he says that's why none of them were successful). I met my uncle for the first time when I was four (1947) after he spent a year in a sanitorium in Switzerland to regain his health.

The camps, or the exodus from homelands, was never talked about in my home: whatever I "knew" I only guessed at, or inferred, so I grew up with the most awful sense of foreboding, and the conviction that it could all happen again. And perhaps one of the original impulses for me to write was in order to "bear witness" in some way to that remarkable and terrible era, to try to make some sense out of it.

***Thomas A. Goldman*** **"Rotterdam—1946":** In my concept of the poem, the focal point is the penultimate sentence: "We buried here one vital organ, hope." Here "we" is "we Americans" but, more specifically, "we consular officials," since I was myself a vice consul in 1946. . . .

What I would like to leave in the reader's mind, without making a specific reference, is the contrast of the generous, even self-sacrificing, attitude of someone like [Swedish diplomat Raoul] Wallenberg, who sought to save as many people as possible, even if it meant disregarding regulations, or even Swedish laws, with the narrow-minded, bureaucratic approach of the American consular service, which sought to admit as few people as possible, presumably on orders emanating from Washington.

***Luba Krugman Gurdus*** **"We Seek You, One and Only God":** This poem was written in hiding, during the Holocaust. Subsequent to my internment at the Majdanek Concentration Camp, I returned to Warsaw. It was April, 1943. The Warsaw Ghetto Uprising was in progress and the Nazis tried to "smoke out the Jewish bandits" [who were] offering fierce resistance. Watching the orgy of smoke, pierced by sporadic flashes, I turned in supplication to God, trying to express my despair in a form which would not incriminate my "aryan" benefactors.

***Leo Hamalian*** **"Boghos Sarkissian, a Watchmaker of Karpet, Remembers the Turkish Atrocities of 1915":** The Turkish genocide in 1915 had an immediate impact on Armenian literature. The first act was to round up the poets and other writers and execute them before the general massacres. And Armenian writing was wiped out because Armenian writers disappeared. That genocide entered the psyche of all survivors and influenced every Armenian writer who was born afterwards because every single family was touched in the small nation . . . every admired writer became a martyr. Even writers with Armenian blood [who are] writing in other languages know that they are writing where they are because of what happened in the "unacknowledged genocide of 1915."

In the poem, "they" refers to the Turks and Kurds, who, no matter how poor and miserable their lives, still are together, spiritually intact, the inheritors of what my father lost. The Armenians lost the contact with *place*, the material reality that must be the groundwork for a spiritual reality. "We" refers to the survivors.

The speaker is legend among the Armenians—my relatives, my cousins, my friends' fathers—I know literally dozens of Boghoses. I feel comfortable in representing his voice because it used to haunt my dreams as a child and I've heard it as a litany more times than I can count. When I was in my twenties and thirties, I dissociated myself from that voice, the voices of my childhood nightmares. I think the holocaust in Germany had some effect on me—I was at Dachau hours after it was taken. Gradually I was drawn back to my heritage partly because I realized that it was not all Boghos, that it could also be joy and warmth and connection as well as the tragic litany howling in the night.

**Cecile Hamermesh "Trilogy"**: "Trilogy" is my testament to my parents, my family, and my people, all of whom have taught me what strength, conviction, compassion, and love means. It is my honor to give them a little something back.

**Deborah Hanan "On Watching *Heritage: Civilization and the Jews*"**: [This series] aired on public television during the fall of 1984 . . . made me wish that at the time of my stepfather's greatest suffering I could have died in his place. Afterwards, I, too, needed to demonstrate what I knew and how I felt.

**Annette Bialik Harchik "Earrings"**: Auschwitz was an extermination camp in Poland where four million Jews were worked, beaten, starved, and gassed to death. And a whole industry was created around the disposal of the bodies. Upon arrival in the camp, prisoners were forcibly stripped, their head hair was shaven off, all their belongings were confiscated, they were branded with blue tattoo numbers and given a striped uniform to wear. Although my mother physically survived the camps, mentally and emotionally she never recovered from the trauma of her tortures and family losses. She was the only survivor of her family, which included two sisters, one brother, parents, grandparents, six aunts, seven uncles, and many cousins. For Franja Bialik, life lost all meaning after her arrival at Auschwitz and she continued lost in her protective mental illness and isolation until age sixty-seven when she died of diseases and conditions induced in the death camp.

**Edward Hirsch "Paul Celan: A Grave and Mysterious Sentence"**: I adore Paul Celan's "Fugue of Death" ("Todesfuge") which may be the greatest Holocaust poem ever written. It stunned me the first time that I read it, and I've carried its music around in my head for years now. I wish I'd written, "Black milk of daybreak, we drink you at nightfall." And the poem's structure is astonishing. Celan himself later renounced the poem for its "simplicity" and "clarity," its easiness. I suppose this is what first got me going on my poem. Celan seemed to me a great voice who was forever haunted and crippled by the experience of losing both of his parents in the death camps and being interned in a camp himself. After the war, he moved to Paris and began to write his first major poems. That's when my own poem takes place, in 1948, Paris. Celan was obsessed by language, by the difficulty (even the impossibility) of writing poems after the Holocaust, by the fact that he wrote in German, a language he both loved and despised, a language infiltrated by history. That's partially why he began to write a poetry which questioned language itself—and which by necessity had to use that language. And that's also one of the reasons that he became such a modern and hermetic poet.

I wanted to write a poem about Celan and his experience. I wanted to help account for his distrust of language itself—and his later hermetic poems—and yet I still love some of his early, more accessible poems—poems which are influenced by surrealism and expressionism. I also wanted to pay homage to "Death Fugue." I didn't at first want my own poem to be written in Celan's voice, from his point of view. I tried lots of other possibilities, but the poem just didn't work out. It always seemed too cool. Finally, I just gave up and decided to write it from inside the speaking subject—to give it intensity. I had to set it at a time when Celan was still writing clear poems. I wanted the poem to be true to its moment (Paris, '48), and also to account for what was going to happen to Celan and to his poetry. I certainly didn't want to use or exploit Celan in any way. I just wanted to write a poem that would speak about the experience from inside—from inside and outside of language, from inside and outside of history, from inside and outside of human life.

I wanted a poem about exile and without transcendence. My grave and mysterious sentence is what came out.

***Barbara Helfgott Hyett*** **"In Some of the Bunks," "And There Were Pits,"** and **"You Know the Funny Thing Is"**: These three poems are based on interviews I conducted with veterans of WWII, U.S. GI's who came upon the camps and who now, forty years later, wanted to tell what they saw.

**David Ignatow "1905"**: The poem, "1905," is a recollection, with contrasting events, such as the Prince Igor opera, which I invented, of my father's extreme poverty and, at the same time, [his] apprenticeship as a skilled binder at the Kiev Monastery. He left Russia immediately after the failure of the 1905 Revolution, when the counterrevolution went on the offensive, attacking members of the Social Democratic Party that had participated in the revolution. My father, as a member, fled before the mobs of the counterrevolution. As a Jew, he was especially vulnerable.

For me, that poem is redolent of the evenings, I, as a child, would listen to my father recount stories of his life in Kiev.

***Laurence Josephs*** **"Passover at Auschwitz"**: I came to write "Passover at Auschwitz" when I read that the people detained in such places did not really have anything like calendars to keep them abreast of days, months, years, and holidays of the religious year. Since for us calendars are so important in the joy of planning holidays like Pesach to which we look forward with such anticipation, I began to think how terrible it must have been for them not even to know—in addition to all the other horrors of their life—what month or year they were suffering through, and that even *that* had been wrenched away from them. Somewhere, too, I felt the extreme irony and bitterness of the fact that this place had become *their* Egypt and [that] they were all suddenly and cruelly the "firstborn" who were terribly in danger.

***Hans Juergensen*** **"The Scar—August, 1934"**: In August 1934, the Jews in my area—provinces of Brandenburg and Silesia—were already isolated. I had to leave the Gymnasium, and my Aryan friends came to see me on the sly (bless them!). The Jews formed their own sports and cultural groups. On the particular Sunday in question, about 100 of us of various ages went on a picnic near the town of Grünberg (Silesia). Our leader was a 38-year-old physician, a veteran of WWI. Late in the afternoon, he and I were standing quite separate from the others, talking about further sports events in the future. I was 14. . . .

As we were standing there, two SS men, in uniform, *black*, walked up to us and said: "Doctor, we want to talk to you, but not here." Then [they] added: "Sonny, you come along, too."

They marched us through some fields and to a forest clearing. Both of us knew what was about to happen. In the clearing, the doctor and I turned around and . . . . [Jurgensen's ellipsis].

I was told to keep this to myself, of course, and was permitted to rejoin the group. People from my town left soon after since we had a distance to travel. How I kept my composure, I cannot tell; but no one in my group had any suspicion of the occurrence.

The body was found later, and the newspapers called it a "hunting accident." The reason for this execution was that he and the district Nazi leader had been comrades in the army; the *gauleiter* had protected him, and the Gestapo did not like it.

The weirdest thing is that the doctor's name has been totally blocked from my memory, though I remember everything else.

My emigration is another story. It had already been initiated before the incident, and I was one of fourteen boys in the first children's transport to the U.S. on a special visa in November of 1934. All the other boys were from prominent families in Berlin. I was chosen, I was told, because of my strange childhood and, also, because my intelligence scores were high. The American "Joint" got us over.

The poem was written—finally—in 1966.

**Rosa Felsenburg Kaplan** "**Kol Nidre**": The first part of the poem refers to the following events: One way of leaving Austria in 1938 was to get a visa to Luxembourg [and] cross the border from there to France where Jews were permitted to remain—provided they did not work, live in Paris, or retain their nationality. Since it was difficult to go through this maneuver with five children, our parents sent us to relatives in Hungary and Czechoslovakia on the passport of people whose children's ages and genders corresponded to ours. Once our parents were settled in Chelles, they located other people who brought us to France. To do so required much ingenuity and luck on the part of our parents and inordinate courage and commitment on the part of the people who did the supporting. For instance, Mrs. Shmuel (Mulo) Cohen, a French woman in her early thirties, transported five children from different families, none of whom spoke French, across Czechoslovak, Hungarian, German, and French borders. Mrs. Cohen is still alive though she lost her husband [who fought] in the French Underground. I do not know what happened to the people who transported me and my cousin Rosa.

Although I considered myself rather sheltered among Holocaust survivors, I found myself having to come to grips with my losses and the unfinished business. It is these areas, rather than so-called survivors' guilt, which I wished to address in my poem—which started on the way home from a Kol Nidre service. I puzzled why it was that Jews who have good mechanisms for dealing with guilt still felt so guilty and concluded that as incest survivors or abused children blame themselves for their victimization, so do we. Our victimization, generation after generation, has been the losses—the unfinished business—which make it necessary to recite *Kol Nidre* three times.

I am currently [1985] a clinical specialist in mental health and substance abuse. Some of my recent experiences at work make me aware of the fact that with all the disruption in my early life, I have been relatively sheltered: I have never been in a situation where the people who were to raise me, teach me, nurture me, were people who abused or exploited me. My Holocaust experiences also taught me that if anybody is not treated decently, nobody is safe.

**Dori Katz** "**Line-up**" : ["Line-up"] was inspired by the last, unfinished, film of the director Andrzej Munk, "The Passenger." It concerns a former German concentration camp guard who is honeymooning with her new husband years later on a cruise ship and recognizes a former inmate among the passengers. The film is her "false" recollections of her experience as a guard in the camp, i.e., the story she feels forced to tell her husband.

"**The Return**": the tattooed number was my father's actual number. In an earlier draft, I had invented a number but when I found out what his actual number had been, I decided to use it and changed the line. I learned as a child that my father had had a leg amputated in Auschwitz; I always pictured him with one leg after that.

**Irena Klepfisz** "**Solitary Acts**": Since the age of 21, I have been writing poetry in which the Holocaust is a recurrent theme. Because I'm a child survivor, my early writing was experiential and very private. Later, I began consciously exploring larger implications. Fearing I might become trapped in the past, I sought connections between the Holocaust of the Jews and the experiences of other groups who lack political power and privilege—women, working-class, Third World, gay. Increasingly, I found that an understanding of the Holocaust broadened my understanding of present political situations and conflicts and of genocides since 1945. These concerns as well as a very strong feminist perspective are, I believe, reflected in my poems "*Bashert*" and "Solitary Acts." So that is one direction of my writing in relation to the Holocaust ["*Bashert*," like "Solitary Acts," appears in *Keeper of Accounts* (Sinister Wisdom, 1982)].

"*Di Rayze Abeym*/ **The Journey Home**": Another, more recent and perhaps less obvious: the use of Yiddish. In 1983, my mother and I returned to Poland after 37 years. Though only seven days long, the trip had enormous impact. Entering the monumental Jewish cemeteries of Lodz and Warsaw (the sole things Jewish left in those former Jewish centers) was like stepping into—not a photograph—but a negative or reverse image. The tombstones, crumbling, overgrown and abandoned, were a reflection to me of the size, diversity, and energy of the destroyed community. I had not, until that trip, realized the full scope of the destruction.

The experience forced me to think further about secular Jewish identity and the fate of Yiddish culture. As a child, I was surrounded by Bundists—secular Jews, socialists, with a deep commitment to Yiddish—and I attended Yiddish schools; later I even taught Yiddish. Yet for all these years I had never thought about language in relation to my Jewish writings. After visiting Poland, I became determined not to forget those creative artists for whom Yiddish had been a life medium and to work towards salvaging something of the language itself. I committed myself to translating Yiddish women writers (e.g., Kadya Molodovsky, Fradl Shtock) and began to experiment with Yiddish in my poetry. "*Di Rayze Aheym/*The Journey Home" is part of a manuscript in progress, tentatively titled *Mame-loshn/Mother Tongue.*

***Norbert Krapf*** "**The Name of a Place**": The time I took my parents to Dachau—it was their first trip to Germany, the only one my father ever took. I was apprehensive about bringing him there, for he was deeply affected by the death of his brother. . . . The camera was frozen against my chest, and we were all frozen in silence. I could see the tension build up in my father, and I was becoming more and more anxious about his reaction as well as overcome with my own complicated and agonized emotions. Finally he turned to me and asked, in a quiet, child-like voice: "Why would anybody want to do this?" All I could say was: "I don't know."

***Carolyn Kreiter-Kurylo*** "**Leaving a Country Behind**": There's a certain amount of truth to the assumption that many German descendants carry with them a collective guilt for the crimes their forefathers committed during World War II. There is also truth to the fact that countless Germans living today are so attached to this guilt that they willingly support whatever efforts they can to prevent similar abominations from occurring. In fact, some of these individuals through documentaries or docudramas have admirably educated Americans about the brutal realities of Hitler's concentration camps. Others on a smaller, though equally important, scale have educated American youngsters about the atrocities of WWII. As a teacher, I belong to this latter group. Interestingly enough, I have gone so far as to take my students to Dachau so they could catch a glimmer of truth about a war that stripped humans of their dignity. I have also spent hours in the classroom familiarizing students with the poems of such caring poets as William Heyen, a German[-American] who shares his own history of the Holocaust in the painful *The Swastika Poems* [later incorporated into *Erika: Poems of the Holocaust* (Vanguard, 1984). See the sequence of Heyen's poems included in Section V.]. And I have written about a personal attempt to leave this collective guilt behind in "Leaving a Country Behind."

I had just returned from Dachau when the initial strains of "Leaving a Country [Behind]" began playing in my head. Having visited the concentration camp with a close Jewish friend [had] emphasized the reality of my German heritage and my inability to ignore these roots while confronting the horrors of Dachau. Once back in America, I came face to face in a recurring dream with an overwhelming sense of collective guilt. This dream initiated the first two segments of the poem. What I hoped to recreate with words was the fragmented nature of this haunting nightmare: the illusive image of my father on a flight home from Munich staring into darkness, his aunt coming into view out of memory, "cupping" fresh flowers, perhaps the last bouquet she'd hold before she lost touch with reality. The second segment provides a glimpse into her past and how her own sense of collective guilt led her eventually to lock herself in an attic "to sketch" the mad giant, Hitler. Flowing out of this image is a vision of my great aunt's funeral, a choirboy, innocent and seemingly unaware of history, singing "as if the past were but a moment he could bury with the dead."

As a young girl, I remember my father telling me I should be proud of my German heritage. I *was* until the day a friend accused me of being kin to Hitler. I can still see her tiny lips pursed as she spoke: *Anyone with a German name like Kreiter must be kin to him!*

**Christine Lahey** **"Dan's Shoe Repair: 1959"**: Dan was our local shoe repairman in a suburb of Detroit where I was raised. As a child, I was fascinated by him, all the more because it was known that he "had been in the camps during the war." The *Life* photos mentioned in the poem I actually saw at home at an earlier age—I still have a mental photo of the one showing hundreds of bodies lying in a pit, twisted, torn beyond recognition. The ghastly horror I felt then (age 7? 8?) is forever impressed in my memory. So, seeing the photo, meeting Dan often (his shop was only about a block and a half from my house) as a local phenomenon, a "witness" to the horrors contained in that *Life* photo, plus my sensibility as a child whose father had passed away when I was just short of two years old, all this years later—in 1979 to be exact—came together in the poem "Dan's Shoe Repair." I should add that early in '79 the image of Dan would come to my mind again and again—the figure from my childhood started to haunt me, and the poem "wrote itself."

**Yaacov Luria** **"There Is One Synagogue Extant in Kiev"**: I never write about the Holocaust itself. I feel that this is the province of survivors, their closest kin, and Holocaust scholars. They have the terrible obligation to bear witness and to record.

Nevertheless, I live with the awareness that I escaped the Nazi murderers only because my grandparents brought their families to the United States at a time when immigration was relatively easy. I become emotional when the lifting of a sleeve reveals a number tattooed on a forearm.

One morning shortly after the Yom Kippur War [fall 1973], I sit with a handful of old Jews in the courtyard of the only synagogue left in Kiev. When I ask how to get to Babi Yar, a woman shows me the palm of her hand. *"Dort iz gornit zu sehen*—there's nothing to see there. It's flat as this hand. Disappeared." How can I avoid expressing this sadness?

**Lois Mathieu** **"Counting Sheep by Night"**: The woman who inspired this poem is named Sylvia. During the war, she and her sister marched through Poland in the cold of winter until their feet were nearly ruined, while in America we were having "blackouts." I feared the man who came through our neighborhood at night with a flashlight ordering my parents to turn off their lights. I don't know what Sylvia and her sister feared. When I got to know Sylvia, she talked a little about the family she lost. She was grateful for her sister. She also showed me her permanently swollen feet and the tattoo on her forearm. For years, I wondered how it was for her to fall asleep and how she experienced art, beauty, love, religion, and intimacy. In "Counting Sheep by Night," I felt each word catch fire as it touched the subject.

**Bernard S. Mikofsky** **"Mame-Loshen, Yiddish"** and **"1945"**: We grieve for the millions lost in our holocaust and in, say, the Cambodian and Armenian holocausts. But whenever I look at the few precious photos we have of my saintly, scholarly uncle, Zalman Moshe Mikowski, his dear wife, and my cousin Bernard and his two sisters (they were married and had children), the Holocaust becomes searingly personal. Bernard was in the Polish army and was killed during the opening weeks in which Nazi Germany cut its bloody swath through Poland. The others were murdered in the concentration camps.

**Aaron Miller** **"Not Dachau"**: I was serving in Germany in 1961 with the U.S. Information Service. In the interest of doing my work with a measure of equanimity, I had avoided visiting places like Dachau. But in the summer of 1961, on a fine Sunday afternoon, with nothing else to do, and with orders to head for East Africa on my desk, I decided to drive out from Munich. The camp and park were swarming with sightseers of all nationalities—French, German, Swedes, Americans, Hungarians, et al. And what struck me very forcibly was that all of them seemed to be on the outside looking in, personally detached from what they were seeing, whereas I was experiencing my own humanity. I mean, at the ovens, I saw myself at both ends of the shuttle. The Nazis had merely been the personification, the incarnation, of the darkness in all of us. At that point, my ethnic identity disappeared; indeed, all of my personae were gone, stripped away to reveal the naked victim, naked killer.

**Gerald Musinsky** "Drawing the Blinds": The actual image of dead beetles and dried leaves spawned the first stanza late one evening. It was winter or late fall, '78/'79, and I was a graduate student studying Hebrew while planning a trip to Israel. PLO supporters, Iranian radicals, White Nationalists (Neo-Nazis), were more prevalent on campus than peace marchers and draft resisters during the Sixties. Local synagogues received terrorist threats, as did Jewish instructors. Later that evening, I was awakened by nightmares of various Holocaust scenes, not in Germany, but here in the U.S. After I awoke, I realized that in order to prevent such a horror from happening again, we must constantly keep it in the public's consciousness.

I suppose I wrote the poem as a personal effort to aid the memories of those who would rather forget. We might draw the blinds, but the horror remains.

**Estelle Gershgoren Novak** "Yom HaShoah": I was born in 1940 while the war was going on in Europe. My parents are Russian Jews who immigrated to America in 1923, escaping from the pogroms that they knew about and, as they now know, escaping from the pogrom of the Holocaust which was yet to come. Twenty years after my father left his village all of the people who lived there and in the surrounding area were shot in a massacre by the Nazis. I myself saw films showing the dead from the concentration camps when I was seven years old and I have never forgotten them.

**Miriam Offenberg** "Reforger": As the public relations officer for the naval unit that would be going to Germany as part of an annual exercise, I was expected to go along and report (favorably) on the activities. The poem was an expression of my feelings at the idea of having to spend a week in that country, and meet and greet its dignitaries. (Fortunately, I never went.)

**Gregory Orfalea** "The Poacher": In 1977-78, while I was living in a provincial city of southwest France called Pau, I chanced to meet a curious person while on a trip in the Pyrenees mountains. The man owned a small, old hotel high in the mountains in a town called St. Engrâce, right before the border to Spain. We visitors for the night were told a story: during the Second World War, this owner and others in the mountains who had been poachers actually (or *braconniers*) had helped smuggle Jews fleeing Vichy France and other Nazi-held lands into Spain. For a time, then, the *braconnier* became a *contrebandier* (or smuggler) of human beings. Many were hid in caves from the police before being taken into Spain.

**Monique Pasternak** "The Witness": The southern part of France, erroneously named "La France libre," had been under the administrative rule of Marechal Petain, a French collaborator of the Nazis, up to 8 November 1942, the night of my birth. The official Nazi military occupation of the south of France had not occurred yet. That particular night was a turning point in the balance of power during World War II. It [was] then that the Allies flew over the south of France on their way to fight the Nazi presence in North Africa. Because the Allied forces were bombing the land, the authorities ordered a black-out and electricity was cut off until the next morning; the German troops quickly moved in and occupied the region, which remained under the control of the Nazis until the liberation. Thus the drama of the light and the dark was vividly acted out during the first twenty-four hours of my life.

**Mark Pawlak** "Unforgettable": I have not written extensively about the Holocaust. The few poems that I have written on the subject, I did not sit down intentionally to write; rather, they are *poèmes trouvé*—unexpected "gifts." As early as January 1985 articles began to regularly appear commemorating the end of World War II and the liberation of the concentration camps (long before the furor over President Reagan's visit to Bitburg cemetery). Several of the news articles I read contained compelling accounts by Holocaust survivors of the horrors they [had] suffered and witnessed. The details of these horrors were described with precision, narrated in a moving and dramatic fashion, and contained startling images,

395

staggering to the imagination. I pared the accounts down into poems modeled after Charles Reznikoff's poems based upon court testimonies [see the excerpts from Reznikoff's *Holocaust* in Section III].

If these poems survive as accounts of second-hand witness to the horrors of the Holocaust, I shall feel that I've achieved my aim in writing them.

***Norah Reap*** **"Numbers"**: "Numbers" is a remembrance of a child's first realization of the Holocaust in terms of an individual survivor who the child knows and cares about. For this child, the tattooed numbers on an arm that embraces her are intuitively understood as a symbol of great suffering and she gently covers them in a futile attempt to erase her friend's pain and regain her own lost innocence.

***Lisa Ress*** **"At Your Table. Vienna V, 1957," "The Family Album," and "U.S. Army Holds Dance for Camp Survivors. Germany, 1945"**: "U.S. Army" and "Family Album," along with many of the other poems in this series in *Flight Patterns* (The University Press of Virginia, 1985), came into being out of the intersection of my own experiences as the child of Holocaust refugees and those recounted in Helen Epstein's book, *Children of the Holocaust* [Putnam, 1979].

"U.S. Army" is based on a combination of an account in Epstein's book and that of the experiences of a Viennese woman, a journalist, who as a child remained hidden by neighbors with her mother in the basement of their apartment building in Vienna during the entire Nazi period. It was in fact she who continued her piano lessons on a board painted to simulate a piano keyboard, and I heard this story from her back in 1958 while in Vienna.

"Family Album" is a kind of quilt pieced together of stories I heard, voices I heard, as a child in Chicago growing up among so many displaced, nostalgic, and bewildered Central Europeans, the continuity of whose lives was so terribly severed by the Holocaust—and again, perhaps, of stories and voices recorded by Epstein. There was, in Vienna's "Stadtpark," a cafe where, in my mother's youth, i.e., in the thirties, one had tea and danced. I've no idea whether it's still there, or whether it is still any sort of café now at all.

***Charles Reznikoff*** from **"Massacres,"** from **"Mass Graves,"** and from **"Inscriptions: 1944-1956"**: (From correspondence with Nathan Pollack): "Charles was my cousin. I have always admired his approach to history. . . . He developed a method of rendering human experience in its atomic form. As an American-born Jew, Charles agonized over the events in Europe while he was safe and comfortable in New York. It took him many years to accumulate and work over the experiences of Jewish victims of the Nazis. It was Charles' way of dealing with a very important aspect of his own life and history."

***Liliane Richman*** **"To My Mother Who Endured"**: In this poem I sought to merge three elements. The first one is an allusion to the Passover meal in which the sufferings of the Jewish people are recounted. In each generation, it is said, some tyrant rises who seeks to annihilate the Jewish race. The Holocaust is recollected in the ritual meal. The second element, the story of Marcelline, was suggested to me as I viewed a *cinéma vérité* film by Chris Marker in which the story of Marcelline is told. The third element inspired the title of the poem, a dedication to my own mother who endured at Bergen Belsen 1942-1945.

***William Pitt Root*** **"Late Twentieth Century Pastoral"**: [My writing of this poem] came from a series of dovetailing circumstances, beginning with my learning that some of the elders in my mother's family, having come from a region that was sometimes Germany, sometimes Denmark, were persecuted by their neighbors in this country during World War II. Because I knew them only as gentle hard-working people, I asked why and the answers, which were not answers, baffled me as a child. Later I learned how Germans had been regarded then, and why, and felt a deep uneasiness about that part of my own blood. Later still, much later, when Jacob Bronowski was narrating [the public television series] *Ascent of Man* [1973] and was touring some of the concentration camps, recalling their horrors, he walked, fully clad, without interrupting his narrative, into a pond in which the ashes of some of those [who had been] cremated had been dumped for years decades earlier. So astonishing was that act, so inexplicably right and so thrillingly healing, that I found myself among the millions weeping at that moment as we witnessed the strange baptismal blessing of that extraordinary man. I wanted to write about it but couldn't find a point of entry, and the act itself far exceeded any gesture of language I might conjure. Later still, in Sitka, Alaska, I was talking with an artist, Diane Katsiaficas, who works with constructions of natural "found" materials. She described finding in Germany, near the Belsen camp, hung on the barbed wire of farmers' fences after the seasonal floods, great patches of natural paper hung drying and curing in the sun. Instantly, I found myself associating those floodwaters with the waters in the pond Mr. Bronowski had walked into, waters in which the ashes of thousands upon thousands had settled, and felt beginning in me the elaborate series of further associations which ultimately took me back to paper again, this time to start the poem which, once begun, nearly wrote itself with my hands.

**Marina Roscher "Going Back" and "The Lanternman"**: I was born and raised in Germany. As a child, I wrote poems in German but, after the revelations of 1945, I knew I would have to grow into another language first before I could hope to write again. Although I have published prose and poetry in English for more than ten years now, I was unable to write about the Holocaust until conversations with the editor of this volume helped liberate feelings and deeply submerged images.

**Larry Rubin "The Nazi in the Dock, at Sixty"**: There was something (is something) grotesque about these old men, being exposed now after four decades and nearing death themselves—hideous crimes are associated generally with younger, more energetic monsters. I wanted to express not only the horror, but the pity of it—to be so old and to have so much to account for. The Fedorenko case in Ft. Lauderdale (Miami Beach is my hometown) is, I think, what triggered the poem; but all the ingredients for writing it were already coming to a boil. . . . [Fedorenko admitted to having been a guard at Treblinka, a major extermination center in Poland, NE of Warsaw and, in March 1981, he was stripped of his U.S. citizenship for failing to disclose his wartime activities during his immigration to the U.S. in 1949.]

**Luada Sandler "The Gift" and "A Scene from *Shoah*"**: Two factors have deepened my interest in the Holocaust: 1. My late husband was born in Latvian Russia and was twelve or thirteen years old at the outbreak of the Russian Revolution. Early in the Revolution, his father was cut off from his family while on a business trip to Riga, and his mother was imprisoned, an alleged political prisoner, leaving four small children to fend for themselves. (My husband was the eldest of the four.) Their mother was sentenced to death, which then was commuted to ten years. Finally, she was released after about a year. The family immigrated to the U.S. when my husband was sixteen. From him and his family, I gained insight into the wanton and destructive use of power in time of war and revolution.

2. During World War II, I served as a staff aide with the American Red Cross in military hospitals in the European Theatre of Operations. Immediately after the end of the war in Europe, I saw emaciated former prisoners of war coming through our hospital in Liège, Belgium, on their way home for further treatment in U.S. hospitals. I remember meeting a man very briefly, a political prisoner who had been at Dachau and was on his way home to New York. Although he did not talk about his years at the camp, one felt the deep tragedy of his experience. In Marseille, I met a family of survivors who were related to one of our staff members, and I spent a day with them. I remember one of them said, "You can't imagine how horrible the camps were, especially for a young woman like me."

The enormity, the depravity, and the monstrosity of the Holocaust seem to me, metaphorically at least, as if an earthquake of cosmic dimensions had struck the universe. I believe the damage it caused is still being felt around the world. Whether that damage can be repaired may be debatable, but I feel it is incumbent on all of us to do our utmost to contribute to the restoration of the world's "balance." When I think how much the world has been impoverished by the Holocaust, not only by those who perished but also by how much the rest of us have been diminished, our task of repair seems extremely formidable.

I am in the process of writing a short story [July 1985] tentatively entitled, "The Changeling," based on the partly true, partly imagined story of a survivor whose baby died as an experiment at Buchenwald. The story concerns my observation of the effect on that mother's life thirty-five years later. Both in that story as well as in my poem, "The Gift," I feel that the telling of the history of even one survivor can help repair at least a small section of the psychic terrain traumatized by the giant upheaval of the Holocaust.

As a Jew, I am alarmed at how soon the world forgets or ignores the Holocaust and how many people are willfully and actively seeking to revise our history, which in turn will invalidate history in general.

***Reg Saner*** **"Aspen Oktoberfest"**: Never having visited Auschwitz (where Lily Tofler died) I transferred her to Dachau, which my family and I did visit. The "record" occurs somewhere amongst testimonies of witnesses at the [Nuremberg] trials. I read selections, not the entire thing—a warehouse of documentation!—in 1967 and found myself adding a Jewish star to our Christmas tree that year, one I made and painted with the name Lily Tofler. I have since put it on our tree every Christmas. She occurs in a poem I included in *So This Is the Map* [Random House, 1981]. And she recurs often when I'm having a glorious day outdoors: I think of Dachau, Treblinka . . . and Lily Tofler. It seems strange that I can be exhilarated by, say, autumn aspens, when a lovely girl like that hardly had a chance. I've made her into a personal heroine showing what courage can do. It didn't save her, yet it did. Her example has often saved me, if not from death (and maybe it has) at least from the blindness of whimpering and whining while standing in the middle of a lucky, privileged life.

***Ruth Lisa Schechter*** **"The Hungarian Mission"**: My poem about the Children's Cadre is based on the experience of Dr. Mary Engel who lives in my area [Croton-on-Hudson, New York] and is a psychologist on [State University of New York] staff. I've been serving as an editor of her book-in-progress, *Marika*. Marika is her Hungarian first name. She was a member of the Children's Cadre and is a survivor of the Holocaust. She is the author of a scientific book, *Psychopathology in Childhood* (Harcourt Brace Jovanovich, Inc.) and other scientific papers about children—also papers about the effect of the Holocaust on children.

***Harvey Shapiro*** **"Ditty"**: Readers of "Ditty" might want to look at "I Sing of a Mayden," an anonymous poem of the fifteenth century.

***Reva Sharon*** **"In the Absence of Yellow"**: When I visited Terezin, the words of Pavel Friedmann's poem, "I Never Saw Another Butterfly," were a constant refrain in my head as I walked through the cells, the prison, the crematoria.

***Steven Sher*** **"Sitting This One Out"**: My parents were still living in Brooklyn, in the downstairs apartment of a two-family attached brick house. The owners (also in their sixties; both of them death camp survivors) lived upstairs. Both apartments shared a common entranceway. Quite often, since my mother and Sally, the landlady, were on friendly terms, they left the interior doors, to both apartments, open. I was seated at my parents' kitchen table this particular afternoon when I heard someone heading slowly down the stairs. I wasn't surprised to see Sally in the entranceway a moment later. But instead of her usual housedress, she wore a formal dress. She'd obviously been to the beauty parlor, too. As I greeted her, commenting on how she looked, I was struck by something incongruous in her appearance. Because she wore short sleeves, I naturally noticed the blue numbers on her arm. But she was dressed for a festive occasion! I stared at her arm as if seeing the numbers for the first time. How, I wondered, could someone who had lived through the death camps again celebrate anything in this life? And so the poem was born out of this disturbing contrast.

***Enid Shomer*** **"Remembering"**: My husband is an Israeli, but has lived in the U.S. since 1967. He is the only Jewish child survivor from his town, Kremenitz, Poland.

His mother fled from Kremenitz with my husband when he was six weeks old. He never knew his father, who was killed right after he was born. He and his mother stayed behind the Eastern Front until the war was over. They ended up in Munich as displaced persons and emigrated to Israel in 1948.

**"Women Bathing at Bergen Belsen"**: I chose the sonnet form for my subject because it is a very demanding form and I wanted to pay homage to the survivors as well as the dead on the day of liberation at Bergen-Belsen. The poem is factual, based on the documentary film, "A Memory of the Camps," which was aired on TV this past spring [1985].

***Maurya Simon*** **"Letter to Vienna from Paris, 1942"**: [This poem and several related poems] arose from stories my mother-in-law, Margit Idelovici Falk, has told me. Both she and my father-in-law were born and raised in Vienna. Most members of their respective families died either in concentration camps, during the fire bombing of Dresden, or in Israel in 1948 during the war there. Margit was sent by her family to Indonesia (in 1940), to stay with Dutch relatives. When the Japanese occupied the country, she was imprisoned in Bandung for four years. I felt not only justified, but compelled to serve as witness for her, and for all those in my extended family—both living and dead—who cried out to be heard. Though one generation removed from the speakers in my poems, I am not at all removed from the anguish of their stories.

***Louis Simpson*** **"The Bird"**: This character study of a Nazi concentration camp guard was written before they started turning up in South America. One critic remarked that the poem was based on my reading of Brecht. This is not true: I had been reading Heine, but the poem rose out of my imagining such a character and situation. The line about the little bird is taken from a German Romantic poem—by Morike, I seem to recall.

In **"A Story about Chicken Soup"**: the mention of my grandmother and the old country are autobiographical. All those people in the old country, southern Russia, were indeed killed by the Germans. The second part is also autobiographical. In 1945, the 101st Airborne Division of the U.S. Army, in which I served, occupied Berchtesgaden. The poem describes exactly what happened: the child with yellow hair, etc. The poem was finished in a curious way. I had written most of it but was having trouble with the third part. A friend, Robert Bly, came to visit. As I explained to him what I wanted to say, he wrote down lines from my conversation. Then he showed them to me, and I had finished the poem.

***Joan Jobe Smith*** **"Hollow Cost"**: An irony that was called to my attention although unintentional on my part is that it is prophesied in the Old Testament that Abraham's descendants would number as many as the stars in the sky [See Gen. 15:1-5]. A devout little churchgoer as a child (although my maternal great-grandparents were Jewish and fled one of the pogroms of the 1800s), I must have retained that image from some Baptist sermon I heard and properly placed the image in my poem. Anyway, when it was called to my attention, I felt quite mystical, if not a little eery. It might be a biblical cliché, that image, but I didn't remember it at all. But the incident described in my poem was one of the major events in my life.

***Deborah S. Snyder*** **"Carolyn's Neighbor"**: I deeply feel that the fact of the Holocaust is important to us as Jews, and as American Jews, also. Not only are we most fortunate to have been in America (especially *as* Jews); but our perspective on the Holocaust has been affected by that fortune. This is an irony that there is no answer for, I think.

That we must "never forget" is vital. However, not only must we not forget, but we must, at the same time, understand that we cannot really comprehend the horror of that time. I've spoken to my parents, who said that people in this country during the years 1933-1945 had no idea of the magnitude of what had taken place in Europe: now, it is like a knight's move in chess. For, not only do we have an altered perspective by place (America/Europe); now [1985], we have one of time: 40 to 50 years.

I found writing [this poem] very difficult. Despite the fact I've been told that some (or most?) of my European relatives perished, my older American relatives would not, for a long time, discuss it. A paternal great-aunt has mentioned some things, but at one or two sentences at a time. Names, dates, and details are lost to me. My aunt's reticence is understandable. I never felt I could pry into a pain as private as hers. . . . I've always felt like an outsider—an American neighbor—unknowing and, therefore, unable to help or prevent.

**Kirtland Snyder** *"City Children at a Summer Camp.* **Slonim, 1936,"** and **"Selma . . . A Pot of Soup . . . A Bottle of Milk. Lodz, 1938":** The Holocaust has haunted my imagination for many years. It has seemed to me to be a central symbol of the human condition, a barbarity that smashes all neat conventions about "civilization." More particularly, it seemed to say something central about the bankruptcy of Christianity. I felt I could discover something essential about myself by writing about the Holocaust. As I wrote, I did indeed discover this essential thing: that I, too, was somehow a victim of the Holocaust. It has to do with John Donne's idea that each man's death diminishes me, because I am involved in mankind. Which, it seems to me, is essentially a Jewish idea.

I felt a deep grief for the Jewish victims of Christian Europe under Hitler, and wanted *to do something* for them, to perform some act of remembrance, to confer some dignity upon their horrible deaths. Just about all my attempts to do so in writing, until *Vishniac's Children* [retitled *A Vanished World*], seemed to fail for one reason or another. The difference, I think, has to do with the fact that the poems of the sequence focus on the living Jews before the Holocaust. This is the beauty of [Roman] Vishniac's photographs. There is enormous dignity in the lives as Vishniac reveals them, no matter how impoverished. These Jews live, even though most of them died.

**Gizela Spunberg** **"Memories of December":** My city Lwów was occupied by the Russians and I wanted to cross the border to Rumania. I never saw my mother again.

**Mary Kathryn Stillwell** **"Dachau":** I visited Dachau in 1980 with my brother and his wife who were stationed (U.S. Army) in Frankfurt, Germany. When we took the train down to Munich, however, I had no idea that Dachau was close by. I spotted the name of the village on a local train map and knew immediately that I must go, that it was in some way necessary.

Dachau, the village, is a pretty town, not very large and, in some ways, like my hometown in rural Nebraska. It was late summer, and all of Germany seemed in full bloom. There were geranium and other bright flowers along curbs and in windowboxes. People walked a little slower and smiled a little easier than they did in Munich and Frankfurt. Although it was raining when we arrived, it was in no sense gloomy.

We caught a local bus to the camp. Once inside those "barbed perimeters," everything seemed to change. Because of the rain, the camp was nearly empty and I became keenly aware of the crunching of the gravel underfoot. We saw the monument, stylized barbed wire and bone, and then made our way through the administration building and the men's and women's barracks that remain standing, then we made our way down the center path. . . .

I have never felt such a sense of empathetic horror and panic before or since: it was as though I was there then. This camp was not exclusively for the extermination of the Jews. Political prisoners, various religious orders, and other "undesirables"—Gypsies and bastards, for example—were also sent here, for labor and detention, perhaps death. This "wider net," I'm sure allowed for my personal entry into the experience of the past. We are all survivors of the camps on some level.

I wanted to write a poem that would express this horror, a *living* horror that must be kept alive, if we are to prevent such a slaughter again in the future.

**Elaine Terranova** **"1939":** [This poem] is based on the Middle Europe of my imagination and Vishniac's camera, a place where my relatives who perished were living. I imagine, too, a child and her mother, in a world that is slipping away from them. The mother is confident that life will remain dependable and pleasant; the child is uncertain and uneasy, for the deeds of fairy tales are more real to her than the superficial calm. As it turns out, she is of course right. All of my mother's family, except for one brother and one sister, were lost.

***Alfred Van Loen*** **"Auschwitz #1," "Auschwitz #5," and "Auschwitz #6":** My Auschwitz poems were originally written in Dutch in 1946 and translated into English in 1948 after I came to this country. My parents, my sister, and I lived in Amsterdam and escaped the Holocaust. I was active in the underground from 1939 to the end of the war. It wasn't until then that we knew the fate of our relatives in Germany and other parts of Europe.

My grandfather, Simon Lowenthal, on the way to his office in Munich, made it his habit to sit on a bench in a nearby park and feed the birds and the squirrels. Early one morning in the fall of 1941, he was attacked by a couple of Nazis and beaten to death. He was seventy-six years old. My grandmother and my father's brother, Hermann, who was a poet, were shortly thereafter sent to concentration camps. Originally Grandmother was held in Theresienstadt, where Father was able to send her packages; later she was moved. From survivors returning to Amsterdam, we heard that Grandmother was seen in Bergen-Belsen, where she died. My Uncle Hermann was in Auschwitz where he was part of the work crew for fourteen months until he, too, was murdered.

These facts and stories told by survivors prompted the writing of these Auschwitz poems. In my dreams, I felt like I had been with my relatives and shared their suffering. As long as I live, I will never be able to forget or forgive the Nazi horror.

***Morrie Warshawski*** **"Sonia at 32":** My mother is a survivor of Auschwitz-Birkenau. My father, too, is a survivor of the camps. Children tend to fix their parents at a certain age and for me "32" is the age that I associate most with my own mother.

***Michael Waters*** **"Dachau Moon":** I was born in Brooklyn in 1949. My father is a Scotch-Irish Catholic and my mother a German-Russian Jew who converted to Catholicism in order to marry my father. I was raised as a Catholic. On Sunday mornings, I'd attend Mass with my parents at St. Martin of Tours Church. Then my Jewish grandmother, Clara Haase, who lived with us, would take me on the subway to the Lower East Side of Manhattan. What a different world! The shops were open, racks of shirts on the sidewalks, women in babushkas jostling each other for bargains. The streets were so loud, so unlike the hushed, empty streets of Sunday afternoons in the parish. My grandmother would sit with her friends on a bench in the park [and] give me some change for a knish or cherry blintz. I loved those Sunday afternoons and still associate them with being Jewish. I was a Catholic six days a week, but on the seventh day—I should have been resting—I was a Jew.

In the 8th grade, I read Shirer's *The Rise and Fall of the Third Reich*, the book in its black cover prominently displayed on my desk so the nun would know I was reading such a large and important book. Surely that reading triggered something—I had begun to wonder about the Jewish heritage, how much of it extended to my mother, how much of it belonged to me. I was a dual citizen in the country of Brooklyn. And when the poems began to come, some couldn't help touching the Holocaust, if only to diminish it enough so that it might be understood, to enlarge it enough so that it might become less real, approach myth. Either way, the task remains impossible, but the mind is a wonder . . . and the closer we come to apprehending the Holocaust, the stronger the soul within us grows. I want to believe this.

***Florence Weinberger*** **"Survivor":** My interest in the Holocaust began in the 1940's, listening to my immigrant parents' well-founded fears that the families they had left behind in Hungary were in danger, then listening to them read aloud the letters arriving after the war from the few survivors.

In 1955, I married Ted (Tibor) Weinberger, a native of Miskolc, Hungary, and a survivor. All the reading and research I have done since then on the Holocaust has been part of an attempt to understand that which cannot be understood. The dedications on all the poems would have to read "For Ted."

"Survivor," of course, is for my husband. It was written last year [1984], prior to our trip to Hungary with our two daughters. My husband had looked forward to this event with great anxiety. Coincidentally, the day we visited Miskolc marked the fortieth anniversary of the day the Jews of the city were removed from the ghetto and put on trains.

**Vera Weislitz "Roses and the Grave"**: Writing is the only way in which I can talk about the past, the Holocaust. My children urge me to do so. For myself, it is a way to talk to my mother, father, grandmother, to ask them questions I had no chance to ask them while they were alive.

**Betty Wisoff "Sanity"**: "Sanity" is the story of a 13-year-old and his experience in a concentration camp. He witnesses a baby being bayonetted and this marks him for life. The boy, now middle-aged, is my grocery store manager. In telling me what he had seen, he prefaced the tale with an account of his dog's illness and the care he gave it. I thought he was rambling, but he was only trying to equate his love of an animal with the German's cruelty to a defenseless baby.

**David Zucker "Entrance to the Old Cracow Ghetto"**: The poem was germinated from the photograph by Roman Vishniac, with the same title. It was from a series he did, many with camera concealed, just before the Germans invaded Poland in 1939. I know it through his book, *Polish Jews: A Pictorial Record*, with an introductory essay by Abraham Joshua Heschel (Schocken Books, 1947, 1965). Most of the photographs were taken in the Carpathian Mountains. I was struck by this stark and beautiful photo, which reminded me of the light and shadow and mysterious depth that I associate with Central European expressionism. The allusions to [Adolphe] Appia and [Max] Reinhardt are meant to indicate how the photo contains a form that suggests to me an aesthetic life beyond its own crumbling and ominous reality. I think the poem has whatever form it has because I am not obsessed with form but with the photograph—its uncanny commentary on what's missing, the people who are about to be exterminated. The scene, decayed and "classic," waits to be invaded by our imaginations.

# Contributors

**Carol Adler** is an instructor at Northwood Institute in West Palm Beach, Florida; an associate of Smart Services, Inc., a public relations firm; and poetry editor of the *Jewish Ledger*. Her poetry, fiction, and translations have been published in more than two hundred periodicals. Adler's fourth book of poetry, *Split Prisms*, appeared in 1989. Her husband escaped from Germany in 1939.

**Fran Adler** teaches creative writing at San Diego State University. Her first book, *Struggle to Be Borne*, was published in 1988 by San Diego State University Press. Adler had two collaborative exhibitions (poetry and photography) traveling the country: "Home Street Home" (1984), which deals with homelessness, and "Struggle to Be Borne" (1987), which concerns childbirth and poverty. Her husband is a survivor.

**Mari Alschuler** is a poet and therapist who lives and works in New York City. Her poetry has been published in the *American Poetry Review*, *Shenandoah*, and *Hellcoal Review*. She has taught writing and Holocaust literature at synagogues and Jewish centers.

**Inge Auerbacher** is the author of *I Am a Star—Child of the Holocaust* (Prentice-Hall Books for Young Readers, 1987), which tells the story of her childhood when, from age seven to ten (1942-1945), she was imprisoned with her parents in Terezin in Czechoslavakia. She was one of only one hundred children—of fifteen thousand—to survive this camp. Auerbacher appeared in "Childhood Memories of the Holocaust," a TV documentary (1985), and gave the memorial speech in Goeppingen, Germany, on 9 November 1988 on the fiftieth anniversary of Kristallnacht.

**Julius Balbin** is a native of Cracow, Poland. He was interned by the Nazis in the Jewish ghetto of that city and then in four concentration camps, including Mauthausen. He was liberated in 1945 by American troops but lost nearly all of his family in the Holocaust. Balbin has published two books of Holocaust poetry in Esperanto, *Strangled Cries* and *The Bitch of Buchenwald* (Cross-Cultural Communications, 1981 and 1986). In 1989, Edistudio (Pisa, Italy) brought out his collected poetry, *Imperio de l'Koroj* (Empire of the Hearts).

**Willis Barnstone** teaches in the Comparative Literature and Latin American Studies departments at Indiana University. His books include *From This White Island*, *China Poems*, and *Sonnetbook: A Rose in Hell*.

**Marvin Bell** is the author of eight books of poetry, a collection of essays, and, with William Stafford, two volumes of poems written as correspondence. Bell's first book, *A Probable Volume of Dreams* (1969) received the Lamont Prize of the Academy of American Poets. Atheneum published his *New and Selected Poems* in 1987, and a book to include new poems and pages from a journal will be published in 1990 by Alfred A. Knopf. He teaches for the University of Iowa, where he is Flannery O'Connor Professor of Letters.

**Lora Berg** currently works for the U.S. Embassy in Tunis, Tunisia. Her first book, *The Mermaid Wakes*, was released by Macmillan Caribbean in 1989. Her father is one of the few survivors on the Glicksberg side of her family.

**Stephen Berg** is the author of *The Daughters*, *With Akhmatova at the Black Gates*, *In It* (University of Illinois Press, 1985) and other books. He edited *Singular Voices* (Avon, 1985) and was cotranslator of *Clouded Sky* by Miklos Radnoti (Ohio University Press, 1972). He coedits the *American Poetry Review*.

**Michael Blumenthal** was born in 1949 to Jewish refugee parents and grew up in a German-speaking home in the Washington Heights section of Manhattan. He is the author of four books of poetry: *Sympathetic Magic* (1980), *Days We Would Rather*

CONTRIBUTORS

*Know* (1984), *Laps* (1984), and *Against Romance* (1987). Blumenthal is director of the Creative Writing Program at Harvard University.

**George Bogin** (1920-1988) was the author of *In a Surf of Strangers* (University Presses of Florida, 1981) and a book-length translation, *Selected Poems and Reflections on the Art of Poetry*, by the Franco-Uruguayan writer, Jules Supervielle (SUN Press, 1985). His poems have also appeared in many literary magazines and anthologies, including the *American Poetry Review, Paris Review*, the *Nation, Ploughshares*, and *Chicago Review.*

**Emily Borenstein** is the author of *Cancer Queen* and *Night of the Broken Glass* (Timberline Press, 1981), a book-length collection of poems on the Holocaust. She is employed as a psychiatric social worker in the Partial Hospitalization Program at Middletown Psychiatric Center (Middletown, New York).

**Van K. Brock** is codirector of the Writing Program at Florida State University in Tallahassee. His books include *The Hard Essential Landscape* and *The Window*, and he has completed a book-length volume of poetry on the Holocaust, *Unspeakable Strangers.*

**Olga Cabral** has published poems in numerous journals and anthologies and, in 1986, a selection of her poems was translated into Russian and published in an anthology of contemporary American writers that was printed in the USSR for Russian readers. Her books include *The Evaporated Man, The Darkness in My Pockets*, and *In the Empire of Ice* (West End Press, 1980). Cabral is the widow of the American Yiddish poet Aaron Kurtz.

**Esther Cameron** was born in New York in 1941, and her background is a mix of Protestant and Catholic influences. She became a Jew in 1978 and, since 1979, has lived mainly in Israel, where a collection of her poems, *A Gradual Light*, was published in 1983—in Simon Halkin's Hebrew translation.

**Joan Campion** is the author of *In the Lion's Mouth: Gisi Fleischmann and the Jewish Fight for Survival.* Campion is contributing editor of *Arts Alive!* magazine and freelances for several other publications.

**James William Chichetto** has published three books of poetry. His work has appeared in many publications, among them the *Colorado Review,* the *Manhattan Review,* the *Boston Globe,* and *Anthology of Magazine Verse and Yearbook of American Poetry.* He is a priest of the Congregation of Holy Cross and currently teaches in the Writing Department at Stonehill College in North Easton, Massachusetts.

**John Ciardi** (1916-1986) was poetry editor of *Saturday Review* and professor of English at Rutgers University. His books include *Thirty-nine Poems, This Strangest Everything, and Selected Poems* (1984). He edited *Mid-Century American Poets* (1950) and translated Dante's *Divine Comedy.*

**Vince Clemente** is a founding editor of *Long Pond Review, West Hills Review,* and *John Hall Wheelock Review* and edited *A John Ciardi Festschrift* (University of Arkansas Press, 1986). His books include *Snow Owl above Stony Brook Harbor* and *Songs from Puccini,* both from Four Rivers Press.

**Helen Degan Cohen** (Halina Degenfisz) was born in Poland. Her family fled to Lida, Byelorussia, when the war began but were soon incarcerated in a ghetto. For a time, she survived with the help of her father and, later, she was hidden by a Catholic woman in the country while her parents worked in the Underground. After the war, they were reunited and returned to Warsaw only to find it demolished. Her work has appeared in *Partisan Review, Concert at Chopin's House: An Anthology of Polish-American Writing,* and in other literary magazines and anthologies. Her novel, *The Edge of the Field,* is based on her childhood during the war.

**Marion Cohen** is a mathematician, mother of five, and author of nine books, the most recent of which are *The Sitting-Down Hug* (The Liberal Press, 1989) and

CONTRIBUTORS

*Counting to Zero: Poems on Repeated Miscarriage* (Center for Thanatology Research, 1989). She is also the editor of three poetry anthologies, one on the loss of babies. Cohen leads a math anxiety workshop at Temple University.

**M. Truman Cooper** has had her work appear in more than forty magazines, including *Poetry Northwest, Blueline,* and the *Bloomsbury Review.* She teaches reading for "Roots & Wings," a literary program for adults.

**R. M. Cooper** has published poetry, short stories, essays, and reviews, and he is the author of three books of nonfiction and a book-length sequence of poems on the Holocaust—from which the Eli and Rebecca sections, included in this anthology, are drawn.

**Stanley Cooperman** (1929-1976) was born in Brooklyn, New York. He taught at Indiana University, the University of Oregon, Hofstra University, and, finally, at Simon Fraser University in Vancouver, Canada. Cooperman published four volumes of poetry and one critical work, *World War I and the American Novel.* He committed suicide in 1976.

**Susan Dambroff** is a poet, performer, and teacher living in San Francisco. Most recently, she has written and presented a one-woman performance piece entitled *Wind, Shoes, and a Paper House* that deals with a woman's struggle with the loss of a friend to AIDS. Dambroff also works as a special education teacher. Her book of poetry, *Memory in Bone* (Black Oyster Press, 1984), includes poems on the Holocaust.

**Sister Mary Philip de Camara,** V.H.M., works with the president of Georgetown Visitation Preparatory School in Washington, D.C., which is where she taught English (1963-1983). With Stephen Hayes, Sister Mary Philip coauthored the Monarch Notes study guide on Conan Doyle's Sherlock Holmes stories and another on the four novels with Holmes. She has written poems and articles for the *Baker Street Journal,* and her poetry also has appeared in the *Christian Poetry Journal,* the *Black Warrior Review, Wings,* and in several anthologies.

**Theodore Deppe** is the author of a collection of poems, *Necessary Journeys* (Andrew Mountain Press, 1988) and has published in *Southern Poetry Review, Beloit Poetry Journal, Kansas Quarterly,* and elsewhere. A new book of poetry, *Children of the Air,* was published by Alice James Books in 1989.

**Diana Der Hovanessian** is president of the New England Poetry Club. She has translated and coedited (with Marzbed Margossian) the *Anthology of Armenian Poetry* (Columbia University Press, 1978), *Sacred Wrath,* poems of Tekeyan, and other books. Her book of poems, *How to Choose Your Past* (Ararat Press), was published in 1978.

**Catherine de Vinck** was born in Brussels and spent four years under the German Occupation. She has published a number of books, including *Ikon, A Book of Common Prayer,* and *News of the World in Fifteen Stations.* De Vinck was a speaker at the Fourth Holocaust Conference at Kent State University in 1985 and, in the same year, was commissioned by Regis College to write the text of "Cantata for Peace."

**Owen Dodson** (1914-1983) was born in Brooklyn, New York. He was professor of drama at Howard University, a lecturer at Vassar, Kenyon College, and Cornell University, and poet-in-residence at the Ruth Stephen Poetry Center of the University of Arizona (1969). His books include *Powerful Long Ladder* (1946) and *Come Home Early, Child* (1977).

**Olga Drucker** is now working on her second book dealing with the generational experience of Jews in Germany. Her articles have been published in numerous periodicals, and her poem, "America, My Home," was included in the New Poetry Forum *Americana Anthology* (1976). In June 1989, she attended the fifty-year reunion in London of the former Children's Transport children.

**Shelley Ehrlich** (1931-1988) was a psychiatric social worker, teacher, and editor, in addition to being a poet. Her poetry was widely published in small press journals, and two books of her poetry, *How the Rooted Travel* and *Dreaming the Ark*, were published by Juniper Press. At the time of her death, she was preparing a third volume of poetry, which will also be published by Juniper Press.

**Kenneth Fearing** (1902-1961) was a poet and novelist whose published work included *Angel Arms* (1929), *Dead Reckoning* (1938), and *New and Selected Poems* (1956), as well as the novels *Dagger of the Mind* (1941) and *The Big Clock* (1946), which was produced as a motion picture in 1948.

**Frederick Feirstein** has published four books of poetry, including *Survivors* (1975) and *Family History* (1986), which won the Quarterly Review of Literature's Colladay Prize. One of the founders of the Expansive Poetry Movement, Feirstein edited *Expansive Poetry: The New Narrative and the New Formalism* (1989). He is a practicing psychoanalyst in Manhattan and a supervisor at the National Psychological Association for Psychoanalysis.

**Irving Feldman** is a professor of English at the State University of New York at Buffalo. His book of poetry, *The Pripet Marshes*, was nominated for the National Book Award, as was *Leaping Clear*. His most recent collections are *New and Selected Poems* (1979), *Teach Me, Dear Sister* (1985), and *All of Us Here* (1986), all from Viking-Penguin.

**Ruth Feldman** lives in Cambridge, Massachusetts, with a long annual sojourn in Italy. She has published three books of her own poetry and ten books of translations from the Italian. Her translations of Primo Levi's concentration camp stories were published in 1986 by Summit/Simon & Schuster with the title *Moments of Reprieve*, and Levi's *Collected Poems* was released by Faber & Faber (England and the United States) in 1989.

**Frank Finale** is editor of *Without Halos* magazine and is one of the founding members of the Ocean County Poets Collective. He teaches in the Toms River Regional Schools in New Jersey. Finale's poems have appeared in *New York Quarterly, Negative Capability, Dekalb Literary Arts Journal*, and elsewhere.

**Charles Fishman** is director of the Visiting Writers Program at the State University of New York College of Technology at Farmingdale and Distinguished Service Professor in the State University of New York. He was series editor of the Water Mark Poets of North America Award (1980-1983) and cofounder of the Long Island Poetry Collective. Fishman's most recent book of poetry, *The Death Mazurka*, was published by Timberline Press in 1987 and reprinted by Texas Tech University Press in 1989.

**Tamara Fishman** wrote the poem included in this anthology when she was thirteen (1985). She is now in the Honors Program at Tulane University in New Orleans.

**Ephim Fogel** was born in Odessa, Russia, in 1920 and came to the United States in 1923. He served in the U.S. Army in World War II and has taught at Cornell University since 1949. Fogel's poems have appeared in *Atlantic Monthly, The Oxford Book of War Poetry, Poetry*, and in other journals and anthologies. He is completing a book of translations from the work of Osip Mandelshtam.

**Carolyn Forché** received the Yale Series of Younger Poets Award for her first book of poems, *Gathering the Tribes* (Yale University Press, 1976). Her second book, *The Country between Us*, was published by Copper Canyon Press in 1981 and reprinted by Harper & Row in 1982. Forché is currently an associate professor at George Mason University. She is at work on a new book, tentatively titled *The Angel of History*, from which the segment included here is excerpted.

**Robert A. Frauenglas** has served as executive director of the Committee for the Absorption of Soviet Emigrés and assistant national coordinator of the Center for Russian Jewry/Student Struggle for Soviet Jewry. He was founder and president of

CONTRIBUTORS

Somrie Press and edited *Brooklyn Prospects: The First Brooklyn Book Fair Anthology* (1984). His book *The Eclectic Musings of a Brooklyn Bum* was published in 1980.

**Florence W. Freed** worked for many years as a clinical psychologist and then as professor of psychology at Middlesex Community College in Bedford, Massachusetts. Her poetry and short stories have appeared in the *Lincoln Review,* the *Jewish Spectator, Agada,* and other periodicals and anthologies. Freed has also published articles on battered wives and on corporal punishment. Her husband is a Holocaust survivor.

**Mike Frenkel** teaches English at George Westinghouse Vocational and Technical High School in Brooklyn, New York. He also serves as associate director for Project Care. Frenkel has written a novel, *The Rest Is Silence,* which deals with the effects of the Holocaust on a child of survivors.

**Sari Friedman** is from a family that escaped from Nazi Germany. She is a poet and short story writer and has published in such magazines as the *Manhattan Poetry Review* and *Stroker.*

**Carol Ganzer** has had her poetry published in *Spoon River Quarterly, Mississippi Valley Review,* the *Madison Review,* and other magazines. She was born and raised in Chicago.

**Patricia Garfinkel** has published work in *Seattle Review,* the *Hollins Critic, Visions International,* and in many other periodicals and anthologies. In addition, she has published a chapbook, *Ram's Horn,* and has translated a series of poems into Korean and published in Korea's literary journal, *Simsang* (Images).

**Kinereth Gensler** is the author of two books of poetry, *Without Roof* (1981) and *Threesome Poems* (1976), both from Alice James Books. She is coauthor of *The Poetry Connection: An Anthology of Contemporary Poems with Ideas to Stimulate Children's Writing* (Teachers & Writers Collaborative, 1978). Her poems have appeared in *Massachusetts Review, Ploughshares, Virginia Quarterly Review,* and in other major literary periodicals.

**Jacob Glatstein** (1896-1971) published sixteen books of poetry—including *Songs of Remembrance* (1943), *Radiant Jews* (1946), and *Down-to-Earth Talk* (1956)—in addition to seven collections of essays and criticism, and four novels. He came to the United States from Poland at seventeen and lived and wrote in New York City until his death. With A. Leyeles and N. B. Minkov, Glatstein was coeditor of the important Introspectivist anthology, *In Zikh* (1930). He was the recipient of numerous literary prizes for his work.

**Gloria Glickstein** is a freelance writer and editor. She lives in New York City and works as editorial director at the Cooper Union for the Advancement of Science and Art. Glickstein is also associate editor of *Boulevard* magazine and has published in *Boulevard, Arrival, Hubbub,* and other literary reviews. Her parents and in-laws are Holocaust survivors.

**Barbara Goldberg** received the 1987 Camden Poetry Award for *Cautionary Tales* (The Walt Whitman Center for the Arts and Humanities, 1989) and is the author of *Berta Broadfoot and Pepin the Short: A Merovingian Romance* (The Word Works, 1986). Her translations of the Israeli poet, Moshe Dor, received the Armand G. Erpf Award from Columbia University's Translation Center (1988), and her own poetry has appeared in the *American Scholar, Antioch Review, NER/BLQ,* and elsewhere. Goldberg's cousins and her maternal grandmother perished at Auschwitz, and her uncle is a survivor.

**Thomas A. Goldman** served as a radar mechanic in the Air Force in World War II, and later he was in the U.S. Foreign Service. As vice consul in Rotterdam, he interviewed survivors seeking to emigrate to the United States.

**Jorie Graham** teaches at the Writers Workshop of the University of Iowa. She has published two books of poetry with Princeton University Press—*Hybrids of Plants* *and Ghosts* (1980) and *Erosion* (1983)—and has a third volume, *The End of Beauty*, from Ecco Press (1987).

**Ber Green** (1901-1989) was born in Russia and came to the United States in 1923. His books of Yiddish poetry include *Flowers Under Snow* (1939) and *Ever-Green* (1965). Green was a founder of the Proletpen, a group of leftist poets of the twenties and thirties. He also founded the Yiddish Cultural Alliance and coedited the anthology *Union Square*. His memoirs, *Blood, Fire, and Pillars of Smoke*, appeared in English in 1985.

**Luba Krugman Gurdus** is an artist, author, and art historian who survived the World War II German occupation of Poland. Her drawings now form part of the permanent collection at Yad Vashem. Gurdus is the author of *The Death Train: A Personal Account of a Holocaust Survivor* (1978) and *Painful Echoes: Poems of the Holocaust* (1985). She lectures on Holocaust art and is coeditor of *Voice of the Woman Survivor*. In 1986, she received the Louis E. Yavner First Citizen Award from the State University of New York at Albany for her "distinguished contributions to education about the Holocaust and other violations of human rights."

**John Z. Guzlowski** is the son of parents who survived the war in a concentration camp in Germany. He came to America with them, as displaced persons, in 1951. Guzlowski's poems have appeared in *Blue Unicorn, Mr. Cogito, Concert at Chopin's House* (New Rivers Press), and elsewhere. He is a professor of English at Eastern Illinois University.

**Nathan Halper** (1908-1983) was an authority on James Joyce and a translator from Yiddish. He served as advisory editor of the University of Oklahoma's *James Joyce Quarterly* and was cochairman of the Second Provincetown James Joyce Symposium (1983). Halper's books include *The Early James Joyce* and *Studies in Joyce* (University Microfilms International, 1983).

**Leo Hamalian** is a professor of English at the City College of New York and editor of *Ararat*, a quarterly of arts and letters. He is the author of *Burn after Reading* and *As Others See Us* and coeditor of *The Roots of Black Drama* (Wayne State University Press, 1989). Hamalian's poems and articles have appeared in a wide variety of national publications, among them the *Journal of Modern Literature* and *Present Tense*. Both his parents escaped from Turkey before the outbreak of World War I.

**Cecile Hamermesh** has published work in several small press magazines and regional journals and newspapers. She is the oldest child of survivors of the Lódz ghetto, Auschwitz, Bergen-Belsen, and Dachau.

**Deborah Hanan** lives in Bronxville, New York, with her two children and husband, and recently began studying Khmer with the hope of translating, with Khmer friends, Cambodian poetry.

**Annette Bialik Harchik** is an administrative assistant in public relations, a Yiddish and Jewish history teacher, and a poet. She has been poetry editor of *Response* and is the house manager of The Writer's Voice Authors' Readings at the Sixty-third Street YMCA in Manhattan. Harchik is an original member of the Jewish Women's Poetry Project and a cofounder of the Poetry Kibbutz. Her poems appear in such periodicals and anthologies as *Ghosts of the Holocaust* (Wayne State University Press, 1989), *Sarah's Daughters Sing* (Ktav Publishing House, 1989), and *Dialogue*. She is the daughter of Polish Jewish survivors.

**Anthony Hecht** was awarded the Pulitzer Prize in poetry for *The Hard Hours* (1967). His other books include *Millions of Strange Shadows* (1977), *The Venetian Vespers* (1980), *Obbligati: Essays in Criticism* (1986), and *Transparent Man* (1990). He currently teaches at Georgetown University in Washington, D.C.

**Leslie Woolf Hedley** has published eight books of poetry—most recently, *Watchman, What of the Night* (Embassy Hall Editions, 1988)—and two books of short stories, *The Day Japan Bombed Pearl Harbor* and *XYZ and Other Stories*. He is publisher of Exile Press, Sonoma, California, and has edited *Contemporary American Satire* and other anthologies.

**Julie N. Heifetz** was cofounder and director of the Child Development Project of the St. Louis Psychoanalytic Institute (1978-1982), and she is currently writer-in-residence for the St. Louis Center for Holocaust Studies. Her books are *Jordie's Present* (fiction) and *Oral History and the Holocaust* (Pergamon Press, 1985).

**William Heyen** is the author of *Lord Dragonfly; Long Island Light: Poems and a Memoir; The Chestnut Rain; Brockport, New York: Beginning with "And"*; and *Erika: Poems of the Holocaust* (Vanguard, 1984). He is a professor of English at the State University of New York at Brockport.

**Edward Hirsch** is the author of *For the Sleepwalkers* (1981), *Wild Gratitude* (1986), and *The Night Parade* (1989), all from Knopf. His poems appear regularly in *Poetry*, the *Atlantic*, the *New Yorker*, and other major periodicals. Hirsch teaches English at Wayne State University in Detroit.

**Barbara Helfgott Hyett** teaches English at Boston University. Her collection, *In Evidence: Poems of the Liberation of Nazi Concentration Camps*, was published by the University of Pittsburgh Press in 1986. A second collection of poems, *Natural Law*, is forthcoming. Hyett's poems have appeared in the *Nation*, the *New Republic*, and the *Women's Review of Books*.

**David Ignatow** has published fourteen books of poetry, including *The Gentle Weightlifter* (1955), *Rescue the Dead* (1968), *Tread the Dark* (1978), and *New and Collected Poems: 1970-1985* (Wesleyan University Press, 1986), and he has also published three volumes of prose. Ignatow is professor emeritus, City University of New York, and president emeritus of the Poetry Society of America.

**Judith Irwin** is a retired teacher of English and humanities. She has completed a book entitled *The Dispossessed: The Cowlitz Indians of Southwest Washington*, and her poetry has appeared in the *Bellingham Review, Bitterroot, Negative Capability*, and other periodicals. Her husband served in World War II with an American military police unit in Germany.

**Katherine Janowitz** was born in Trencín Teplice, Czechoslovakia, in 1946. Her parents were sent to a labor camp in 1942, but they escaped in 1944 and hid in the woods of Slovakia until the war ended. Janowitz's poetry and short stories have appeared in *Ms., Partisan Review*, and elsewhere.

**Randall Jarrell** (1914-1965) was born in Nashville, Tennessee. His books of poetry include *Blood from a Stranger* (1942), *Losses* (1948), and *The Lost World* (1966). He taught at Kenyon College, Sarah Lawrence, and the Women's College of the University of North Carolina (Greensboro). Jarrell's highly regarded book of criticism, *Poetry and the Age*, was published in 1953.

**Laurence Josephs** has published four collections of poetry: *Cold Water Morning, Six Elegies, The Skidmore Poems,* and *New and Selected Poems* (Copley Publishing Group, 1988). His work has appeared in various anthologies and in *Southern Review, Poetry*, the *New Yorker*, and elsewhere. He is a professor of English and resident poet at Skidmore.

**Hans Juergensen** is a professor of humanities at the University of South Florida and the author of fifteen books of poetry, including most recently *Testimony: Selected Poems, 1954-1986* (University of South Florida Press, 1989). From 1976 to 1980, he was a consultant to the Nobel Prize Committee on Literature. Juergensen served in the U.S. Army during World War II; saw combat in Italy, including Sicily; and was buried alive and left for dead at Anzio.

**Marc Kaminsky** has published *Daily Bread* (University of Illinois Press, 1982), *A Table with People* (Sun Press, 1982), and *The Road from Hiroshima* (Simon & Schuster, 1984). He is director of the Institute on Humanities, Arts, and Aging at the Brookdale Center on Aging at Hunter College in Manhattan.

**Peretz Kaminsky** is the author of *Reflections in the Eye of God* (1969) and *The Book of Questions* (1972). From 1952 to 1967, many of his poems written in Yiddish appeared in a variety of Yiddish publications in North and South America.

**Rosa Felsenburg Kaplan** was born in Vienna and is a Holocaust survivor and the child of survivors. She is a social worker and mental health educator. Kaplan's poems have appeared in *Shirim, Jewish Frontier, Voices Israel,* and other periodicals, and in *Women Speak* (Women's Institute for Continuing Jewish Education, 1987).

**Laura Kasischke** was a student at the University of Michigan when she wrote the poem included in this anthology. She is from Grand Rapids, Michigan.

**Dori Katz** is a professor of French and comparative literature at Trinity College in Hartford, Connecticut. She has translated poetry by Norge, Guillevic, Eluard, and Max Jacob, as well as three books by Marguerite Yourcenar. Katz was born in Belgium in 1939 and survived the war in hiding with a Catholic family and in a home for orphans. Her father died in Auschwitz. She and her mother immigrated to America in 1952.

**Melanie Kaye/Kantrowitz** is the author of *Some Pieces of Jewish Left: Secular Tales for Modern Times* (1990). Her poems, essays, and stories have appeared in *Nice Jewish Girls, Off Our Backs, Lesbian Poetry,* and elsewhere. She edits *Sinister Wisdom* and, with Irena Klepfisz, coedited a special double issue, *The Tribe of Dina: A Jewish Women's Anthology* (1989). Kaye/Kantrowitz is active in Middle East peace work.

**Miriam Kessler** has published poems in the *Alchemist* (Canada), *Peregrine,* and *River Styx,* and in a variety of anthologies. She trained as an actress at Hedgerow Theatre, the oldest repertory theater in the United States, and she has worked as a staff writer for the *Patriot* and *Evening News,* in Harrisburg, Pennsylvania. She is currently at work on a biography of the late Isabella Gardner.

**Irena Klepfisz** was born in Warsaw in 1941 and is a Holocaust survivor. She came to the United States in 1949. Klepfisz is the author of *Keeper of Accounts, Different Enclosures: The Poetry and Prose of Irena Klepfisz* (Onlywomen Press, 1985), and coeditor of *The Tribe of Dina: A Jewish Women's Anthology* (Beacon Press, 1989). An activist in both the Jewish and lesbian-feminist communities, she has taught English, Yiddish, and women's studies and, in 1989, she served as translator-in-residence at YIVO Institute for Jewish Research in Manhattan.

**David Koenig** is the author of a book of poetry, *Green Whistle* (William Caxton, Ltd., 1988), and has taught English and creative writing at Oakton Community College in Des Plaines, Illinois, since 1971. Koenig was a Fulbright lecturer in West Germany in 1975. His parents fled from Vienna in 1939.

**Yala Korwin,** author of *To Tell the Story: Poems of the Holocaust* (Holocaust Library, 1987), was born in Lwów, Poland. She spent from 1942 until 1945 in a German labor camp and, with her family, immigrated to the United States in 1956. She has worked in New York as a commercial sculptor. Her index to reproductions of art in books was selected by the American Library Association as one of the outstanding reference works for 1981.

**Aaron Kramer,** author of *On the Way to Palermo, Carousel Parkway, In the Suburbs* (Ali Baba Press, 1986), and other collections of poetry, is also a translator from German and Yiddish. He has published *The Poetry and Prose of Heinrich Heine* and *A Century of Yiddish Poetry* (Cornwall Books, 1989). Kramer also translated *The Emperor of Atlantis,* a death-camp opera that premiered in 1977. He is professor of English at Dowling College on Long Island.

**Norbert Krapf** has published seven poetry collections, including *Lines Drawn from Dürer* and *A Dream of Plum Blossoms.* He is also the editor of *Under Open Sky: Poets on William Cullen Bryant; Stories They Wanted to Tell,* a collection of materials dealing with the German heritage of his native area in southern Indiana, and *Beneath the Cherry Sapling: Legends from Franconia* (Fordham University Press, 1988).

**Carolyn Kreiter-Kurylo** is a painter, sculptor, and poet, who works as a language arts and writing resource teacher for Fairfax County Public Schools and as an adjunct professor for George Mason University, where she teaches graduate poetry courses to teachers. Her poems and articles on writing have appeared in numerous publications, including *Antioch Review, Prairie Schooner,* and *Mid-American Review,* and her first volume of poems, *Contrary Visions,* was published in 1988 by Scripta Humanistica.

**J. L. Kubicek** is a disabled World War II veteran, who has worked for a quarter of a century in the fields of correction and welfare. His poems have appeared in many U.S. and Canadian journals, including *Arizona Quarterly, Bogg, Colorado North Review,* and *Jewish Spectator.* His chapbooks are *Flemish Light* (1984) and *From the Olduvai* (Pentagram Press, 1989).

**Maxine Kumin,** author of *Up-Country: Poems of New England* (1973), which received the Pulitzer Prize in poetry, has also published *To Make a Prairie: Essays on Poets, Poetry, and Country Living* (1979), *Closing the Ring* (1984), *In Deep: Country Essays* (1987), and *Nurture* (1989), the last two from Viking-Penguin.

**Aaron Kurtz** (1891-1964) was born near Vitebsk, Russia, and immigrated to the United States in 1911. He published eight books of Yiddish poetry, including *Khaos* (Chaos) in 1920, *Marc Chagall* in 1947, and *Lider* (Poems) in 1966. He was associated first with the *Insichist* group of modern Yiddish poets and later with the proletarian poets. Kurtz died of cancer in 1964.

**Christine Lahey** is a composition specialist and an adjunct assistant professor at the Center for Creative Studies at the College of Art and Design in Detroit. Her chapbook *Sticks and Stones* was published in 1980 by Urban Despair Press. Other work has appeared in the *Ohio Journal, Michigan Quarterly Review,* and *All's Normal Here: A Charles Bukowski Primer* (Ruddy Duck Press, 1985). Lahey is the former editor of the *Wayne Review* and (with Kurt Nimmo) coeditor of *Planet Detroit: An Anthology of Urban Poetry* (1983).

**Carole Glasser Langille** has published work in *Partisan Review, Centennial Review,* and *North Dakota Quarterly.* She lives with her husband and children in rural Nova Scotia.

**Cornel Adam Lengyel** has written *Four Days in July: The Story behind the Declaration of Independence, Fire Watch* (poetry), and *The Shadow Trap* (drama). He lives in Georgetown, California.

**Denise Levertov** was born in Ilford, Essex, England, and came to the United States in 1948. Her many books of poetry include *The Jacob's Ladder, Relearning the Alphabet, Candles in Babylon,* and *Breathing the Water* (New Directions, 1987). She has also published a translation of Guillevic's poetry, *Selected Poems,* and two prose works, *The Poet in the World* and *Light Up the Cave.* Levertov helped initiate the writers and artists protest against the Vietnam War.

**Philip Levine** has published *Not This Pig* (1968); *The Names of the Lost* (1976); *Ashes: Poems New and Old,* which received the National Book Critics Circle Award in 1979; *A Walk with Tom Jefferson* (Knopf, 1988), which won the Bay Area Book Reviewers Association Award for best poetry book of the year; and other books. He teaches creative writing at California State University at Fresno.

**Leatrice H. Lifshitz** has edited *Her Soul beneath the Bone* (University of Illinois Press, 1988) and was the founder of Rockland Poets and the Rockland County Haiku Society. Her poems have appeared in such journals as *Dragonfly, Parnassus, Stone Country,* and *Shirim,* and in a variety of anthologies, including *I Name Myself Daughter* (1981), *Poets for Africa* (1986), and *The Women's Encampment* (1987).

**Abraham Linik** is a Holocaust survivor, whose parents, brother, and sister were all victims of the Holocaust. His poems have appeared in such periodicals as *Bitterroot, Hadoar,* and *Judaism.* He is a school principal and real estate agent and lives in Needham, Massachusetts.

**Geraldine Clinton Little** is past vice president of the Poetry Society of America and past president of the Haiku Society of America. Her work has been published in about 350 literary journals, and she is represented in *Eigo Haiku,* by Hiroaki Sato, the first book on English-language haiku poets published in Japan. Little's books include *A Well-Tuned Harp; Heloise and Abelard: A Verse Play; Hakugai: Poem from a Concentration Camp,* a book-length narrative on the incarceration of Japanese-Americans during World War II; and *Contrasts in Keening: Ireland.*

**Alan Lupack** edits the *Round Table: A Journal of Poetry and Fiction* and *Avalon to Camelot,* a journal devoted to Arthurian studies. His poems and stories have appeared in dozens of literary magazines, including *Aileron,* the *Third Wind,* and *Slipstream.* Lupack is also curator of the Rossell Hope Robbins Library of medieval studies at the University of Rochester in Rochester, New York, and editor of *Arthur, the Greatest King: An Anthology of Modern Arthurian Poetry.* His wife lost members of her family during the Holocaust.

**Yaacov Luria** served in the Army Air Corps (1943-1946). He has taught courses in creative writing and contemporary literature at Fordham University and has worked as the New York theatre critic for the *Baltimore Jewish Times.* Luria is the author of one book of poetry, *Not a Piano Key,* and has published short stories, poems, essays, reviews, and other work in a wide range of periodicals and anthologies, including the *New Yorker, Harper's,* the *Saturday Review,* the *Christian Science Monitor, Moment,* and the *Los Angeles Times.*

**Arnost Lustig** was born in Prague in 1926 and, as a teenager, was sent with his parents to Theresienstadt, then to Auschwitz, where his father died in the gas chamber, and then to Buchenwald. He came to the United States in 1970 and is now a citizen. His books published in English include *Darkness Casts No Shadows* and *Dita Saxova.*

**Josef Lustig** has published essays, reviews, and translations in *Yale Review, World Literature Today* (University of Oklahoma, 1983), *Encountering the Holocaust* (1979), and in other books and periodicals. Lustig is well known as a film researcher, screenwriter, cinematographer, and director. His credits include work on documentaries, including *Precious Legacy* (1985), *The Mafia on Trial* (1986), and *Arab and Jew* (1988), as well as on Hollywood productions, including *The World According to Garp* and *Ragtime.*

**Arlene Maass** has published poems in Israel and the United States, in *Jewish Currents, Voices Israel,* and *Concert at Chopin's House: A Polish-American Anthology.* With her husband, the Rev. Eliezer Maass, she resides in Skokie, Illinois, where she is a contributing editor at *Cornerstone.* Recently, she created a newsletter for young writers called *Chicago Poetry Factory.*

**Lois Mathieu** has published poetry in *Calyx,* the *Portland Review,* and other periodicals. She is employed as manager of customer documentation for Konica Business Machines.

**David McKain** is a professor of English at the University of Connecticut. His books and monographs include *Christianity: Some Non-Christian Appraisals* (1965), *The Common Life* (Alice James Books, 1982), and *Spellbound: Growing Up in God's Country* (University of Georgia Press, 1987), which was nominated for the National Book Award and the Pulitzer Prize.

**Bert Meyers** (1928-1979) was born in Los Angeles. He taught English and comparative literature at Pitzer College in Claremont, California. Meyers's books include *The Wild Olive Tree, Sunlight on the Wall,* and *The Dark Birds.*

**Robert Mezey** teaches at Pomona College and the Claremont Graduate School. His first book, *The Lovemaker,* won the Lamont Poetry Award in 1960. Other books include *White Blossoms, The Door Standing Open, Selected Translations,* and, most recently, *Evening Wind* (Wesleyan University Press), which was awarded the Bassine Citation and a special prize from PEN West. Syracuse University Press published Mezey's translation of César Vallejo's 1931 novel *Tungsten* in 1989.

**Richard Michelson** has published *Tapdancing for the Relatives,* which was published in 1985 by the University Presses of Florida. He has taught in the Goddard MFA writing program at Vermont College and has published work in *Nimrod, Bellingham Review, Jewish Currents,* and other magazines. Michelson is the owner of art galleries in Amherst and Northampton, Massachusetts.

**Bernard S. Mikofsky** has taught Russian and other Slavic languages and also Romance languages, at Kent State, Indiana University, and elsewhere. From 1943 to 1946, he served as a Signal Corps intelligence officer. He has published articles on Slavic philology and linguistics and currently writes op-ed pieces for the Bethlehem, Pennsylvania, *Sunday Globe* and other newspapers.

**Aaron Miller** is executive director of Universities Field Staff International, an educational corporation engaged in research and publication in international affairs. He has lived and worked abroad for extended periods and is the author of three books of poetry.

**Marilyn Mohr** was formerly managing editor of Aesopus Press, Woodstock, New York. She was coeditor of *The Catskill Poets' Series* and the *Woodstock Poetry Review* and edited *Rising,* an anthology of New Jersey poets (1987). She is the author of a chapbook of poems, *Running the Track,* and is represented in the anthology, *Sarah's Daughters Sing* (K'tav, 1989) and in other anthologies and periodicals. Mohr is currently coordinator of The Poets' Forum in West Orange, New Jersey.

**Teresa Moszkowicz-Syrop** was born in Poland. Except for her only brother, her family perished in concentration camps. After the war, she was reunited with him in the USSR and later emigrated, with her husband, to the United States. Her poem "In the Park" was published by J. Campbell in *Most Beloved Poems.*

**Elaine Mott** has published poems in *Cincinnati Poetry Review, Black Ice, Cutbank,* and *Wind.* She lives in Bayside, New York.

**Gerald Musinsky** has taught writing at the University of Pittsburgh Writing Lab, the University of Arizona, and elsewhere. He also has served as an assistant editor of *Israel Perspective.* His collection of poetry, *Steel Living,* was published by Compad International (Pittsburgh).

**Mark Nepo** won the 1987 Ithaca House Series competition for his first book of poems, *God, the Maker of the Bed, and the Painter,* (Greenfield Review Press, 1988). His second book, *Fire without Witness* (British American, 1988), is an epic poem centered on Michelangelo and the stories of the Biblical characters he painted in the Sistine Chapel ceiling. Nepo's poems have appeared in *Antaeus, Kenyon Review, Sewanee Review,* and in other literary journals.

**Amos Neufeld** is an Israeli-born child of survivors and considers himself a dislocated Israeli writer who happens to write in English about home and exile. His poems have appeared in many literary journals and anthologies, and his film reviews and articles—often concerning the Holocaust—have been published in a variety of magazines and newspapers.

**Estelle Gershgoren Novak** was born in 1940 in Detroit, the child of immigrant parents from the Russian Pale. Most members of her father's family who remained in the USSR were murdered in the Nazi massacre at Kamenets-Podolsky (1941). Novak's poems have appeared in *West Coast Poetry Review, California Quarterly,* and elsewhere.

413

**Miriam Offenberg** has been a teacher, community relations coordinator, audiovisual specialist, writer, and editor. She serves as president of the Chaucer Guild in New Jersey.

**Gregory Orfalea** is the author of *Before the Flames: A Quest for the History of Arab Americans* (University of Texas Press, 1988) and coeditor (with Sharif Elmusa) of *Grape Leaves: A Century of Arab American Poetry* (University of Utah Press, 1988). His collection of poems, *The Capitol of Solitude*, was a winner of the 1987 Ithaca House Series poetry competition. Orfalea is an editor with the U.S. Small Business Administration in Washington, D.C.

**Gary Pacernick** is a professor of English at Wright State University in Dayton, Ohio. His poems have been published in *American Poetry Review, North American Review, Voices within the Ark: The Modern Jewish Poets,* and *Traveling America with Today's Poets.* His play, *I Want to Write a Jewish Poem,* has been performed on various stages and on public television, and his book of criticism, *Memory and Fire: Ten American Jewish Poets,* was recently published by Peter Lang.

**Linda Pastan** has published seven books of poetry, including *The Five Stages of Grief; PM/AM: New and Selected Poems* (1982); *Fractions of Darkness* (1985), which won the Maurice English Award; and *The Imperfect Paradise* (W. W. Norton, 1988). She lives in Potomac, Maryland, and is on the staff of the Bread Loaf Writer's Conference.

**Monique Pasternak** was born in France in 1942 during the German Occupation and spent the first few years of her life in hiding with her family, some members of whom survived. She is the author of *Flying on the Wings of Aleph, A Poem Is the Sum of a Good Many Prayers,* and *The New Siddur for Co-creators,* and her poems have appeared in a variety of publications. She is a transpersonal therapist and educator and leads workshops at Ocean Star Center on the Mendocino Coast in northern California.

**Mark Pawlak** has been an editor of *Hanging Loose* magazine since 1981 and is a founding member of the October Poetry Theater. His poems and his translations from the German of Brecht and others have appeared widely in magazines and anthologies. Pawlak is the author of two poetry collections—*The Buffalo Sequence* (Copper Canyon) and *All the News* (Hanging Loose)—and he is coeditor (with Dick Lourie) of *Smart Like Me: High School Age Writing from the Sixties to Now* (Hanging Loose, 1989). He teaches mathematics at the University of Massachusetts at Boston.

**Edmund Pennant** has written *I, Too, Jehovah* (Charles Scribner's Sons), *Dream's Navel,* and *Misapprehensions* (1984), both from Lintel, and *The Wildebeest of Carmine Street* (Orchises Press, 1990). Pennant's poems have appeared in *New York Quarterly,* the *American Scholar, Moment,* and numerous other periodicals and anthologies. He teaches creative writing at Adelphi University on Long Island.

**Louis Phillips** is a poet and playwright whose most recent book of poems is *The Time, the Hour, the Solitariness of the Place,* published by Swallow's Tale Press. Broadway Play Publishers has issued his full-length play, *The Envoi Messages.* Phillips teaches creative writing at the School of Visual Arts in New York City.

**Ronald William Pies** is associate clinical professor of psychiatry at Tufts University School of Medicine. He is the author of *Inside Psychotherapy: The Patient's Handbook;* a chapbook of poems, *Lean Soil;* and several short stories on Jewish themes. Pies is currently writing a novel involving the role of women in Jewish scholarship.

**William Pillin** (1910-1985) is the author of *To the End of Time: Poems New and Selected,* published by Papa Bach Editions in 1980. His earlier books include *Theory of Silence* (1949), *Pavane for a Fading Memory* (1963), and *Everything Falling* (1971). He was born in the Ukraine and died in Los Angeles.

**John C. Pine** is a retired librarian who lives with his wife in the Sierra foothills of California. He is the author of five books of poetry, *Block Island, Cliff Walk,*

*Ice-Age, Chinese Camp and Other California Poems,* and, most recently, *Silhouettes at Eventide,* all from Moveable Feast Press.

**Ginger Porter** was a high school student when she wrote "I Am Babi Yar." She was editor of her high school creative writing magazine, *Metanoia,* and received a number of awards for her efforts in the graphic arts.

**David Ray** has published more than a dozen books of poetry. *Sam's Book* (Wesleyan University Press) won the Maurice English Award for 1988. Wesleyan also published his poems about India, *The Maharani's New Wall,* in 1989. Ray's poems have appeared in many literary journals, including *Ploughshares, Poetry,* and the *Iowa Review.* He is professor of English at the University of Missouri—Kansas City, where he edited *New Letters* from 1971 to 1985.

**Richard C. Raymond** (d. 1980) was born and raised in Boston. He joined the United Nations Relief and Rehabilitation Agency in Germany during World War II and helped in the rescue efforts in the camps following liberation. His book, *A Moment of Bells,* was published by Plowshare Press in 1970.

**Norah Reap** is a former English teacher who has been employed as a social worker since 1988. She has been a member of the United States Senate staff, writing speeches on health and education issues, and she currently practices psychotherapy, treating individuals, couples, and families. Reap is a convert to Judaism.

**Naomi Replansky** is a poet whose first book, *Ring Song,* was published by Scribners in 1952 and nominated for the National Book Award in Poetry that year. In 1988, her chapbook, *Twenty-one Poems, Old and New,* was published by Gingko Press. Replansky's poems have appeared widely in anthologies, most recently in *Women on War* (Simon and Schuster, 1988).

**Lisa Ress** was born (as Anneliese Reiss) to Viennese parents in Tangier, Morocco, in 1939. Her first book, *Flight Patterns,* won the 1983 Associated Writing Programs Award in Poetry and was published by the University Press of Virginia in 1985. Ress has taught creative writing at Cornell; the University of California, Irvine; and Hollins College. She is currently an assistant professor of English at Knox College, Galesburg, Pennsylvania.

**Charles Reznikoff** (1894-1976) was one of the Objectivists of the thirties and, for a time, was poetry editor of *Jewish Frontier.* His book-length volume of poetry, *Holocaust,* was published by Black Sparrow Press (1975), which also issued a two-volume definitive edition of Reznikoff's *Complete Poems* (1976-1977).

**Liliane Richman** was born in Paris, the child of a survivor. She moved to the United States in 1959. Her poetry and prose have been published in *Response,* the *Smith, Sackbut Review,* and elsewhere. Richman's doctoral disertation was "Ideology and Themes in the Vietnam Films, 1975-1985." She teaches language arts at the arts magnet high school in Dallas.

**Michael D. Riley** has taught English at Floyd Junior College in Rome, Georgia, where he coedited *Old Red Kimono* (1976-1978). Currently, he is an assistant professor at the Berks Campus of Pennsylvania State University. Riley's poetry has appeared in *Southern Humanities Review, Texas Review, Arizona Quarterly,* and in many other periodicals. His first book-length collection of poems, *Scrimshaw: Citizens of Bone,* was published by Lightning Tree Press in 1988.

**Nicholas Rinaldi** teaches literature and creative writing at Fairfield University. His published books include a novel, *Bridge Fall Down,* and three volumes of poetry. "Auschwitz" is taken from his latest collection, *The Luftwaffe in Chaos,* which deals with the Holocaust and other events of World War II. Rinaldi's poems and short stories have appeared widely in literary journals.

**Charlz Rizzuto** has translated two volumes of Holocaust poetry by Julius Balbin, *Strangled Cries* (1981) and *The Bitch of Buchenwald* (1986), both published by Cross-Cultural Communications.

# CONTRIBUTORS

**Martin Robbins** is a cantor who also teaches writing and editing at the Radcliffe Seminars and the Harvard Extension. Among his books are *A Reply to the Headlines* (Swallow, 1965) and *A Week Like Summer* (X Press, 1979). His dramatic works include "In Praise of Light" and "A Tenor's Vocalise to the Morning in the Century of the Holocaust."

**William Pitt Root** grew up in rural Gulf Coast Florida but has lived in the West ever since. His recent books include *Reasons for Going It on Foot* (1981), *Selected Odes of Pablo Neruda* (Translations, 1986), and *Faultdancing* (1986). He teaches in the University of Montana's MFA program.

**Marina Roscher** was born in Regensburg, Germany, and has worked as a professional translator here and abroad. She is a founding member of the *New York Quarterly* and a contributing editor of other periodicals. Her poetry, translations, scholarly articles, and fiction have appeared in many publications, including *New Letters, Southern Studies,* and *Poetry Canada Review.*

**Max Rosenfeld** has translated about a dozen books of Yiddish poetry, most recently the story of Jewish resistance in the Minsk ghetto, written by Hersh Smolar, a leader of the Jewish underground in that region. He teaches classes in Yiddish culture for Gratz College and for Jewish community centers in Philadelphia.

**Menachem Z. Rosensaft,** an attorney, was born in the displaced persons camp of Bergen-Belsen, West Germany, in 1948. Both his parents survived Auschwitz and Bergen-Belsen. Rosensaft is the president of the Labor Zionist Alliance and founding chairman of the International Network of Children of Jewish Holocaust Survivors. On 5 May 1985, he led the only demonstration at Bergen-Belsen in protest against President Ronald Reagan's visits to both the mass graves of Bergen-Belsen and to Bitburg Cemetery, and he was a key participant in subsequent international actions.

**Larry Rubin** teaches English at Georgia Tech in Atlanta and has published three books of poetry: *The World's Old Way* (1962), *Lanced in Light* (1967), and *All My Mirrors Lie* (Godine, 1975). Since 1956, about 800 of his poems have appeared in a great number of literary journals and in 43 anthologies, including *A Geography of Poets, The Norton Introduction to Poetry* (third edition, 1986), and *The Made Thing: An Anthology of Contemporary Southern Poetry* (University of Arkansas Press, 1986).

**Luada Sandler** has worked as a teacher and social worker and, during World War II, served as a staff aide with the American Red Cross in military hospitals in the European Theater of Operations. More recently, she has been engaged in recording the oral histories of Soviet Jewish emigrés to the United States.

**Reg Saner** won the first Walt Whitman Award from the Academy of American Poets and the Copernicus Society of America (1975) for *Climbing into the Roots* (Harper & Row). His next book, *So This Is the Map* (Random House) was an open competition winner of the National Poetry Series. Saner's most recent collection is *Essay on Air* (Ohio Review Books, 1984). He is Distinguished Research Lecturer at the University of Colorado.

**May Sarton** is the author of over fifty books in four genres: poetry, novel, journal, and memoir. Her most recent titles are *After the Stroke,* a journal, and *The Silence Now,* a volume of poetry, both 1988, and a novel, *The Education of Harriet Hatfield* (1989), all from W. W. Norton. In 1985, *At Seventy: A Journal* was selected for the American Book Award of the Before Columbus Foundation. She has been a Fellow of the American Academy of Arts and Sciences since 1958. Sarton was born in Belgium and came to the United States with her parents in 1916 as refugees from World War I.

**Ruth Lisa Schechter** (1927-1989) was the author of ten books of poetry, the most recent of which is *Many Rooms in a Winter Night* (1989). She was the founder and editor of *Croton Review.* Schechter lived in Croton-on-Hudson, New York.

**David Shapiro** is the author of six volumes of poetry, including *January, Lateness,* and *To an Idea.* His poetry, art, and literary criticism appear regularly in such places as *The New Yorker, Partisan Review,* and *The Paris Review.* A professional violinist in his youth, Shapiro is currently an associate professor of art history at William Paterson College in New Jersy.

**Gregg Shapiro** was born in Chicago and raised in Skokie, Illinois, among survivors of the death camps. His poetry has been published in *Gargoyle, Pearl,* the *Grolier Poetry Prize* anthology (1985), and *Folio,* and in other journals and anthologies.

**Harvey Shapiro** is the author of eight books of poetry, including *Battle Report; This World, Nightsounds,* and *The Light Holds.* His most recent collection is *National Cold Storage Company: New and Selected Poems* (Wesleyan University Press, 1988).

**Reva Sharon** is an American poet living in Jerusalem. Her grandparents emigrated from Europe to the United States, but most of the family who remained in Europe perished in the Holocaust. Sharon's work has appeared in many journals and anthologies, including *Under Open Sky* (Stone House Press and Fordham University Press). Her first book of poetry, *Berekhat Tzefira: Pool of the Early Morning Wind,* was published in Jerusalem in 1989.

**Steven Sher** is the author of four books of poetry, of which *Trolley Lives* (Wampeter Press, 1985) is the most recent. A collection of his short stories, *Man with a Thousand Eyes and Other Stories,* was published in 1989 by Gull Books. Sher was coeditor of *Northwest Variety: Personal Essays by 14 Regional Authors* (Arrow Books, 1987). He has taught at Brooklyn College, the University of North Carolina at Wilmington, and elsewhere.

**Pearl B. Sheridan** is a Wilmette, Illinois, teacher and writer whose classes and readings of poetry have often centered around the Holocaust. Her work appears in *Mother Poet* (1983), in *Zachor, a Compendium of Materials and Guide for Teaching the Shoah,* and in curriculum units on *The History of the Jewish Woman in America* (Board of Jewish Education of Greater Metropolitan Chicago). She is an editor of Thorntree Press in Wilmette.

**Enid Shomer** is the author of *Stalking the Florida Panther,* which won the poetry book prize of the Word Works. Her poems and stories have appeared in numerous magazines and anthologies, including *Poetry, Ploughshares, New Letters,* the *Women's Review of Books,* and *New Visions: Fiction by Florida Writers* (Arbiter Press, 1989). Shomer's husband, an Israeli, is the only Jewish child survivor from his town, Kremenitz, Poland.

**Maurya Simon** has had poems in *Poetry, Grand Street,* and the *Literary Review.* Her first book, *The Enchanted Room,* was published in 1985 by Copper Canyon Press. She is the daughter-in-law of survivors.

**Louis Simpson** was born in Jamaica, British West Indies. His books of poetry include *The Arrivistes* (1949); *At the End of the Open Road* (1963), winner of the Pulitzer Prize in poetry (1964); and *People Live Here: Selected Poems* 1949-1983 (BOA Editions). Recently, Paragon House published Simpson's *Collected Poems* and *Selected Prose* as well as his newest volume of poetry, *In the Room We Share* (1989). He teaches at the State University of New York at Stony Brook and lives in Setauket, New York.

**Frieda Singer** has been a creative writing teacher in the New York City high schools and a book reviewer for Rand McNally. Her work has appeared in various journals and anthologies, including *Negative Capability, Z Miscellaneous,* and *Anthology of South Florida Poets* (1988-1989).

**Myra Sklarew** teaches at the American University in Washington, D.C. Her books of poetry include *From the Backyard of the Diaspora* (Dryad Press, 1976) and *The Science of Goodbyes* (University of Georgia Press, 1982).

**Joan Jobe Smith** is a Dust Bowl descendant, born in Paris, Texas. She has taught creative writing, writes both fiction and poetry, and is the editor of *Pearl,* a literary magazine.

**Deborah S. Snyder** received and MFA in poetry from George Mason University in 1989, and her work has appeared in a number of periodicals and anthologies. She resides with her husband in Stafford, Virginia.

**Kirtland Snyder** has published a chapbook, *Winter Light,* (Innerer Klang, 1987), and has had poems, stories, and nonfiction pieces appear in *The Ardis Anthology of American Poetry, Exquisite Corpse, Midstream, Ms.,* the *Hampden-Sydney Poetry Review,* and elsewhere. In 1981, Snyder converted to Judaism.

**J. R. Solonche** has published in the *American Scholar,* the *Literary Review, Wisconsin Review, Anthology of Magazine Verse and Yearbook of American Poetry* (1985), and elsewhere. He lives in Blooming Grove, New York.

**Gizela Spunberg** was born in Lwôw, Poland, and received her master's degree in law and political science at the University of Jan Casimirus, prior to practicing law (before World War II) as a *referendar* of VIII degree in government service. She survived as a political prisoner in Karaganda and Siberia and arrived in the United States in April 1946. Her entire family perished in the Holocaust.

**Martin Steingesser** performs his poems, stories, and small shows with music, using folk forms, such as a miniature box theater. He has published work in the *American Poetry Review, Witness,* and the *New York Times. Hauling Up Morning,* his anthology of poems and short prose about Central and South America, was published by the War Resisters League in 1990.

**Gerald Stern** is the author of *Lucky Life,* which won the Lamont Poetry Selection of the Academy of American Poets (1977); *The Red Coal; Paradise Poems; Love Sick; Leaving Another Kingdom: Selected Poems* (Harper and Row, 1990); and other books. He teaches at the Writers Workshop at the University of Iowa and lives part of the year in eastern Pennsylvania.

**Mary Kathryn Stillwell** has had poems in the *Paris Review, Confrontation, Nimrod,* and other literary journals. A book-length collection of her poetry, *Moving to Malibu,* was published by Sandhills Press in 1988 as part of the Plains Poetry Series. Stillwell is director of communications and marketing at Long Island University.

**Bradley R. Strahan** is the director of Visions International Arts Synergy and publisher and editor of *Visions International, Black Buzzard Review,* and the Black Buzzard poetry chapbook series. His most recent books of poetry are *Crocodile Man* (1988) and *New Love Songs for an Age of Anxiety* (1989). Strahan's poetry has appeared in a wide range of periodicals, including the *Christian Science Monitor, Poetry Australia,* the *Salmon* (Ireland), and *Midstream.*

**Yuri Suhl** (1908-1986) was born in a small town in the Polish Ukraine. He left Poland at the age of fifteen and settled in New York City. Suhl was the editor and translator of, and contributor to, *They Fought Back: The Story of Jewish Resistance in Nazi Europe,* and he also published four volumes of Yiddish poetry and other works.

**Harriet Susskind** is professor of English at Monroe Community College in Rochester, New York, where she teaches creative writing and women's studies. Her poetry and criticism appears regularly in such journals as *Prairie Schooner, Georgia Review,* and *Choice.* Recently, Susskind served as an advisor to the public television series "Voices and Visions," and she is on the executive poetry committee of the Modern Language Association.

**Marie Syrkin** (1899-1989) was born in Bern, Switzerland. Her books include *Blessed Is the Match: The Story of Jewish Resistance* (1947), *Woman with a Cause* (1963), and *Gleanings: A Diary in Verse* (Rhythms Press, 1979). Syrkin served as editor of *Jewish Frontier* and was professor emeritus, Brandeis University.

CONTRIBUTORS

**Marilynn Talal** was a poet in the schools in California for ten years, serving as Marin County coordinator. She has taught writing at the University of Texas in San Antonio, at the University of Virginia—Arlington, and elsewhere. Her poems have appeared in *Poetry, California Quarterly, Southern Poetry Review*, and in other literary magazines and anthologies.

**Elaine Terranova** has been an "Artist in Education" for the state of Pennsylvania, and she teaches writing at Community College of Philadelphia. Her poems have appeared in *American Poetry Review, Ploughshares, Earth's Daughters, Poetry Northwest*, and other magazines, and her chapbook, *Toward Morning/Swimmers*, was published in 1980 by Hollow Springs Press. Nearly everyone in her mother's family was lost in the Holocaust.

**Susan Tichy** teaches in the writing program at George Mason University. Her poems, reviews, and essays have been published in a wide variety of literary journals and anthologies, including the *American Voice*, the *Antioch Review, Crazyhorse, Crossing the River: Poets of the Western United States* (Mesilla Press, 1987), and *Early Ripening: American Women's Poetry Now (Pandora Press, 1987)*. Tichy's most recent book is *A Smell of Burning Starts the Day* (Wesleyan University Press, 1988), and her collection, *The Hands in Exile* was a selection in the National Poetry Series for 1983.

**William Trowbridge** is a professor of English at Northwest Missouri State University and an associate editor of the *Laurel Review*. His books are *The Book of Kong* (Iowa State University Press, 1986) and *Enter Dark Stranger* (University of Arkansas Press, 1989). His poems have also appeared in *Poetry*, the *Georgia Review*, the *Kenyon Review, New Letters*, and many other journals.

**Alfred Van Loen** was born in Oberhausen-Osterfeld, Germany, in 1924. He was sent to school at a Dominican cloister in Holland and later was active in the Underground. Van Loen moved to the United States in 1947. He is internationally recognized as a sculptor, and examples of his work may be seen at the Louvre, the National Museum in Jerusalem, the Metropolitan Museum of Art in Manhattan, and in other major museums and galleries in this country and abroad.

**Doris Vidaver** has written poetry, fiction, and essays that have appeared in the *Literary Review, Poetry*, the *American Scholar,* and many other publications. Her latest book is *Arch of a Circle* (Swallow Press/Ohio University Press). Vidaver is an assistant professor and director of the Humanities Program at Rush University, Rush-Presbyterian-St. Luke's Medical Center, Chicago. Her translations from the Yiddish, both prose and poetry, received a Translation Award from the Lamed Foundation for the Advancement of Hebrew and Yiddish Literature.

**Anneliese Wagner** won the Eileen W. Barnes Award for her book of poems, *Hand Work. Fish Magic,* translations of Elisabeth Borchers's poems, will be published in the United States and England. Wagner teaches writing at Sarah Lawrence College and at the New School for Social Research in Manhattan, and she serves as a consultant to individuals writing personal testimony about the Holocaust. She is a survivor.

**Derek Walcott** was born in St. Lucia, West Indies, and now lives in Trinidad and Brookline, Massachusetts. He is the author of more than ten books of poetry, including *The Star Apple Kingdom* (1979), *Midsummer* (1984), *The Arkansas Treatment* (1988), and *Collected Poems 1948 to 1984,* all from Farrar, Straus & Giroux, which is also publisher of his drama collection, *Three Plays* (1985).

**Morrie Warshawski** is a freelance writer and media arts consultant. His articles on the arts have appeared in such magazines and newspapers, as the *San Francisco Examiner* and *American Film,* and in Jewish periodicals nationwide. His poems have been published in *Modern Poetry Studies, Cutbank, Yellow Silk,* and other literary journals. Warshawski's parents are survivors of the camps.

**Burton D. Wasserman** has published in a variety of poetry magazines, including *Kiosk, Tempest, Earthwise,* and *Undinal Songs.* He lives in Mount Vernon, New York.

**Michael Waters** has published four books of poetry: *Fish Light* (1975), *Not Just Any Death* (1979), and—from Carnegie-Mellon University Press—*Anniversary of the Air* (1985) and *The Burden Lifters* (1989). He has edited *Dissolve to Island: On the Poetry of John Logan* (Ford-Brown & Company, 1984). He teaches at Salisbury State University in Maryland.

**Florence Weinberger** had her first collection of poetry, *The Invisible Telling Its Shape,* published by Ambrosia Press in 1989. She lives in Encino, California, and is the wife of a Holocaust survivor.

**Vera Weislitz** is a poet, sculptor, and teacher who was born in Moravia. She and her sister are among the hundred children, of fifteen thousand imprisoned at Theresienstadt, who returned alive. Her mother died during the war; her father died at Dachau. After the war, she met and married the novelist Arnost Lustig, who was also a survivor. They emigrated to the United States with their two children in 1970. Weislitz's poems were part of the exhibition *Precious Legacy,* which traveled around the United States—and around the world.

**Theodore Weiss** is the author of eleven books of poetry and three books of literary criticism. His most recent title is *From Princeton One Autumn Afternoon: Collected Poems of Theodore Weiss* (Macmillan, 1987), which received the Shelley Memorial Award from the Poetry Society of America. Weiss was Paton Foundation Professor of Ancient and Modern Literature at Princeton, before his retirement in 1987, and he was a fellow at the Institute of Advanced Studies in Princeton (1987-1988). With his wife, Renee, he has published *Quarterly Review of Literature* for more than 40 years.

**Ruth Whitman** is the author of seven books of poetry, the most recent of which are *The Testing of Hanna Senesh* (Wayne State University Press, 1986) and *Laughing Gas: Poems Selected and New 1963-1988* (Wayne State, 1990), and she has also published three books of translation from Yiddish poetry. Whitman teaches poetry at Radcliffe College and at the Massachusetts Institute of Technology. She has been the recipient of the Kovner Award of the Jewish Book Council of America.

**C. K. Williams** has published eight books of poetry, including *A Day for Anne Frank* (1968); *With Ignorance* (1977); *Flesh and Blood* (1987), which won the National Book Critics Circle Award in Poetry; and *Poems: 1963-1983* (1989). He has been a professor of English at George Mason University and currently resides in Paris.

**Betty Wisoff** is the founder and chairperson of the Long Island Writer's Network and a retired corporate executive. Her grandfather and other members of her family were killed by the Nazis.

**Carolyne Wright** is a poet whose books are *Stealing the Children* (1978), *Returning What We Owed* (1980), *Premonitions of an Uneasy Guest* (AWP Award Series, 1983), and *From a White Woman's Journal* (Water Mark Press Award Series, 1985). Her poems, translations, reviews, and essays have appeared in *Poetry, Virginia Quarterly Review, Stand, New American Poets of the 80's* (Wampeter Press), *The New Generation* (Doubleday), and many other journals and periodicals. Wright spent 1986-1988 in Calcutta, India, translating the work of Bengali women poets.

**Jeffrey A. Z. Zable** has published poetry, fables, and prose in over two hundred magazines and anthologies. His most recent collection is *Zable's Fables* from Androgyne Books.

**David Zucker** is a professor of English at Quinnipiac College in Hamden, Connecticut, where he teaches Shakespeare and modern American poetry and modern drama. He has published *Stage and Image in the Plays of Christopher Marlowe* (Salzburg, 1972) and edited (with D. A. Dike) *Selected Essays of Delmore*

*Schwartz* (Chicago, 1971). His poetry and criticism have appeared in *American Poetry Review, Shenandoah, Modern Poetry Studies, Iowa Review,* and other journals.

## Sources Cited

Adorno, T. W. "Engagement." In *Noten zur Literatur III.* Frankfurt am Main: Suhrkamp Verlag, 1965.

Arlen, Michael. *Passage to Ararat.* New York: Farrar, Straus & Giroux, 1975.

Artaud, Antonin. *The Theater and Its Double.* New York: Grove Press, 1958.

Cattley, S. R., and George Townsend, eds. *Acts and Monuments.* 8 vols. New York: AMS Press, Reproduction of 1849 edition (no date given).

Dante. *The Inferno.* Translated by John Ciardi. New York: Mentor, 1954.

Dawidowicz, Lucy S. *The War against the Jews 1933–1945.* New York: Holt, Rinehart and Winston, 1975.

Gilbert, Martin. *The Holocaust.* New York: Hill and Wang, 1978.

Hersh, Gizelle, and Peggy Mann. *Gizelle, Save the Children.* New York: Everest House, 1980.

Hilberg, Raoul. *The Destruction of the European Jews.* Rev. and definitive ed. 3 vols. New York: Holmes & Meier, 1985.

ICP Library of Photographers. *Roman Vishniac.* New York: Grossman Publishers (Viking), 1974.

Jewish Black Book Committee. *The Black Book: The Nazi Crime against the Jewish People.* New York: Jewish Black Book Committee, 1946.

Kaplan, Chaim. *The Warsaw Diary of Chaim Kaplan.* New York: Macmillan, 1965.

Kogon, Eugen. *The Theory and Practice of Hell.* Translated by Heinz Norton. New York: Farrar, Straus & Co., 1950.

Langer, Laurence. *The Holocaust and the Literary Imagination.* New Haven: Yale University Press, 1975.

Lipstadt, Deborah E. "What Is the Meaning of This to You?" *Tikkun* 4 (May/June 1989): 67-69.

*Response.* The Wiesenthal Center's World Report. 10 (April 1989):10.

Rosten, Leo. *The Joys of Yiddish.* New York: McGraw-Hill, 1968.

Sachar, Abram L. *The Redemption of the Unwanted: From the Liberation of the Death Camps to the Founding of Israel.* New York: St. Martin's/Marek, 1983.

Stine, Peter. "German Complicity in the Armenian Genocide." *Witness* 1 (Spring 1987):98-106.

Vishniac, Roman. *A Vanished World.* New York: Farrar, Straus & Giroux, 1983.

Volavkova, Hana. *I Never Saw Another Butterfly: Children's Drawings and Poems from Terezin Concentration Camp 1942–1944.* Translated by Jeanne Nemcova. New York: McGraw-Hill, 1964.

Young, James E. "Holocaust Memorials: Memory and Myth." *Moment* 14 (June 1989): 20-29, 59.

# Index of Poets

## Index of Translators

# Index of Titles